Digitization and Digital Archiving

PRACTICAL GUIDES FOR LIBRARIANS

About the Series

This innovative series written and edited for librarians by librarians provides authoritative, practical information and guidance on a wide spectrum of library processes and operations.

Books in the series are focused, describing practical and innovative solutions to a problem facing today's librarian and delivering step-by-step guidance for planning, creating, implementing, managing, and evaluating a wide range of services and programs.

The books are aimed at beginning and intermediate librarians needing basic instruction/guidance in a specific subject and at experienced librarians who need to gain knowledge in a new area or guidance in implementing a new program/service.

About the Series Editor

The **Practical Guides for Librarians** series was conceived by and is edited by M. Sandra Wood, MLS, MBA, AHIP, FMLA, Librarian Emerita, Penn State University Libraries.

M. Sandra Wood was a librarian at the George T. Harrell Library, The Milton S. Hershey Medical Center, College of Medicine, Pennsylvania State University, Hershey, PA, for over 35 years, specializing in reference, educational, and database services. Ms. Wood worked for several years as a Development Editor for Neal-Schuman Publishers.

Ms. Wood received a MLS from Indiana University and a MBA from the University of Maryland. She is a Fellow of the Medical Library Association and served as a member of MLA's Board of Directors from 1991 to 1995. Ms. Wood is founding and current editor of *Medical Reference Services Quarterly*, now in its 35th volume. She also was founding editor of the *Journal of Consumer Health on the Internet* and the *Journal of Electronic Resources in Medical Libraries* and served as editor/co-editor of both journals through 2011.

Titles in the Series

1. *How to Teach: A Practical Guide for Librarians* by Beverley E. Crane
2. *Implementing an Inclusive Staffing Model for Today's Reference Services* by Julia K. Nims, Paula Storm, and Robert Stevens
3. *Managing Digital Audiovisual Resources: A Practical Guide for Librarians* by Matthew C. Mariner
4. *Outsourcing Technology: A Practical Guide for Librarians* by Robin Hastings
5. *Making the Library Accessible for All: A Practical Guide for Librarians* by Jane Vincent
6. *Discovering and Using Historical Geographical Resources on the Web: A Practical Guide for Librarians* by Eva H. Dodsworth and L. W. Laliberté
7. *Digitization and Digital Archiving: A Practical Guide for Librarians* by Elizabeth R. Leggett

Digitization and Digital Archiving

A Practical Guide for Librarians

Elizabeth R. Leggett

PRACTICAL GUIDES FOR LIBRARIANS, NO. 7

ROWMAN & LITTLEFIELD
Lanham • Boulder • New York • Toronto • Plymouth, UK

Published by Rowman & Littlefield
4501 Forbes Boulevard, Suite 200, Lanham, Maryland 20706
www.rowman.com

10 Thornbury Road, Plymouth PL6 7PP, United Kingdom

British Library Cataloguing in Publication Information Available

Library of Congress Cataloging-in-Publication Data

Leggett, Elizabeth R., 1985–
    Digitization and digital archiving : a practical guide for librarians / Elizabeth R. Leggett.
      pages cm. — (Practical guides for librarians ; 7)
    Includes bibliographical references and index.
    ISBN 978-0-8108-9207-1 (pbk. : alk. paper) — ISBN 978-0-8108-9208-8 (ebook)
  1. Archival materials—Digitization. 2. Archival materials—Conservation and restoration.
3. Digital preservation. 4. Records—Management. 5. Electronic records—Management.
I. Title.
    CD973.D53L44 2014
    025.8'4—dc23
                                        2014009307

For my parents

Thank you to Ben and Kopana,
for teaching me about librarianship and practical digital archiving,
and to Sandy, for this wonderful opportunity

Contents

List of Figures

List of Tables

Preface

In today's world, people are reliant on their computers. Computers are so important and so necessary to communicating in the modern world that many people even carry them around in the form of smartphones, tablets, or laptops. Some people are connected to their digital data all the time. A computer could contain everything about a person's life: his or her thoughts, letters in the form of e-mail, important documents, photos, home videos—even a person's preferred entertainment, such as recorded television programs, movies, music, or games.

You've probably heard horror stories of people who were about to finish their dissertations, then their computer crashed and they realized that they hadn't backed up their work, or maybe their computer crashed and they lost years and years of family photos. Computers are pretty delicate things to entrust your life and your memories to, but a lot of people do, and it's considered pretty normal.

Similarly, the Internet is prevalent in everyday life. A lot of people turn to the Internet for all kinds of information, from reading the news to finding funny jokes to trying to figure out exactly what that rash is. For some people, the Internet is their only source of information because it is so fast and convenient.

Some people think that all of this means that libraries are dying out, since so much information is online and it's so readily accessible without any help or guidance. This is not true at all. In fact, libraries and archives are probably going to become more important as time goes on and people become more dependent on computers and digital information.

Not all information is available in a digital format, and there is plenty of valuable information out there that has only a tangible format. These materials can't be accessed from a computer of any kind. There is also plenty of information that is in the reverse situation—it has only a digital format and is entirely dependent on a delicate computer for its survival.

Librarians and archivists can be part of an effort to address these issues through digital archiving: the archiving of digital items. Digital archiving can involve storing digital versions of tangible objects, such as a scan of a photo, as well as items that have only a digital format, such as a website.

Right now, it may seem as though digital items are less worthwhile to preserve than tangible ones, but this is not true. For example, in the past, when a great writer died, he or she might have left behind notes, original documents, or letters that future generations could study. These are easily archived; the paper can be preserved and stored in safe conditions. A writer whose works make a great impact now, though, might leave behind a stack of CDs, a laptop, or, even worse, an outdated method of data storage, such as a box of floppy disks. What do you do with these kinds of items? The storage methods of this author would require the efforts of a digital archivist.

There can be a lot of confusion that goes along with digital archiving, though. Some people find computers intimidating. You might not know why a TIFF file is better than a JPEG for archiving but not for viewing over the Internet. You might not understand the difference between a 150-ppi image and a 300-ppi image. You might not know what the difference is between a CD and a Blu-ray disk. You might not know why you need metadata for your patrons to successfully find information in your archive or why there are copyright laws specifically aimed at digital items. You might not understand why backups are important or why you can't treat digital items the same way that you do tangible ones.

Creating a useful digital archive doesn't have to be hard. *Digitization and Digital Archiving: A Practical Guide for Librarians* is designed to guide you through the basic knowledge that you should have to make informed decisions about your archive and your archiving project.

In this book, you will learn why digital archiving is important to a modern, technology-dependent society and why it is useful to your archive. You will also learn about archival-friendly file formats and how to choose the best storage methods for your archival data. *Digitization and Digital Archiving* covers the basic equipment that you'll need, including a simple explanation of how computers work. In addition, you'll gain an understanding of how the Internet and the World Wide Web function and how they are important to your digital collection, why metadata is essential for a functioning archive, and why copyright laws for digital and tangible materials differ. You'll learn about the limitations of digital archiving as well so that you can plan for problems that may arise. The final chapter puts it all together, guiding you through a basic plan for your own archiving project.

Organization

Digitization and Digital Archiving: A Practical Guide for Librarians is divided into 15 chapters. Each chapter covers a practical aspect of digital archiving and helps you to make decisions about how to go about forming your own archive.

In chapter 1, you'll start by learning what digital archiving is, why it is important, and why it is becoming more prominent in modern times; then in chapter 2, you'll move on to learning the basics of how a computer operates and stores data, along with the meanings of basic computer terminology.

In chapters 3–5, you'll learn about the optimal archiving formats for images, text, and audio/video data, and you'll learn how computers perceive and store these types of data.

Chapters 6–10 teach you about the common methods of data storage available today, which methods are best for your archive and why, and how the different common methods of data storage work on a physical level. Optical disks, magnetic tape, hard drives, flash memory, and cloud storage are all discussed in these chapters. Chapter 10 also gives you an overview of how the Internet works.

You'll most likely need equipment for an archiving project, and chapter 11 teaches you about the basic equipment that you may need for your project, how it works, how to use it, and in which situations it is optimal. You'll also learn what to look for in any software that you need for your project.

Metadata is an important aspect of any digital archiving project, and chapter 12 discusses what metadata is and why it is necessary; it additionally addresses concerns that you may have about how your patrons access your files and how much access they will have. Chapter 13 helps you avoid legal issues in regards to copyright law, and chapter 14 teaches you about the limitations of digital archiving. At the end, you'll review the important parts of this book, putting it all together in chapter 15.

◎ Using This Book

If you have experience with computers, then you've got a good start on things. But if you don't, that's okay. This book assumes that you're not an expert, and it will explain the basics of everything that you need to understand. All you need to know when you start is a general understanding of how to use a computer. If you can type a word document, look at an image, play a game, listen to some music, and open a website, then you probably know enough to use this book. If you want to create databases or put your collection online, then this becomes more complicated, but anyone can create a digital backup of nearly any kind of information and store it under safe conditions to preserve it for the future.

This book does not tell you *everything* that you need to know to start your digital archive, because you'll have questions and needs specific to your situation and collection, and if every possible situation were addressed, this book would be large, confusing, and difficult to read. Instead, this book is an overview of the practical knowledge that you should be aware of and the general steps that you'd need to take to create a digital archive. Ideally, once you reach the end, you will know what additional questions need to be answered for you to proceed with your project.

This book also contains generalized information so that you can easily adapt it to your needs. You may have an immense collection and be overwhelmed with the prospect of digitizing it all. You may have a minute collection and need to know how to best manage your limited budget and resources.

You also do not have to be a librarian to use this book, although it is helpful. If, for instance, you're trying to create a genealogical archive for your community or just for your family, this book can help you, too. Even if you know next to nothing about computers, you can create a digital archive. This book will guide you, step by step, through the process of how computers work, what file formats are and which ones to choose, how to store your data, how to select your equipment, and even how to avoid the legal issues that may arise with digital archiving.

You don't have to read this book in order. If you have questions about, say, the copyright issues arising from digital materials, then you could just skip straight to chapter 13. The chapters build on one another, though, so if you have questions about everything, you really should read them in order.

Computers and digital information do not need to be difficult or intimidating—anyone can make a difference and help preserve the digital present for the future and make the past easily accessible by those who seek their information through the Internet.

CHAPTER 1

Why Use Digital Preservation?

── IN THIS CHAPTER ──

▷ What is digital archiving?

▷ What is the difference between digital archiving and traditional archiving?

▷ What are some current large digital archiving projects?

▷ How can you start your own digital archive? What do you need?

▷ How should you use this book?

IF YOU'VE PICKED UP THIS BOOK, then you've probably been hearing some buzz about digital archiving. Maybe you've been hearing about it from your colleagues, from a presentation at a conference, or from the publications that you read. You could have read about it from an article online, too, if you like to use the Internet. Perhaps you're already involved in a digital archiving project and would like to learn more. Or maybe the title of the book merely interested you, and now you're wondering—what exactly is *digital archiving*? The quick and easy answer is the archiving of electronic materials as opposed to physical ones.

It's a little more complicated than the concept of regular archiving in that digital archiving can mean a couple of things. First, digital archiving can involve creating and storing digital copies that have a physical, tangible form. For instance, an e-book could have a tangible equivalent. An electronic copy of a journal article and a scanned copy of a photograph are other examples of digital copies of tangible items. Digital archiving can also involve storing copies that have no physical forms and never have—otherwise known as *born-digital* materials. This would include, for example, web pages and digital images. Finally, digital archiving can involve storing items that are somewhere in between these two concepts. For example, a CD containing software sort of has a physical format (the disk), but it's really digital in nature. Software is also something that can be archived.

Digital archiving has recently become rather prominent among librarians and archivists, for a few important reasons:

- In the past, computers were too large, expensive, and slow to make digital archiving viable. Only large companies and organizations could use computers for large amounts of data storage, and even then, the amount of data that could be stored was tiny compared to what is possible now.
- Modern computers and the equipment needed to create a digital archive, such as scanners, are affordable and easy to obtain today, even for an archive with a small budget.
- Owing to the rise of personal computers as everyday items and to the rise of the Internet, more and more information is being created that has no original physical format and is solely digital. This information is quite vulnerable for reasons that are explored later; therefore, archiving efforts are needed to preserve the history being made right now.
- Also owing to the rise of personal computers and the Internet, your patrons are expecting to have the information that they desire rapidly and possibly without ever entering your archive. For example, a college student can now write a perfectly good research paper without ever leaving his or her dorm room, using online databases, journals and magazines that post articles online, e-books, textbooks, and blogs written by professionals.

So, digital archiving is a trend, but it's not trendy, and unless everyone spontaneously decides to stop using computers and the Internet, it's something that will need to be addressed in the future as more and more digital materials are created and people continually turn to the information found online rather than that found inside a building.

At this point, though, you may be wondering—why it is necessary to have an entire book devoted to digital archiving. Isn't it just like regular archiving? In some ways, yes, it is, and in some ways, it's quite different.

◉ Archiving

People have been attempting to record information for millennia. Images, which can be a form of recorded information, have been around as a form of communication for tens of thousands of years. Images are nice in that they don't require a particular language for one to understand the meaning, but they can't be particularly specific about meaning, either. Sometime in 3200 BCE, people were using small tokens to indicate numbers or amounts of goods, which were important for a developing economy and civilization. Writing, perhaps logically, followed not too long after that (Valentine 2012).

Ever since then, writing has been a major form of sharing information among civilizations across the world, and it persists today. Consider the Internet, for instance, which has an unprecedented amount of written information that can be shared nearly instantly all across the globe, along with other forms of information (videos, photographs, etc.).

Writing was initially used on tablets of stone or clay to express rather simple concepts, just tallies of goods and similar data that could replace the token system. With the invention of more complex writing and objects more convenient to write on, such as parchment and papyrus, people were needed to store and maintain all this information, leading to the rise of libraries.

In the past, the concepts of an archive and a library were pretty much the same (Harris 1995), probably because books were massively expensive and rare, given that they were written and illustrated by hand. There might be only one copy of a book in existence as well, and such a book would be extremely valuable. If a person could afford to have books, then that person would also be able to afford the expenses involved with storing and maintaining those books, blurring the line between a library and an archive.

Over time, however, the cost of books has gone down, and their accessibility has gone up. Libraries are now less involved with maintaining information (as an archive is) and more interested in distributing it. Libraries even have to make decisions about which books are worth keeping in their buildings. There are books around today that are not valuable or have so little value that they can't even be given away; consider outdated encyclopedia sets, for instance. There are instructions on the Internet for art and craft projects that describe how to turn old books into lamps and tables, and there are people who fold or carve the pages of books to turn now valueless items (at least as far as the ability to sell them goes) into works of art. This was pretty unthinkable not that long ago, which may be the reason for the current need to distinguish between a library and an archive, at least in part.

An archive is different from a library in that the point of an archive is to preserve materials from the past—in essence, to save a record for the future. Archives don't weed the same way that libraries do, and archives don't consider items to lack value, because everything created by a culture is a record of its past. Information in an archive does not become outdated.

It may be sobering to archivists, though, to think of preserving the massive amounts of written materials along with the invention of photography and the invention of ways to record moving images and sounds, since you can't save everything. You'll always be limited by the amount of space and time that you have, your funding and other resources, and the number of people whom you have to do the work of preserving information.

This limitation changes somewhat with digital archiving, though. There's a reason why people prefer e-mail and digital photography over snail mail and printed photos. You can save huge amounts of information using the technology available today, but physically, it will take up practically no space at all.

For an example of just how much the technology of today can store in comparison to that of the recent past, the floppy disk was the main method of storing data outside a computer not very long ago (it's since fallen largely but not entirely into disuse). A typical floppy disk could store about 1.44 megabytes of data (you'll learn more about what exactly this means in the next chapter). By contrast, some modern storage devices can hold terabytes of information, a not uncommon amount for current computer hard drives. A terabyte is 1,048,576 megabytes of information.

So, suppose that you were able to store one high-quality image on that floppy disk. Modern storage devices could hold about 728,178 images of the same quality—more than what most people will ever need. But for you, the need to store that many images could well be within the realm of possibility. Remember: this is part of why digital archiving is becoming much more prevalent—storing 728,178 floppy disks would be exceptionally inconvenient, not to mention expensive to buy that many floppy disks. But buying and storing one hard drive is not difficult at all.

Think of it this way. You could have a paper version of a book, which will take up a couple of inches of shelf space, or you could have a CD with the same information on it but in a digital form. CDs are a fraction of an inch in thickness, and the scenario of a CD only holding one book is an inaccurate situation—a CD could actually hold quite a few books, depending on how long they are, what kinds of files they are, and whether or not they are illustrated. The digital copies of items take up far less space than the tangible ones.

What this means to you is that going digital brings you closer to the ultimate dream of an archivist: saving everything. But before you get too excited, you need to remember a few things. Digital archiving is not the same as traditional archiving. If you're trying to turn a physical collection into a digital one, then this is a time-consuming process, even if you have the best and most optimal equipment for your collection. It's also rather dull and tedious work. So, you'll be restricted both by your available staff and by that ever-limiting factor: time.

Even if you're trying to preserve items that have no physical format and are already digital in nature or are born-digital materials, you'll run into some troubles. For example, the copyright laws in regard to digital materials are much less clear-cut than those for physical materials, meaning some possibly tricky legal navigations for your archive.

There's another issue as well. Archivists traditionally work at preserving physical items. Even though writing has been around for thousands of years, no one's created a truly stable method of saving information, although some people and organizations have made an excellent effort. There's still a struggle to prevent written materials from decomposing. But no matter what kind of material you use to record information, it is all subject to decay. The various writing materials of the past, such as papyrus, bark, paper, and parchment, are all subject to decay or damage caused by the passage of time. Even materials that one would think are nearly impossible to damage or that would withstand the test of time are deceptively delicate. Clay tablets can be eaten by worms, strangely enough. Stone can break, crumble, or simply wear away. Metal is subject to corrosion (Kathpalia 1973).

Electronic information is no more stable than any of these. In fact, it's even less stable. A book printed on acidic paper (the bane of archivists everywhere) has a longer projected life span than stored digital materials (Lazinger 2001). And, as mentioned before, digital archiving and physical archiving are *not* the same.

Consider this: archivists know a lot about how to keep a book from falling apart. All the typical ailments of a decaying book have treatments. Rot can be stopped, for instance, and pages and covers can be glued back together. If you have a book with highly acidic pages, the pH can be altered with chemicals. There are quite a variety of materials and methods that can be used to preserve all kinds of information with physical formats. After all, archivists have had thousands of years to perfect the art, and there's been a continuous production of new material during that time available for experimentation. You can easily determine from a visual examination that something is wrong with an item such as a book and address it accordingly. This is not true for digital materials.

The bits and bytes of a digital item are not as easy to deal with as tangible items. You can't touch them. You can't stitch a corrupted file back together or add a chemical to prevent a file from decaying. While computers are a part of everyday life for many people and become more user friendly all the time, understanding exactly what they are and how they work is not so simplistic. Even an expert might struggle to understand what is wrong with a file that has gone bad.

It's not as easy to determine what is wrong with a storage device for digital items as it is with tangible ones, nor is it so simple for you to fix it yourself. Part of the challenge of dealing with digital materials is determining how to preserve information that doesn't exactly have a physical format, information that doesn't depend on the preservation of a specific object, or even information that has never had a physical format.

The difficulties with digital archiving are discussed throughout this book and are explored in-depth in chapter 14. For now, consider the positive aspects of digital archiving. It's an excellent space saver, and your collection will likely see more use if you digitize it, especially if you make it available over the Internet. Even if you don't—that is, you make your digital collection solely available inside of your archive—your patrons will likely appreciate a digital collection, particularly if you work to make it easily searchable, a topic touched on in chapter 12. Searchability greatly improves the speed with which patrons will be able to locate meaningful information in your collection.

Even if you don't want to make your collection available to the public at all, a digital archive can be useful and of great benefit to future generations. It can serve as a backup to your physical collection, for instance. Or, you may simply want to contribute to the overall goal of preserving a culture that is becoming owners of bits and bytes or usage rights rather than physical objects. There are many benefits to wanting digital collection for your archive and many ways in which it will benefit others.

ⓖ Goals of a Digital Archive

While there are many organizations creating digital archives right now, the ultimate purpose for each program may not be quite the same. Therefore, you may need to approach matters a bit differently according to your collection, the goals of your archive, and, to some extent, your philosophies in regard to what an archive should achieve.

It may be that you just want to make your collection more available to the public, which is a simple goal with a clear and useful purpose for your archive. For example, suppose that your archive has a lot of genealogical records on microfilm—which is really handy and a great space saver but tedious to use and to locate and put back into place. You could scan the images on your microfilm reels and create digital images instead, which don't have to be filed away and can be retrieved with a keyword. If your collection is available online, you might find that your patrons are not only increasing in number but coming from places far away from your archive. This scenario might mean fewer patrons physically coming in through your doors, so you'll need to think about how to show that your archive is getting plenty of use when it comes to getting funding. Although this is a common scenario, there are many other goals that you could have.

Are you interested in preserving the vast amounts of information that are available through the Internet? In the past, to share information, you'd need to print a book, flyer, newspaper, newsletter, or similar item that was limited in number and could be kept as part of an archive. Now, many websites make publishing all kinds of materials online easy and accessible—and not just written materials, either. YouTube, for instance, makes it possible for anyone to share videos of nearly anything, while websites such as Flickr and Photobucket make it possible to share photos. Anyone can make something and share it with the world through the Internet. Is it the goal of your archive to preserve this kind of information?

More information is being produced every day that can be meaningfully sorted and organized by librarians. The difficulty is made even greater by the fact that some people steal materials from others online, effectively creating illegal duplicates of the same information, and the fact that people can easily change, move, or erase information that they have created. Do you want your archive to be part of an effort to organize, track, and record this kind of information?

As an example of a similar possible goal, if your archive is part of a university, you might want to collaborate with the IT department to archive web pages created by the faculty or organize and create backups of papers written by professors. If something ever goes wrong with your university's servers or if faculty members stop maintaining their pages or move on to another university, you have the information that they created, and you can put it back online if desired. You've probably encountered a "dead link" before—that is, a link that went to a web page that is no longer there. Your archive could address issues such as this by preserving web pages.

Another problem with digital information is the fact that it's so easily changed. It's impossible to accidentally erase a book out of existence, but it's quite possible to destroy an e-book in this manner in just a few seconds, leaving nothing of the original. It's also impossible to go in and erase a paragraph out of a book (even the most meticulously placed White-Out will leave a noticeable gap on the page), but this is perfectly possible with an electronic document, leaving no one the wiser. Are you interested in ensuring that born-digital materials have a backup to protect against accidental loss or that they have a master copy to which they can be compared for integrity? The second goal is one that's actually being addressed right now, as discussed further in chapter 14.

Although being changed or erased will obviously make information unavailable, there's another scenario in which data can be lost: obsolescence. This is one of the most difficult issues in regard to digital archiving and is addressed throughout the book, particularly in chapter 14. You're probably aware of some computer technologies that are considered obsolete, such as 8-in. floppy disks, 5.25-in. floppy disks, punch cards, and some forms of magnetic tape.

Your archive may be interested in ensuring that data does not become obsolete due to file formats or equipment that is no longer practical to use. This means focusing on transferring information from old methods of data storage (e.g., a floppy disk) to ones that are more current (e.g., a CD) or converting old file formats to new ones. This is a more abstract goal, in a way, because your archive doesn't necessarily gain anything or achieve better patron access by moving files around. However, it's an important goal. Much information has been lost during the rise of computers as a method of information storage due to obsolete methods of data storage or by not properly caring for methods of data storage.

As a rather infamous example of this happening, the 1960 census was recorded onto a UNIVAC tape drive, which was probably efficient at the time; computers are excellent when it comes to efficiency. However, when the U.S. Census Bureau attempted to access

POSSIBLE GOALS FOR A DIGITAL ARCHIVE

- Making it easier to access the archive's information
- Preserving modern digital culture and information
- Assisting other archives with their preservation projects
- Protecting a collection that is unique to your organization
- Making information available while protecting the original object from wear caused by use

the stored files a mere 16 years later, it discovered that the data could not be accessed because the UNIVAC tape drive became obsolete. While the bureau was able to transfer many records onto new tapes, not everything could be recovered (Lazinger 2001).

If your archive decides to focus on this as a goal, then it's certainly a useful and worthwhile one. Regardless of what you do, though, guarding against obsolescence is something that you'll need to address to protect your collection. While this might not be the major focus of your project, it is something that will certainly need to be a part of your plans.

ⓖ Digital Archives

If you create a digital archive, you're certainly not alone in your project. There are varieties of organizations that are attempting to preserve all kinds of materials. When you begin planning your archive, you can look to these organizations for guidance by seeing what they preserve and how and even by asking questions. There are many digital archiving projects, and this book touches on just a few of the ones that may be of particular interest to you.

If you haven't heard of it already, American Memory—which is part of a larger project known as the National Digital Library—is something that is sure to interest you. The aim of this program is to digitize the Library of Congress's (2013) historical collections and make them available to the public. While the program originally distributed its digitized materials via CD-ROM and gave copies to schools and libraries, the cost of this method became prohibitive. Today, the collection is available to the public via the Internet, which is much less costly and much more convenient to patrons. The collection holds a variety of materials, such as sound recordings, photographs, maps, sheet music, videos, and writings.

Apart from having an interesting online collection, the Library of Congress is a good place to turn to in general for ideas about how to preserve your information. The Library of Congress has many recommendations online for good file formats to use for preserving digital materials. If you don't quite understand what that means or implies, this is covered later in this book.

Another interesting example of a large-scale project is the Internet Archive (2013). It is exactly what it sounds like: an archive of the Internet. While not fully complete (such a thing would be nearly impossible), the project records and archives many online web pages, something that may prove useful to historians in the future, possibly even now. But the project doesn't just store web pages; it also stores many other materials, including digitized text, audio, and video files.

The Internet Archive promotes itself as an "Internet library," and in a way, it is; but there are a growing number of these today, with many projects attempting to fulfill the same ideal. For instance, Project Gutenberg (2013) is yet another digital archiving project, the main aim of which is to digitize classic literature and make it available to the public. Literary works that are no longer under copyright in the United States are digitized and made freely available to U.S. citizens. Works such as Frank L. Baum's *The Wonderful Wizard of Oz* and Louisa May Alcott's *Little Women* are among the numerous offerings available through this project.

All kinds of things can be archived, so if you have an unusual collection or a specific goal, this should not deter you from making a digital archive. For example, the National Digital Newspaper Program (2013)—which is part of a partnership between the National

Endowment for the Humanities and the Library of Congress—has a very fine-tuned goal: provide Internet access to historical newspapers from all across the United States as well as information about those newspapers. Many organizations participate in building the collection by digitizing their archival newspaper collections and contributing both the files and the information about the newspapers to the program. This is something that you may want to consider as well while you read this book. If you have similar goals to another archive or organization, then you may want to collaborate or consider participating in a larger program.

◎ Starting a Digital Archive

You may be starting completely from scratch with your digital archive. That's okay; this book assumes that you don't have a program or that something about your program could use an overhaul. But you may be wondering if you really have the things that you need to get started; for instance, you may wonder if your budget is capable of handling this, if you have enough people to devote to the project, or if it will take too much time away from your other projects.

There's a lot of confusion when it comes to digital archiving. The standards that you should follow aren't particularly clear. There are multiple groups out there with suggestions for how you should go about your project, for instance, which computers you need to use and at what resolution you need to scan items. Some of what these groups have to say is confusing. Part of the problem, too, is trying to make standards for creating digital information when the software that you need and the capabilities of computers keep changing every year.

Looking at what other people are doing and investigating standards for data creation is a good thing. However, the truth of the matter is this: You can make a digital archive with a fleet of brand-new computers, armies of cameras and scanners, the latest software, and magnetic tape recorder with a state-of-the-art robotic tape-retrieval system. You can also make a perfectly useful archive with an older computer, a scanner, some software that you downloaded free off the Internet, and a package of CDs that you got from an office supply store. Everything depends on what you have to work with and what you need to get done.

When you read this book, keep a couple of things in mind regarding your archive.

Budget: What kind of a budget do you have to work with? Do you have a lot of money, or will you need to make do with what resources the archive already has available? Do you have a donation that will give you a onetime opportunity for equipment that you may not be able to replace soon?

Time frame: Are you on a time limit, or do you have an indefinite amount of time to add to your collection?

Scope: What kinds of things do you want to archive? Books, music, images, web pages, software programs? Are you preserving the past or the present?

Staff: How many people are available to work on your project? Do you have armies of student workers at your beck and call, or will it only be you working on this project?

Collaborating: Do you want to collaborate with another archive?

There is no answer to any of these questions that will indicate that you don't have the means or ability to create a useful digital archive—that is, unless you do not have computers or someone to work on the project. Those you must have: a computer and a worker. Thinking about these questions as you read, however, will help you make some decisions or determine if a proposed method of data storage is not for you.

A single untrained person can make a usable archive. There are instructions online designed to assist people doing personal genealogy so that they can create a digital archive. In fact, if you are a genealogist making a personal archive or if you are working at a single-librarian archive or library, this book can help you, too. While it's optimal to use the best equipment and resources available and the standards indicated by groups researching the topic, sometimes that's not possible. Your ultimate goals should be to create a digital archive that suits the needs of your organization and your patrons. If it meets your needs and is accessible, then you've reached your goals.

Ⓖ Key Points

- Digital archiving is a new trend among archivists and librarians that will become more prevalent and more important as time goes on and society relies more and more on information that is solely digital in nature.
- Digital archiving offers many benefits to you, your archive, and your patrons, although there are drawbacks as well.
- Although the goal of preserving the past and present for the future is the same with both digital archiving and traditional archiving, how you should approach achieving your goal is different.

In the next chapter, you'll learn about computers, including an overview of what they are, how they work in general, what binary is and why it's important in computer science, and what some of the common terminology is in regard to computers. You'll also learn about many of the physical components of a computer and what features you can look for to purchase the optimal machines for your archive.

Ⓖ References

Harris, Michael H. 1995. *History of Libraries in the Western World.* 4th ed. Metuchen, NJ: Scarecrow Press.

Internet Archive. 2013. "About the Internet Archive." http://archive.org/about/.

Kathpalia, Yash Pal. 1973. *Conservation and Restoration of Archive Materials.* UNESCO.

Lazinger, Susan S. 2001. *Digital Preservation and Metadata: History, Theory, Practice.* Englewood, CO: Libraries Unlimited.

Library of Congress. 2013. "Mission and History." http://memory.loc.gov/ammem/about/index.html.

National Digital Newspaper Program. 2013. "About the Program." http://www.loc.gov/ndnp/about.html.

Project Gutenberg. 2013. http://www.gutenberg.org.

Valentine, Patrick M. 2012. *A Social History of Books and Libraries from Cuneiform to Bytes.* Lanham, MD: Scarecrow Press.

How Do Computers Store Information?

MANY BOOKS WRITTEN ABOUT THE BASICS OF COMPUTERS start off with a history of computers. Oftentimes, this includes a paragraph or two about the abacus, sometimes accompanied by a colorful photograph. This seems rather peculiar, considering that an abacus really bears no resemblance at all to a laptop, a smartphone, or any other computerized equipment. Certainly you can't text anyone with an abacus, and Google is not abacus compatible. So, if an abacus is so unlike a modern computer, then why do so many books mention them just before discussing devices that do seem much more like a modern computer?

It's better not to think about how an abacus is like a computer but rather how a computer is like an abacus. An abacus is a set of beads on posts that can be moved to help the user make calculations quickly. It is a calculator. A computer is, in essence, a glorified calculator. The basic definition of a computer is that it is a device that can compute, or make calculations. The word can even refer to a person who is making calculations, "one who computes," which means that it's the calculations that are the essence of what a computer is.

Since modern computers can allow the user to do a variety of tasks that don't seem like calculations at all, such as playing games or watching movies, it's not so obvious that the computer is only making calculations. From a computer's perspective, the world is solely made of numbers. Every function that it does is essentially a calculation, and it can assign a numerical value to anything, such as words, music, or photographs. You'll learn more about exactly how a computer can do this in the next few chapters.

While a typical archivist doesn't need a computer to make complex calculations, knowing a little about how a computer works and how it interprets data is helpful to understanding what digital information actually is and how it can be kept safe. Computers are capable of performing many tasks, some of them extremely complex, but there are still many things that computers cannot do. Knowing about these limitations is useful so that you don't make assumptions about computers' potential and so that you can make plans for how to deal with problems should they arise.

This chapter covers some of the basics about how a computer works, starting with a brief discussion about how computers view data; it then explores the components of basic computers. When you need to purchase computers, either for yourself or for your patrons, a lot of jargon gets thrown around, most of which involves nonintuitive numbers and acronyms for the hardware that you find inside a computer. Knowing what these parts are and what they do can make decision making much simpler and make it easier to purchase a computer that is optimal for your archiving projects.

Binary System

So, how exactly do computers process information? While a computer user might see an image of a bunny or a sunset on the computer's monitor, there isn't a tiny picture of a bunny or a sunset inside the machine. If a user listens to a song, there isn't a miniature copy of a band inside the computer (although that might be more interesting). As mentioned before, everything in a computer's world is numbers. Everything that can be seen on a computer monitor or heard through the speakers has a numerical value of some kind. A computer can assign a numerical value to a color, for instance, and all the numerical values for colors can combine to make that aforementioned bunny picture.

Modern computers work in binary, which means that they only use two numbers—ones and zeroes—to make all their calculations. In movies, television shows, and other media, artists and directors use screens of ones and zeroes to symbolically represent "incomprehensible computer technology stuff," such as in the movie *The Matrix*. But that's not what the inside of a computer looks like. There are no dripping walls of neon green text anywhere inside a computer, in spite of what special-effects artists would have the public believe.

From a computer's perspective, there aren't even ones and zeroes. The calculations inside a computer are actually done through high and low frequencies of electricity. There are no ones or zeroes floating about inside—it's all just electricity. A high frequency represents a one, or *on*, and a low frequency is a zero, or *off*. Think back to the abacus. The beads can symbolically represent different numbers or multiples of numbers. So, in a computer, pulses of electricity symbolically represent numbers, but there are only two possibilities: one and zero.

A computer doesn't "know" what a one or a zero is any more than an abacus does. A computer is not capable of understanding these concepts; all that a computer can do is follow commands programmed by a human, who does know what the concepts of one and zero are. What a computer can do is detect high and low frequency, which humans interpret as ones and zeroes. A modern computer only seems more complex than an abacus because it can do so many calculations in a short period, which it does through the use of the binary system. *Binary* means "two," referring to the two possible numbers in the system: one and zero.

But a computer doesn't have to use binary at all. It's possible to create a computer that uses the much more familiar decimal system or an octet system, a hexidecimal system, or essentially any system at all. In fact, the people who designed early models of computers attempted to have values of 0–9 and even letters represented in transistors. It was only in 1940 that the current binary model was proposed (Andrews 2006).

People tend to prefer the decimal system of dealing with numbers, which uses the numbers 0–9. So, why would you want to program a computer to use a system that's not intuitive to human users? The reason is that the binary system is easier for computers to handle. Remember, the ones and zeroes for a computer are pulses of electricity. How this works in a computer is that, as mentioned, a high frequency of electricity is a one, and a low frequency is a zero. From a computer's perspective, this makes things easy to interpret. Anything with a high frequency is a one; anything with a low frequency is a zero.

If a computer engineer used a number system with eight numbers instead, which is an octet system, this would require the computer to be able to detect a variety of signals. It would need to be able to detect whether an electrical signal is low, a little higher, a little higher than that, and so on for eight different frequencies. That leaves a lot of room for inaccuracy and interpretation on the part of the computer. As indicated earlier, computers don't "know" anything, and so they can't make guesses in the way that a human can about information, either.

A binary system doesn't need guessing. It reduces things to essentially yes or no. Is the frequency high, yes or no? Is it on or off? There is no "sort of on" for a computer to interpret. So, even though it's not intuitive for humans, using the binary system greatly improves the accuracy of the computer and leaves little gray area for interpretation. It also helps when the electrical signal needs to be strengthened. Even over an area as short as an inch, the electrical signals can begin to degrade, losing the distinction between the high and low frequencies. This means that as the signals travel around the computer, they can lose their strength. If there are only two possibilities, this signal can be "reclocked," or reset to the original frequency, thus eliminating data loss. Doing this to a signal that has multiple interpretations is difficult or even impossible without data loss, whereas strengthening this yes/no signal is much easier (Dale and Lewis 2013).

Since a computer is designed for calculating, everything in a computer's world is a set of calculations. Although the human user may perceive what he or she is doing with a computer as playing a game or typing up a notice or listening to a song, the computer is making calculations and interpreting numerical values. Binary can represent and calculate any number with just two numbers. To show you how this works, Table 2.1 has the decimal numbers 1–10 and their binary equivalents.

This set of ones and zeroes is equal to 49 in the familiar decimal system: 110001. The two numbers are really the

Table 2.1. Decimal and Equivalent Binary Numbers

BINARY	DECIMAL
1	1
10	2
11	3
100	4
101	5
110	6
111	7
1000	8
1001	9
1010	10

same thing and mean exactly the same amount; it's just that the system of representing it has changed.

In school, when you first started learning about math and numbers, you almost certainly learned about "places," or the slots used to represent and understand numbers. Thinking back on this can help you understand how binary works.

Suppose that you have 2,156 items. You know, intuitively, that this number does not mean that you have a set of 2 items, a set of 1 item, a set of 5 items, and a set of 6 items for a total of 14 items. You can see this number as meaning that there are two thousand, one hundred, and fifty-six items present—because you know that each place for each number actually represents a multiple of a number, not the number itself.

2 Thousands
1 Hundreds
5 Tens
6 Ones

When in the tens place, five doesn't mean five. It means five multiplied by ten, or fifty. The one in this example is not one item—it's one set of one hundred items. Binary can be thought of in exactly the same way, but it doesn't have the same places. For instance, the number 1011 has these places:

1 Eights
0 Fours
1 Twos
1 Ones

This number isn't 3, nor is it 1,011. It has one set of ones, a set of twos, no sets of fours, and one set of eights for a total, in the decimal system, of 11. While the places for decimal numbers keep going up in multiples of ten, for binary, each new place is double the place before it. So in this sequence, the next place beyond the eights place would be the sixteens place.

You can produce any number with the binary system using any type of mathematical function, although it gets a little more complex when a computer starts working with decimal places and negative numbers, and all computers are limited in the highest number that they are able to calculate (Dale and Lewis 2013).

Binary can represent only two numbers at a time, and just as in the decimal system, it's necessary to have multiple numbers grouped to express a larger amount. For instance, a person needs the numbers 1 and 9 to express the number 19. It's like that in binary, too, and so there are terms in computer design for these larger, more useful collections of binary numbers.

Bits and Bytes

The term *byte* is one that's unavoidable when learning about and discussing computers. If a person tries to buy a blank CD, for instance, there will be a marking indicating how many MB it holds, standing for *megabytes*. It's pretty easy to interpret from all this that a byte is some sort of storage unit. But what exactly does it mean?

USEFUL TERMS FOR STORAGE CAPACITY

Bit: 1 binary unit

Byte: 8 bits

Kilobyte: 1,000 bytes

Megabyte: 1 million bytes (1,000 kilobytes)

Gigabyte: 1 billion bytes (1,000 megabytes)

Terabyte: 1 trillion bytes (1,000 gigabytes)

Computers work in binary. So, the smallest unit of information possible for a computer is either a one or a zero. The term for this unit is a *bit*, which stands for the longer term *binary digit*. Think of a bit as kind of being like a coin—the coin itself is a single unit with two possibilities: heads or tails. A bit also has two possibilities: one or zero. A single number doesn't really do much. In this case, a single bit can represent only two commands. That's not particularly useful, so there are larger units of information in regard to a computer.

One of the most commonly used and useful of these is the *byte*, a set of eight bits that together form a single unit of information. Why eight? It may seem somewhat random, considering that, again, people like to think in tens—probably because humans come with an easy method of keeping count (10 fingers). However, eight bits is a rather useful unit of information for a computer. Eight bits can be used to create enough numerical combinations to use one binary number for every letter of the alphabet for English, including capital and lowercase letters, some characters, and numbers. Eight bits is also handy for encoding color information, as you'll learn in the following chapter. Because eight provides a significant number of useful number combinations, eight and multiples of eight are often used for computers when they are storing data. It's not entirely arbitrary.

However, a byte is still really a very small unit of information. Talking about how many bytes a modern computer is able to store would be cumbersome, because the number would become very large. That's why, in many cases, there's a prefix to the term *byte*, such as *kilobyte* or *megabyte*. The term *kilo* means "one thousand," so there are about 1,000 bytes in a kilobyte. This is not perfectly accurate; there are actually 1,024 bytes in this amount of data. The exact numbers of bytes are rounded for the sake of convenience for programmers and consumers.

One of the popular methods of portable data storage in use today is the flash drive, which is discussed in detail in chapter 9. If you were to put a flash drive with a four-gigabyte capacity into a USB port and examine how much data it can hold, you might notice that it's not exactly four gigabytes. This is due to the rounding effect; the description on the product packaging and what you actually get will be close, but not exactly the same. A megabyte, by the way, is about a million bytes; a gigabyte is about a billion bytes; and a terabyte is about a trillion bytes.

For a little comparison between these amounts, this chapter has about 7,500 words and uses about 77 kilobytes to store in a digital format. It would take about 12,987,012 copies of this chapter to fill a single-gigabyte flash drive, which is considered pretty small by today's standards. Images and sound files require a lot more space than do words, so it's possible to store a lot of word files in a modern computer. When digitizing collections, however, a photo of an item is oftentimes required, even if the item contains text (consider a photo of a book page, for instance). Knowing how much space a computer needs to store a photo, as an example, can help you determine how much storage is optimal to preserve your archival collection, as well as how large of a photo is practical for you to store, given that larger photos require more information and, thus, more storage.

As mentioned in the beginning of this chapter, bits and bytes don't float around inside a computer. They are composed of pulses of electricity, and this electricity needs physical materials to conduct the signals from one area of a computer to another. Hardware and software programs are actually needed to do something useful with all these numbers and signals. All computers need the same basic parts to do this.

◎ A Basic Computer

Every personal computer, no matter what kind or which company made it, has three basic components: hardware, software, and firmware. Just about anything that makes up a computer, short of the casing and screws that hold it together, falls into one of these three categories. Although these terms sound similar, there are definite differences among them.

Hardware is composed of the parts of a computer that can be touched; that is, they're tangible in nature. The motherboard, hard drive, monitors, mice, and keyboards—these all constitute the hardware of a computer. These parts allow the all-important electrical currents to run throughout the device. However, these items all do nothing that is of any use without software.

Software refers to the programs that run on a computer and make the hardware components actually do something. The operating system, word-processing programs, and solitaire games are all examples of software.

Firmware is a little trickier to define because it's a mixture of both hardware and software. Firmware items are physical in nature, like hardware, but have software permanently embedded into the item. ROM chips are a type of firmware. However, firmware items are not usually something that concerns an average user; they are more important to people who program and design computers.

Of these components of a basic computer, two are visible and tangible: the hardware and the firmware. The hardware, or "guts," of the majority of personal computers is hidden inside a little metal and plastic box, so many people may have no idea of what is actually in there, what it looks like, or how it works. Even if it were possible to see inside, through a clear casing, looking at the parts wouldn't lend much information about how the computer works just by observation. There aren't many moving parts, and those few moving parts are often hidden inside their own casings for the sake of safety.

For all the mystery and complexity involved, the insides of a computer comprise a limited number of items. If you've never seen the inside of a computer, opening one up can be very educational. While all personal computers are made of essentially the same parts, it's best to look at a desktop-style computer, as more compact models, such as laptops, require a lot of disassembling to see the parts, and reassembling them correctly can be difficult. A typical desktop is easy to open and to look at the inside, in most instances by simply removing a panel; that is, you don't need to take it apart to see most of the

TYPICAL COMPUTER COMPONENTS

CPU (central processing unit)

Hard drive

Motherboard

Ports

RAM (random access memory)

ROM (read-only memory)

components. If you do want to look at the inside of a real computer, back up your files, take precautions against the hazards of static electricity for the safety of the computer, and be sure that the power is off and disconnected for your own safety. Never attempt to disassemble the power supply of a computer, either; this is a box behind the power socket that connects your computer to an electrical socket. Otherwise, opening a computer is typically safe to do and, in fact, can be a good thing, as it gives you an opportunity to clean out the dust that collects inside. Consult your owner's manual for more instructions about how to safely clean out a computer to avoid harming it or yourself. If you're nervous, though, try working on an outdated or "dead" computer.

Central Processing Unit

One of the most important items in a computer is the central processing unit, or CPU. If you open a computer, this item may not be visible to you, however. This little device is typically hidden behind a fan, as the CPU gets hot and needs to be cooled.

The CPU does all the calculations, interprets all instructions for the computer, and coordinates input/output operations. When a user taps a key or clicks a mouse, the action gets processed through the CPU, which can then determine what needs to be done. For instance, if a user hits "A" on the keyboard with a word-processing program open, the keyboard sends a signal that gets processed through the CPU, which ultimately determines that what it is supposed to do is to display "A" on the computer monitor.

Everything that a computer does, all the calculations needed to do anything, is processed through the CPU. As a result of handling all those electrical pulses, the CPU heats up rapidly. The CPU usually has a fan over it to dissipate the heat and protect it from damage. You may also see a block of metal strips or prongs around the CPU that don't appear to do anything and don't seem very electronic in nature. This is a heat sink, which also helps to dissipate heat and keep the CPU cooler. It doesn't do any calculating or storage, but it serves an important function for keeping the CPU safe. You can see the CPU by removing any fans or heat sinks, but be careful and don't use a screwdriver with a magnetic head. Also don't forget to replace everything when you're finished.

The fan and the heat sink help the CPU operate, but a few other components of the computer affect CPU speed or its operation.

Clock

How fast a computer is able to process information is highly dependent on the speed of the CPU, and several aspects of the CPU affect the speed. One of these is the clock speed. The *clock* on a computer is not quite like the one that you check to see when it's time to go to lunch or when a movie will start. A computer's clock is actually a crystal which vibrates, or creates a series of pulses at an extremely high frequency. The pulses are carried to all the components of the computer, enabling it to synchronize its activities, sending information and stopping at the same intervals. It's a little like how a traffic light directs the flow of traffic. The CPU can't have two "cars" entering at the same time. The clock ensures that all data is transmitted in an orderly way.

The rate at which this crystal vibrates is represented in hertz, abbreviated to Hz. One megahertz, or MHz, is a million cycles of this crystal per second. A gigahertz, or GHz, is a billion hertz. The higher this number, the faster the computer can function. This number is also sometimes represented in MT/s, or megatransfers per second, which is 1 million bytes transferred per second over a bus (Andrews 2006).

Bus

CPUs, along with working at a certain speed regulated by the clock, can transfer certain amounts of information each time the crystal vibrates. For instance, a computer may have a 32- or 64-bit processor. This is the number of bits that can be transferred to and from the CPU simultaneously; you'll notice that these are both multiples of 8, the number of bits in a byte. The electronic lines that transfer these bits to different parts of the computer are known as *buses*. You can think of them like an actual bus, driving information to a certain destination in the machine. If a processor is 32 bit, then it can carry 32 passengers (bits) at the same time. A 64-bit processor can take 64. Older machines had smaller buses, but 32 and 64 are the common sizes now.

Front Side Bus

The front-side bus, or FSB, is sometimes mentioned with a computer's specifications. This is a particular type of bus that enables the CPU to communicate with the outside world. This bus's size is also represented in hertz, just like the clock, indicating how fast it can transmit data (Dale and Lewis 2013). The front-side bus connects the front side of the processor to the rest of the computer. Other buses are used with the CPU, such as the back-side bus, which connects the processor to the internal memory cache, and the internal bus, which enables the CPU to communicate with itself (Andrews 2006). However, the FSB is usually the one mentioned in a computer's specifications, as it has a big impact on the speed of the processor (Dale and Lewis 2013).

Cache Memory

A CPU has its own memory solely for the CPU, referred to as the *cache*. This is memory that a CPU can use to temporarily store data that has been recently processed or accessed, which makes further processing faster. For example, suppose that you were reading this book and you had to do something else for a few minutes. It would be more efficient for you to just put the book down on your desk rather than put it away. Cache memory works on a similar principle, temporarily storing data that will be needed again soon rather than storing it elsewhere in the computer and retrieving it again. The more cache memory that is available, the more information that can be stored in this manner.

Multiple CPUs

There are some terms that go along with the CPU, such as *dual core* or *quad core*. In older machines, there was a single CPU chip in the machine. However, having more than one makes the calculations required for computer function go much faster.

A speedy CPU makes processing faster and reduces the downtime that occurs when a user is waiting for a computer to finish running a program. However, a fast processor often uses more electricity and is more expensive. Look at the specifications carefully when comparing the CPU on different models; your decision may require some balance and compromise to get the optimal combination.

While the CPU does all the calculating for a computer, other essential parts are required that largely involve memory storage. The CPU is not able to communicate with these parts on its own, however. It needs something else to do this—something that allows the results of its calculations to travel throughout the machine, a way to get the information to make those calculations in the first place. That something is the motherboard: the largest circuit board in a computer.

Motherboard

The motherboard is easy to spot inside a computer. It typically looks like a large green sheet of metal, usually at the bottom or side of the computer's casing, with a variety of circuits and small plastic pieces sticking out of it. Most or all of these pieces will have something plugged into them. Everything in the computer connects to the motherboard at some point, and the motherboard is what enables communication among different parts of the computer.

However, it's likely that not all the slots will have something plugged into them when you buy a new computer. Motherboards often have room for more components than are actually installed during the manufacturing process. This can be a good thing, as it enables you to add parts to the computer, and it allows for some customization. You could therefore purchase an inexpensive machine with your budget, then upgrade it as funds allow. One of the easiest ways to upgrade a machine is to add more RAM, which is a type of memory.

RAM and ROM

RAM chips are long, rectangular objects that fit into little plastic slots on the motherboard. *RAM* stands for "random access memory." This is temporary memory in the computer, the contents of which vanish as soon as the user turns off the power. Another term for this is *volatile memory*. These chips have an important purpose in the computer. They serve as a temporary storage for the CPU, containing data until the CPU can process it. Once information has been processed by the CPU, the new information can also be stored temporarily in the RAM chips. If a person types a document in a word-processing program, for example, while that person works on the document, both the information needed to operate the program and the information about the document itself are stored in the RAM chips.

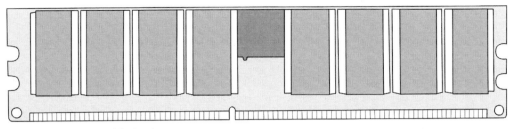

Figure 2.1. A typical RAM chip.

Unlike the CPU, in which more is not necessarily better, having more RAM has a noticeably positive effect on computer function, and more RAM is typically better up to a point. If a computer that you are considering doesn't seem to have enough RAM for your needs, find out if the RAM is expandable. Computers don't always come with as much RAM as they can actually use; that is, you may find that some slots for RAM chips inside a computer are in fact empty. You can buy more RAM chips and put them into these slots. While the computer will need to configure itself to accept new RAM and while you need to be sure that your RAM chips are compatible with your computer, installing new RAM essentially involves putting an object into a slot and is very simple. Figure 2.1 shows what a RAM chip generally looks like.

There are three types of random access memory in general. DRAM and SRAM—dynamic and static RAM, respectively—are typical for older machines. DRAM chips lose the information stored on them if they are not continually refreshed with electricity. SRAM chips don't need refreshing but are more expensive than DRAM chips.

Current computers are more likely to use SDRAM chips, or synchronous DRAM. This divides the information in the RAM chips into two memory banks. You may also see a computer advertising something called DDR SDRAM, which is similar to SDRAM but is able to transfer data in a computer twice as fast as ordinary SDRAM. This type of RAM reads data twice per cycle of the computer's clock.

The benefit of RAM memory for the computer is that the memory is changeable. What has been stored in the RAM chips can be erased, altered, or replaced. However, memory that is not changeable is also valuable; this is the kind that is present in ROM chips.

ROM stands for "read-only memory." These chips don't lose their memory once the user turns off the computer, which is essential for the function of the computer and its operating system. For instance, once you turn on a computer, the computer requires instructions about what to do next, such as how to look for the operating system software. You may have heard terms such as *BIOS*, or basic input/output system, and *POST*, or power-on self-test. These are both programs that run as soon as the user turns on the computer. The BIOS is the first program that runs when the computer starts, and it controls communications among components of the computer, such as the keyboard. The POST is a test that the computer conducts on itself to ensure that the hardware components are functioning properly. The information for these programs is stored in a ROM chip. Without this information, a computer can't do anything at all.

While an essential part of the computer, the ROM chips are typically not an aspect that you use to compare one computer to another when making a purchase. However, there is a kind of memory that can have a great influence on your decision—the hard drive memory, which is the location of long-term memory for the computer.

Hard Drive

In a computer, the RAM chips have temporary, changeable information storage, and ROM chips have permanent, nonchanging information storage. The hard drive is therefore where information is stored that must not be erased once the computer has been turned off but which needs to be able to be rewritten. For instance, if you were writing a letter and wanted to save the data, once you click the Save button, the information needed to re-create that letter is stored in the hard drive.

The hard drive in a computer looks like a plain plastic box, most likely black with a sticker that contains information about its specifications. It likely has a cord coming from the box that connects to the motherboard, enabling other parts of the computer to access the hard drive information, although some hard drives connect more directly to the motherboard. While putting the hard drive inside a box may seem inconvenient—given that a person can't see the inside of the hard drive to find out what it looks like—this setup is important for the safety of the hard drive.

A hard drive consists of a set of metal disks, or platters, which rotate at an incredibly high speed. The information on each platter is stored in concentric circles on the face of the drive, known as *tracks*. Each track is in turn divided into sectors, little sections that each contain specific information. To access these sectors, there is an actuator arm over each platter, the end of which has a read/write head. As can be guessed from the name, this head can read information and write new information onto the hard drive.

To find information, the platter spins at an extremely high rate to position the correct sector under the actuator arm. At the same time, the arm can move up and down the platter to locate the correct track and read or write information to the sector. In a way, a hard drive is like a very small, very high-tech record player. While a hard drive doesn't record information in little pits that are read by a needle and while it can record much more than sound information, the process by which an arm seeks information on the disk is somewhat similar.

The rapid speed of the hard drive platters and the movement of the arm means that a computer can find the necessary sector rapidly, making hard drives an efficient method of long-term storage. However, that there are moving parts presents a problem. For instance, one of the major reasons that the hard drive is in a case is so that the platters are protected. If they jostle and crash into one another, they can scratch one another, causing permanent damage to the data they contain. There is a good alternative option to the traditional hard drive, a solid-state drive with no moving parts. However, this type of storage has some unique problems of its own and is more expensive than a traditional hard drive.

When you purchase a computer, you should look at how large the hard drive is. Hard drive space is typically represented in gigabytes, although terabyte hard drives are becoming increasingly available. In the case of a hard drive, bigger is always better. You'll learn more about traditional hard drives as well as storage without moving parts in chapters 8 and 9, respectively.

Many parts inside a computer enable it to communicate with itself. However, this is all fairly useless if the computer is not able to communicate with the user as well—thus enter the ports.

Ports

The outside of a typical computer has some vents along the sides and back to circulate air; a slot or two for CDs or DVDs; and a number of smaller slots, holes, holes with pins, or raised areas with small holes on the front and back. These slots and raised areas are ports, which serve an important function—enabling the inside of the computer to communicate with the outside world and vice versa. Without this, computers cannot receive information from the user about what to do, and the user cannot see the results of a computer program. Peripherals are used for communication between the user and the computer, with the keyboard and mouse being the major methods of putting data and commands into the computer. The computer can in turn communicate with the user through the monitor and other output devices, such as printers. The type, number, and location of ports may be important to you when purchasing materials for your library or archiving project.

The variety of ports that a computer may have is quite large. Some ports are specialized or uncommon, and some ports have gone out of use over time. Some common ports on computers include the following:

Universal serial bus: USB ports are some of the most frequently found ports on modern computers and can enable a variety of peripherals to communicate with the computer, such as mice, printers, keyboards, cameras, and drawing tablets. Storage media, such as flash drives or external hard drives, also plug into USB ports to communicate. Devices designed for USB ports can be inserted into the port while the computer is on.

IEEE 1394: Also known as FireWire, a device in competition with the USB port that has similar functions and abilities. When the two types first came out, USB ports were less expensive to manufacture, and so they are more common today. Although both types are still in use, the two are not interchangeable. Devices designed for use with FireWire will not work in a USB port and vice versa, so it's important to know if a peripheral that you want to use requires a FireWire port or a USB port before purchasing computers or peripherals.

Video graphics array: The VGA port is used for monitors, and it connects the graphics card in the computer to the monitor. The graphics card is what controls the output that goes to the monitor. The card goes by several other names, such as *video card* or *display adapter.* This port is blue, which allows the user to match the blue end of a monitor cord to the correct port. Other ports can be used to connect a monitor to a computer, but this is a common method.

Ethernet: This port enables computers to communicate with one another in a small location, as within a library or an archive, or it can connect to a modem or router to enable communication via the Internet.

High-definition multimedia interface: The HDMI port enables audio and video communication between the computer and another device, such as a flatscreen television, which is useful if you want to use the computer to play media or make presentations.

Audio: Typical computers have ports for speakers, headphones, and microphones. These may or may not be important, depending on whether your archive includes audio or video materials.

PS/2: This port is specialized for mice and keyboards. It is round and usually color coordinated to the end of the mouse or keyboard so that the user doesn't accidentally put the wrong peripheral into the wrong port, since they're the same size. This type of port is more common on older computers, however, and modern mice and keyboards typically plug into a USB port or are wireless.

Serial: This port connects peripherals to the computer and has either 25 or 9 pins. The 25-pin version was phased out for the more convenient 9-pin version. A variety of peripherals can be used with this type of port, such as mice or external modems. These can transmit only one bit of information at a time, and so are not very common anymore, although they were used often on older machines (Miastkowski 2004).

Parallel: Parallel ports have two series of small holes rather than pins (Schmidt 2000). They are able to transfer 8 MB per second, which is far superior to a serial port but pales in comparison to a USB or FireWire port. These ports can connect to a variety of devices, such as printers or scanners, but, like serial ports, they are more common on older machines (Chen and Mills 2002).

Figure 2.2 illustrates these common ports.

Ports often require a cable that connects the port to the peripheral. To download photos from a digital camera, for instance, you need a cable that plugs into a port. On many computers, though, there is another option. Secure digital, or SD, cards are a source of memory storage for digital cameras, and some computers have a slot specifically for these cards, enabling the user to take the card out of the camera and put it into the computer so that the computer can access the photos. This eliminates the need to connect the camera itself to the computer, which can be appealing if the camera is difficult to move, as it might be if you have a permanent photography setup for digitization. Since ease of access is important to working efficiently, you may want to see where the ports are located on a computer as well.

While using cords is the typical means for a peripheral to communicate with a computer, it should be noted that some peripherals are available in a wireless format. For instance, keyboards and mice are commonly available as wireless peripherals, meaning that they are able to communicate with the computer without the need for a cord, instead using a transceiver, which not only receives signals from the device but also sends them to it. Normal peripherals draw power from the computer, but wireless peripherals require a power source external to the computer and so require batteries or charging. Not needing

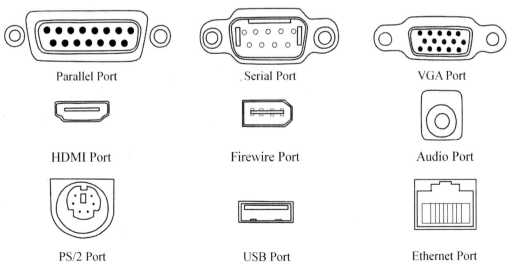

Figure 2.2. Common computer ports.

wires doesn't mean that wireless peripherals don't need ports, though—the transceiver plugs into a port in the computer.

Many ports will be at the back of the computer, but some may be at the front. Take the location of these ports into consideration—USB ports on the front of a computer can be convenient if you plan on using flash memory to transfer information, for instance. Another feature on the outside is a CD drive, and you may have more than one on a single computer. Floppy drives are another possible feature, but these are uncommon on new computers and are typically found only on custom computers. If you have information on floppy disks that need converting to another format, you may want a custom computer or a peripheral that can read floppies.

Key Points

- Modern computers use the binary system for calculation. Any number in the decimal system, which is what people normally use for everyday tasks, can be represented with a series of ones and zeroes in the binary system. All functions of a computer are simply a set of calculations or numerical values.
- All computers have the same basic, essential parts—such as the central processing unit, buses, motherboard, memory chips and hard drives, ports, and peripherals for communication.
- Choosing the optimal computer for your archiving project depends on a number of factors, such as what type of equipment you plan to use, what kind of software you want to run, and how much money you have in your budget.

Deciding what kind of computer is best suited for your archiving project is only the beginning of the decisions that need to be made to ensure that your project goes smoothly. Whether you are archiving born-digital materials or digitizing nondigital materials, you'll most likely need to know about image formats. In the next chapter, you'll learn how computers store image data, what the different common formats for images are, and which ones are best suited for digital archiving. Images are stored in different ways according to their formats, and some lend themselves better to archiving than others.

References

Andrews, Jean. 2006. *A+ Guide to Managing and Maintaining Your PC.* 6th ed. Boston: Course Technology.

Chen, Li, and Joyce White Mills. 2002. "What's under Your PC's 'Hood': A Primer for Today's Machines." *Computers in Libraries* 22 (7): 14.

Dale, Nell, and John Lewis. 2013. *Computer Science Illuminated.* 5th ed. Burlington, MA: Jones & Bartlett Learning.

Miastkowski, Stan. 2004. "No More Cable Confusion." *PC World* 22 (8): 158.

Schmidt, Cherry A. 2000. *The Complete Computer Repair Textbook.* 2nd ed. El Granada, CA: Scott/Jones.

Storing Images

NOW THAT YOU HAVE AN IDEA of how computers work, the next step is to learn how this information has practical relevance to your archive. All files are stored in the form of bits and bytes of information, using binary encoding. Exactly how a computer uses this to encode data varies somewhat, depending on what kind of data you want to store. Image files are one of the many kinds of data that you may need to archive.

People generally like pictures and photographs. They can be attractive and are often helpful toward understanding a variety of information. Chances are good that you'll need to deal with images at some point with your archive, regardless of what kind of information you need to store.

It's in the instincts of an archivist to save every bit of information possible, and while it is possible to save a lot of information digitally, it's impractical to store everything. Learning more about how computers store and interpret images will help you decide how to achieve a compromise—storing as much information as you possibly can without making it impossible to store the information in a practical way. The more information that you store, the more space you require for storage. While it's not quite the same, the principle is similar to how physical items work; you can keep only so much data on a storage device, and large data files take longer for a computer to retrieve and process than do small ones.

Each type of data is stored a little differently than the next. In the case of data for images, the information is stored in a series of small, finite amounts that form a picture when viewed together.

Although the real world is made up of tiny particles known as atoms, people don't see the world this way. Humans can't distinguish atoms, since they are far too small, but the human brain does have the ability to see light and color from many atoms together to perceive an entire object. The real world is a continuum of information, with infinite variations in color and light.

Computers aren't like humans, though. Computers don't like continuums. Continuums can't be saved in a file with an intrinsically limited size. Computers instead work with small, distinguishable pieces of data, stored as bits and bytes. So, rather than trying to preserve information about the entire world, a computer stores tiny bits of data that form meaningful information when put together. For images, this little bit of data is the pixel, which stands for "picture element."

Talking about pixels can get a little confusing because the term *pixel* can mean slightly different things when referring to different topics. When talking about an image file, a pixel is the smallest amount of information that a computer can store about an image. The more pixels, the bigger the image, and the more information that is available to the user about it.

Resolution refers to the number of pixels that an image has. As an example, imagine that you have two identical images of a mountain. They are the exact same image, but the second one has a higher resolution with more pixels. The second image will be larger from the computer's perspective, have a bigger file size, and have more information about that mountain. Details that can't be distinguished on the first photo—individual trees, for example—might be able to be seen on the second photo because there is more information available.

Pixels can also be used to describe a monitor's size and its resolution. As you might already know, the images on televisions and computer screens are made up of many tiny bits of light arranged in a grid. It's a little like a mosaic but made of light instead of tiles. One of these tiny bits of light is a single pixel. Pixels take advantage of how the human

---

USEFUL TERMS FOR VISUAL DATA

Color depth, bit depth: the number of bits used to store a color

Compression: removing unnecessary information to make a file smaller

Compression ratio: the ratio between the size of the full and compressed images

High color: color encoding that uses 16 bits per pixel

Lossless compression: compression that loses none of the original data

Lossy compression: compression that discards some of the original data

Pixel: the smallest amount of data for an image

Resolution: the number of pixels in an image

True color: color encoding that uses 24 or 32 bits per pixel

brain works—humans are able to take shortcuts, to fill in blanks or make abbreviations in their minds. So, when a person looks at an image on a television that is composed of many tiny dots, he or she can interpret the picture, not as those many dots, but as a whole image to see what it is supposed to represent.

When scanning images, you may see terms such as *ppi* and *dpi*, which stand for "pixels per inch" and "dots per inch," respectively. These are measurements of the image's resolution, as mentioned earlier. Again, the resolution of a digital image refers to how many pixels there are in an image—that is, the density of the pixels. Although this is usually measured in pixels per inch, it is possible to measure it in other ways, such as pixels per centimeter. The higher the resolution of an image, the higher the quality, the clearer the image, and the more information there is available about it. While dpi and ppi are both used as measurements of resolution, ppi is more accurate in terms of preserving images; dpi generally relates to the capabilities of a printer (Bioinformatics and Research Computing 2008).

Although they are sometimes used interchangeably when speaking of image resolution, dpi and ppi are not really interchangeable, and using them interchangeably is not technically correct. If you have a choice, it's better to work with ppi as a measurement for preserving your images, for the sake of simplicity. Note that the higher the resolution, the more data is needed to store the information for the image; that is, there are more pixels. Thus, information needs to be stored for all those extra pixels.

For your archive, once you've determined how much storage you have available and what kind of information needs to be stored, it's best to use the same resolution or to have a standard for all images for the sake of consistency. Choosing the optimal resolution is a bit of a balancing act, as a higher resolution is better and captures more information, but a resolution that is too high results in an image that is extremely large and cumbersome to store, retrieve, and view. The Library of Congress's (2007) American Memory Project uses 300- to 400-ppi resolution, depending on the size of the item and how necessary it is to have high resolution. You can use a higher resolution if you think that your archive would benefit from it. For instance, you might be specializing in archiving images; however, you probably don't want to use a lower resolution than this. While a number of factors are involved with choosing your ideal scanning resolution, the size of an image file depends in part on how much information is needed to store the colors in that image.

⑥ Colors

As discussed in the previous chapter, computers encode information using bits. A bit essentially reduces things to a yes/no situation, since each bit can be either a one or a zero. Color information can be encoded using bits, too. If there is one bit available for colors, then a computer can display two colors because a bit has two choices—for instance, black and white. A zero could mean black, and a one could mean white. In many cases, as in the case of displaying text, black and white is perfectly acceptable, and a computer can display quite a bit of information using only two colors.

The world isn't in black and white, though. To replicate the real world, more bits are needed to assign more colors. As an example, if there are two bits, then there are four possible combinations for bit values. A programmer could assign a color to each one of these bit values, and the computer would therefore display the colors that the programmer assigned when interpreting an image. This kind of situation might look like this:

Bit value	Displayed color
00	black
01	cyan
10	magenta
11	yellow

The more bits that are used to encode colors, the more possible colors that a computer can display, assuming that the monitor is able to display the colors as well, although this isn't much of a problem in modern times. This quality is known as the *color depth* or *bit depth*, and it refers to how many bits are being used and how many possible colors can be displayed. Eight bits allow for 256 total bit combinations, which can therefore represent 256 different colors. Use of eight bits and 256 colors was common in computers in the past. This number of colors is adequate to display images in a fairly faithful manner, but it doesn't come close to the variety of colors available in the real world.

Modern computers can use quite a few more bits for each pixel. There is 16-bit color, called *high color*, which allows for 65,000 colors. The first five bits are for red, the next six for green, and the last five for blue (Orr 2003). The extra bit for green is due to humans being more sensitive to green light than to red or blue light, and so the extra bit allows for more shades of green. That makes an image appear to be more true to life to the human viewer (Cambridge in Color 2013). While this produces a sufficient number of colors for many images, there is an even higher level of color for computers, called *true color*.

True color can have either 24 or 32 bits per pixel. Using 24 bits per pixel allows for around 16 million possible colors. Although no computer can quite replicate the real world, true color comes pretty close, and humans can't really tell the difference. With 24 bits, each color—red, green, and blue, in that order—gets eight bits, or a full byte. It works the same way with the 32-bit version, but the last eight bits are for controlling transparency, or an area that is clear or has no color. This is important for computer-generated graphics, particularly those intended for use online.

Using 24 bits per pixel has some serious disadvantages, though, notably with file size. With 24 bits, a computer could encode the information for three alphabet letters (an entire word in some cases, such as *cat* or *dog*), or those same 24 bits could store the information for one tiny dot of color in a picture, a pixel. This quickly becomes cumbersome and takes up a lot of storage space. Fortunately, programmers have come up with some ways to make image files a little smaller.

Compression

There's a saying that "a picture is worth a thousand words." With digital images, this is true in a literal sense; image files are big, and a great deal of text can be stored in the same amount of space as a single photograph. With 24 bits of information needed for every pixel in an image that uses true color, images can become very large, very quickly. For example, the digital version of this chapter requires about 68 KB of data to store. In contrast, figure 3.1, found later in this chapter, uses 23,621 KB of data.

So, what is compression? It's possible for a computer to eliminate redundant information about an image and still display it correctly from the information that is retained. This is known as *compression*. Compressed files still have the necessary information to reproduce a file, but they don't need as many bits as the full file and thus need less space to store. There are different methods of compression, depending on the file type. There are two general types of compression: lossless and lossy.

With lossless compression, the computer looks for patterns or redundancies in an image. For instance, it may detect that a large block of plain black pixels in the image. Rather than save the data for each pixel, it instead saves a mathematical code, or an algorithm, that lets the computer know what was in the original. When a person wants to look at the image, then a decompression algorithm decodes this information and displays the correct pixels on the monitor. As a simple example, suppose that a person was grocery shopping and wanted three cans of soup. Rather than write "can of soup" on the grocery list three times, that person could write "can of soup × 3" or "3 cans of soup." Both phrases have the same information and are interpreted in the same way, but the second method saves two lines of space. This method of compression is known as *lossless* because even though the information is compressed, there is no loss of information, and the displayed image is exactly like the original.

Lossy compression methods can further compress files. These methods are a little less precise in that they essentially abbreviate the pixels in an image, removing information that's not necessary for a human to understand the overall image, such as minute color variations. If the compression is low or an image hasn't been compressed repeatedly, the viewer might never notice that an image has been compressed. However, because information is lost during compression, the image essentially becomes less accurate and less true to the original every time that it is compressed. For archiving, lossless compression is more desirable. Understanding the difference between lossy and lossless compression will help you choose the best balance between saving file space and having accurate information preserved in your archive. However, a few other terms are useful to know when it comes to compressing files.

The term *compression ratio* refers to the ratio of the full-size image to the size of the compressed image in regard to how much data is required to store the image. The larger the difference between the first and second numbers in a compression ratio, the smaller the compressed image is in comparison to the full-sized image. So, if an image had a compression ratio of 1:10, the compressed image is 10 times smaller than the original, and if an image had a compression ratio of 1:32, then the second image is 32 times smaller.

The term *nonadaptive* means that the software compresses every image in the same way using the same method. *Adaptive* therefore refers to software compressing based on the unique characteristics of an image. Compression can be symmetric or asymmetric. This is important for images viewed online. If a compression method is symmetric, then compression and decompression of an image both take the same amount of time and work for a computer. If a method is asymmetric, then decompressing an image is much faster than compressing it. This makes for faster loading when patrons want to see an image that your archive might offer online (Orr 2003).

Many options are available when it comes to compression, and different types of file formats offer different possible methods. The type of compression that a particular file format uses can make a difference in which one you find most suitable for your archive.

When looking at an image file, you might notice some letters at the end that you did not type when naming the file, such as JPG or PNG. These are called *file extensions*. Their function is to let the computer know how the information is encoded. Without the extension, a computer isn't able to figure out what it should do with the data. While a computer uses different combinations of bits to encode color data, it also needs information about the order of those bits so that the colors can be displayed correctly to the user. There's a little more to saving an image than just encoding color.

There are quite a few different formats for images, which might seem a little strange. Why isn't there one universal format for every kind of image data? Wouldn't that make things easier for everyone—computer designers, users, and the computers themselves? It would no longer be necessary to convert formats, and any image program on any computer would be able to open any kind of image, since they're all in the same format. Not every type of software can open every type of image file.

It's true that a universal format would make things easier. However, image formats have different virtues that make them appealing for different purposes—and different drawbacks that make them unappealing for other uses. For your archive, some of these formats may have features that seem more useful to you than others. For the purpose of archiving, formats that encode a lot of information are likely to be the most desirable. However, if you need images that can be transferred over the Internet, you might want to consider a different format. Most image formats have potential uses for you, and so each should be considered carefully. You may also want to save the same item in multiple formats to gain the virtues of different file types; for instance, you might use a file type with a lot of information for storage but offer a type that creates a smaller file to patrons viewing your collection online.

BMP

A bitmap file, or BMP, is one of the more basic file types, and it works in a simple manner: the information for the color of each pixel is encoded from left to right and top to bottom. The BMP format has some virtues from the perspective of archiving in that it is fairly old and well established and BMP files can be opened with a variety of programs. However, BMP files are not as suited for compression as some other file types, nor are they well suited for transmission over the Internet.

COMMON IMAGE FILE FORMATS

BMP: bitmap file

GIF: graphics interchange format

JPEG, JPG: Joint Photographic Experts Group format

PNG: portable network graphics

SVG: scalable vector graphics

TIFF, TIF: tagged image format

TIFF

TIFF, or tagged image file format, has the ability to be either lossless or lossy, although it's typically used for lossless storage. TIFF files are usually not compressed, and they contain a lot of information; thus, they are often quite large. For the purpose of archiving, though, more is often better, and so a TIFF format can have a lot of appeal. The TIFF format is one of the preferred formats for images for the Library of Congress's (2013) collections, and it is one of the best choices for digital image storage. However, TIFF is not a good format for displaying images online, since they take a long time to download and most web browsers can't display TIFF files at all; as such, this is not a useful choice for sharing your collection online.

GIF

The graphics interchange format, or GIF, has a rather unusual method of storing color compared to other formats. A GIF image is limited to 256 colors, but it doesn't have to be the same set of 256 colors for each GIF image; each image can use 256 colors from 16 million possible colors. If a person saves an image as a GIF, the program that creates the GIF uses algorithms to determine the optimal colors needed to save the image as faithfully to the original as possible (Matthews 2013). This is a technique known as *indexed color* (Dale and Lewis 2013). GIF images are also capable of having transparent backgrounds, whereas some other formats aren't able to store information for transparent or clear pixels.

Since they only use 256 colors, GIF images need only a few bits per pixel to represent all 256 colors. This makes GIF images naturally small. GIF can also compress large areas of uniform color by indicating that there are a certain number of pixels with the same color, rather than saving the information for each individual pixel (Matthews 2013).

GIF images work best in situations in which there are only a few colors, such as line art, logos, or grayscale images, and do poorly for full-color photographs. They can also be used effectively for the web. Because less information is needed for the image, it takes less time for the image to load. As another bonus, GIF images can be interlaced or noninterlaced. This feature is designed for web use in particular. If an image is interlaced, then it can load in stages. The lowest-resolution image loads first, so the viewer is able to get an idea of what the final image will look like. The picture then reloads in increasing stages of resolution until the highest resolution is achieved. If it is noninterlaced, then it loads in stages from the top of the image down. Making an image interlaced increases the file size (Lake and Bean 2008).

While this format is considered acceptable by the Library of Congress for storing images, it's likely to be of best use to you if it is the original format of an image, if you are storing web pages, or if you are making your collection available over the web due to the color limitations; that is, it won't faithfully reproduce a scan of a complex full-color photo or similar image (Library of Congress 2013).

PNG

A portable network graphics, or PNG, file is another image type designed for use on the Internet. It was designed to improve on the GIF format, offering more colors and higher compression (Dale and Lewis 2013). PNG files are smaller than GIF files and allow for true color, whereas GIF files are limited to 256 colors. PNG files are compressed according to patterns within the image. This compression is lossless, which makes it a desirable format for displaying images on the web, even complex images such as full-color photographs. Like GIFs, PNGs can have transparent backgrounds.

PNGs do have a few drawbacks. GIF images can be animated, whereas PNGs cannot; PNGs are also not supported in as many software programs as GIFs (Dale and Lewis 2013). Furthermore, PNG files are not supported in older web browsers, although it is not an issue in new ones. For archiving, PNGs are preferable to GIFs according to the Library of Congress (2013).

JPEG

JPEG, also known as a JPG, stands for Joint Photographic Experts Group. This is a commonly used file format. Rather than storing information pixel by pixel, a JPEG file takes averages of a range of colors to form the image. This is handy from the perspective of storage, since JPEG files can be highly compressed. JPEG images use lossy compression, and the amount of compression can be controlled. However, because JPEGs lose information after each edit and save, their quality can become poorer over time. JPEGs are a good choice for photographs but aren't a good choice for any images with large patches of uniform color or images with sharp, precise lines. For instance, it wouldn't be a good choice for a simple logo.

JPEGs are a good choice for complex images that are intended for use online, such as photographs. JPEG files have a feature similar to GIF's interlaced images. For a JPEG, this is known as *progressive encoding*, and it allows an image to be loaded in stages on a web page. Images without this feature have what is known as *standard encoding* (Lake and Bean 2008).

SVG

An SVG, or scalable vector graphics, file is much less commonly used than the other file types. The other image formats discussed so far are all what are known as *raster graphics*. This means that the information for the image is stored pixel by pixel, encoding the color and number of each pixel. An image doesn't have to be stored that way, though. Instead, an image can be stored on the basis of its shape. This is known as a *vector graphic*.

If you've ever tried to make a standard photograph very large or very small, you'll notice that there are some problems. Shrinking an image involves essentially taking averages of all the pixel color values. Expanding the image can lead to a "pixely" look. An image file can't create more information than what is available, so it creates an estimate, which leads to the pixely look.

A vector graphic is saved by its shape rather than by individual pixels. This has one major benefit—scalability. A vector graphic looks exactly the same regardless of how big or, up to a point, how small it is. There are a few ways to store vector graphics, but the SVG format is the preferred format for the Library of Congress (2013). Vector graphics can also be converted into a raster image. This process is known as *rasterizing*.

Native Formats

The formats listed here are general image formats. Many programs are able to read these files and display the images back to the user. However, it's important to note that many image files are able to be read only by the software that created the file or by specific types of software. If you don't have the right software, then you can't see the image that is stored with such a format. For instance, the extension PSD is the extension for a file created by the photo-editing program Photoshop. A general program can't read the information in this file; only programs that are able to open Photoshop files can read the information contained in the file (many painting or photo-editing programs can).

A format that is specific to a program like this is known as a *native format*. There are many instances in which you might need to work with native formats—when using editing software, for instance. The need to work with a native format is an issue that may arise when working with digital photography in particular, and many cameras have their own file formats used for capturing images. This can also be referred to as a "raw" format. These formats often have more data than the format to which they are converted, which is another important consideration to keep in mind (London and Stone 2012). Digital negative, or DNG, files are a type of raw format sometimes used with cameras that is preferred by the Library of Congress (2013).

Every file type has potential uses as well as drawbacks. Table 3.1 summarizes the features of the image file types discussed so far.

Determining the optimal format for your collection is not the only matter that must be considered when creating your archive. Just because an image is saved at the optimal resolution with the best format for your archive doesn't mean that the quality is inherently good. In some instances, images can benefit from adjustment.

◎ Editing Images

If you have a physical format for an image, such as a photo or a painting, it needs to be copied with a scanner or a camera to convert it to a digital format. After capturing images, you may want to adjust the quality of the image. For instance, if you scanned a 100-year-old

Table 3.1. Benefits and Drawbacks of Image Formats

FILE TYPE	BENEFITS	DRAWBACKS
BMP	Usable with a variety of programs	Low compressibility
TIFF	Stores a lot of information, has lossless compression, preferred by the Library of Congress	Creates large files
GIF	Small files, good for web pages and sending information over the web, can be used for animations and images with transparent backgrounds, can load on a web page in stages, lossless compression	Limited colors
PNG	Appropriate for the web, lossless compression, more colors available than a GIF	Cannot be animated like a GIF, not supported in as many programs as GIFs
JPEG	Usable with a variety of programs, compression can be controlled, good for photos on the web, can load on a web page in stages	Lossy compression, loses noticeable amounts of information after repeated saves
SVG	Useful for storing vector graphics, can be rasterized	Usefulness is limited to vector graphics
Native formats	Often have a lot of information about an image	Limited by the types of programs that can open the file

photo of the inside of an office and there wasn't enough light available to get a good photo in the first place, it's possible with modern technology to get a clearer image from a muddy one by digitally altering the contrast. It's important to use methods that don't permanently alter or remove information, however.

Many photo-editing programs have something called a *histogram*. This may not be labeled as such in the program, so you may need to browse around your particular program to look for this option. A histogram looks like a tiny graph.

As mentioned earlier, 8 bits can produce 256 colors. When a computer is using true color, each color channel—red, green, and blue—gets 8 bits for color. This means that each color can have 256 different levels of intensity, essentially ranging from very dark to very light. A histogram shows these levels. Histograms can also display the general range of darks and lights in an image, which is particularly handy for black-and-white images.

In a histogram, pure black is represented by a value of 0, and pure white is 255. A program with a histogram gives a person the ability to adjust these values in an image. As an example, suppose that the aforementioned office picture is in grayscale. If an image's histogram shows that there are no white values, this indicates that the image has a lot of grays but no strong white points. There are usually some arrows beneath a histogram that allow the user to manually adjust it. If a person moves the arrow to where the histogram levels start, then the brightest grays present in the current photo will become white. This is a good way to get better contrast, which both improves the aesthetics of a photo and makes it easier for the user to interpret a photo; it also offers a little more control than the more common brightness/contrast adjustment option. This method doesn't lose information from the image file, but it does change the file so that it doesn't look exactly like the original. Figure 3.1 shows a grayscale photo with its histogram, as well as the same photo adjusted for higher contrast.

Color photos sometimes have histograms for each color: red, green, and blue. These show the amounts of each color in the photo, and adjusting them will change that amount, making it more or less intense. This may be of use to you in some situations; for instance, if you find that your scanner captures a particular color poorly, you can adjust things to be more true to the original image. The equipment that you use can have a large impact on the quality or faithfulness of the images that you capture and store.

⊚ Key Points

- Image files require a lot of space to store all the information needed to save and reproduce an image. The more colors that are available in an image, the more space that is needed for storage.
- For archiving, choose a resolution for your collection that is high enough to be useful but not so high that it's difficult to store and retrieve images in a practical manner.
- Numerous file types are available for images, all of which have different practical uses for an archive.
- Along with choosing color, resolution, and file type, it's possible to adjust images to make them clearer or more faithful to the original image.

Figure 3.1. Using a histogram.

In the following chapter, you will learn how computers store text and what file types are available for text storage. Because archiving text sometimes involves capturing images of printed text, there is some overlap between storing images and storing text. In addition, you will learn why computers sometimes have difficulty "reading" text, as your patrons will likely be interested in searchable text.

References

Bioinformatics and Research Computing. 2008. "Resolution." http://jura.wi.mit.edu/bio/graphics/scanning/resolution.php.

Cambridge in Color. 2013. "Digital Camera Sensors." http://www.cambridgeincolour.com/tutorials/camera-sensors.htm.

Dale, Nell, and John Lewis. 2013. *Computer Science Illuminated.* 5th ed. Burlington, MA: Jones & Bartlett Learning.

Lake, Susan, and Karen Bean. 2008. *The Business of Technology: Digital Multimedia.* 2nd ed. Mason, OH: South-Western Cengage Learning.

Library of Congress. 2007. "The Library of Congress Technical Standards for Digital Conversion of Text and Graphic Materials." http://memory.loc.gov/ammem/about/techStandards.pdf.

———. 2013. "Still Image: Preferences in Summary." http://www.digitalpreservation.gov/formats/content/still_preferences.shtml.

London, Barbara, and Jim Stone. 2012. *A Short Course in Digital Photography.* 2nd ed. Upper Saddle River, NJ: Prentice Hall PTR.

Matthews, Rick. 2013. "Digital Image File Types Explained." http://users.wfu.edu/matthews/misc/graphics/formats/formats.html.

Orr, Genevieve. 2003. "Image File Formats." http://www.willamette.edu/~gorr/classes/GeneralGraphics/imageFormats/index.htm.

Storing Text

IMAGES ARE LIKELY TO BE AN IMPORTANT PART of your archive, but they're only part of the information that you might want to store. If you want to store books or manuscripts, then this is text information, which must be handled slightly differently. Text information for your digital archive will essentially fall into two categories: text information in the form of a scan or a digital photo of a printed text item, such as a book, and text information that was "born digital" and whose original format is an electronic text file. While understanding how text files are stored is somewhat simpler than understanding the methods for image files, choosing an appropriate file format to store your text information is somewhat less clear-cut and a little more complex than selecting a format for an image.

Encoding Text

Just like any other kind of data, text data is encoded with bits. Rather than colors, as in image files, the bits represent characters, like the letters in the alphabet. One bit has the possibility to represent two characters, with a 0 standing for one letter and a 1 standing for another. That's not particularly helpful. More bits are needed to encode more letters to encompass the entire alphabet.

Whenever you type on a keyboard, each little key is sending an electrical signal to the computer. You're communicating that you want the particular key to activate a command in the computer. In the case of a word-processing program, the key press is an instruction to display a letter or a character. The computer decodes the electrical signal generated by the key and converts it to a binary sequence, which is then stored and displayed back to you on the screen.

When images are encoded for color, there's a basic method to how the bits are encoded that's pretty logical. In true color, there are three sequences of eight bits. Each bit sequence tells the computer how much red, green, or blue there is in a pixel, with 0 being none of the color and 256 being the greatest possible amount of that color. For example, 256 red and 0 blue and green would be pure red, while 150 red and blue and 0 green would be purple. It's fairly logical, and so all computers can easily interpret color information in the same way.

Determining how many bits and what sequence of numbers represents each letter in a text file, however, is essentially arbitrary. Any combination of zeroes and ones could represent a letter. This leads to some compatibility problems among systems in terms of encoding letters in binary.

In the past, there have been numerous ways to encode characters, called *character sets.* However, if different computer and software manufacturers use different methods of encoding text characters, then files for text information are incompatible among computers and among software programs. One software program will not be able to determine what the characters mean from another program, or it will display characters incorrectly. For example, if the letter *A* is coded as 001001 for one computer and 100100 for another, then word-processing files created with one computer can't be interpreted correctly by the other. You can't share the information, and you're limited to which kinds of computers your files will work with.

In 1960, there were at least 60 character sets in use, 9 of which were in use by IBM's computers alone. Because the ideal situation is to use formats for digital information that can be opened with a variety of software programs, this situation would be a nightmare for archivists. To avoid problems like this, computer manufacturers eventually agreed to use some particular character sets for text to increase compatibility (Dale and Lewis 2013).

One of the first standard character sets was the ASCII set, or the American Standard Code for Information Interchange, which is intended for use by personal computers. Another standard set, EBCDIC, or the Extended Binary Coded Decimal Interchange Code, is intended for use by larger computers, such as servers and mainframes. The two do not overlap as far as encoding characters goes. For instance, in ASCII, the letter *A* is represented by the sequence 01000001, while *A* in EBCDIC is 11000001 (Fuller and Larson 2008).

The ASCII set originally used seven bits to represent each character, with an eighth bit used as a "check" bit to check for accuracy as the data was transmitted through the computer; this allowed for 128 characters total. This encodes all the letters of the alphabet for English (lower- and uppercase), numbers, and basic punctuation. Having separate sequences for upper- and lowercase is necessary because a computer doesn't perceive upper- and lowercase letters as being the same. While a person could read *T* and *t* as being the same letter, a computer doesn't distinguish this. The bit combinations for these two letters are completely different, depending on whether they are capitalized or not (Dale and Lewis 2013).

A later version—the Latin-1 Extended ASCII set—used all eight bits and had 256 characters. This allowed for some accented characters and extra symbols. As with capital and lowercase letters, computers are not able to tell that a normal letter is essentially the same as one with an accent; they are composed of two entirely different sets of bits (Dale and Lewis 2013).

There's a problem with using only eight bits and 256 characters, though. It works just fine for words in English and other languages that use the same alphabet. However, it doesn't work well for every language. More characters are needed to represent all the languages of the world. The Unicode character set is designed to address this problem. Unicode uses 16 bits per character rather than 8, allowing for 65,536 possibilities. This set includes characters in languages other than English and a wider variety of symbols (Fuller and Larson 2008). This system can also use more than 16 bits if needed for a character, so it's a flexible method of encoding text data (Dale and Lewis 2013). For convenience, the Latin-1 ASCII set is encoded in the same way in the Unicode set; that is, the first 256 character codes in Unicode are encoded exactly the same way as the corresponding characters in the ASCII character set. This makes the two sets compatible from a programming perspective (Fuller and Larson 2008).

With this level of compatibility between computers and software programs, you might suppose that choosing file formats for storing text is incredibly simple. Unfortunately, this is not the case at all. In some ways, deciding how to store text can be even more challenging than determining how to store images.

◎ Text Formats

Storing text can be a complicated process for an archive. In essence, there are two types of text that your archive might need to store. The first kind is a text file: text information that has been encoded by a computer and is born digital. The second is text that originally had a physical format. Even though it is text from the user's perspective, it can't necessarily be stored as a text file. Instead, it needs to be treated like an image.

COMMON TEXT FILE EXTENSIONS

DOC, DOCX: Microsoft Word documents (DOC is the older version)

HTML: hypertext markup language file

ODT: open document text

PDF: portable document format

RTF: rich text format

TXT: plain text file

WPD: WordPerfect document

WPS: Microsoft Works document

XML: extensible markup language file

Text File Formats

There are a number of formats for text files, and choosing an appropriate format can be a tricky process. Many formats and extensions for text files are proprietary and belong to a specific software company. For instance, the extension DOCX indicates a file created with the software program Microsoft Word. A proprietary file like this is typically compatible only with the program that created it; that is, another copy of the program is able to open a file with this extension, so you can't use just any word-processing program to open a DOCX file. It must be opened with Microsoft Word or another program that is specifically designed to open this file format. This is a little like using a native format for photos, as discussed in the previous chapter.

To make things even more complicated, files created by one version of a particular type of software might not be compatible with newer or older versions of the same software. For instance, older versions of Microsoft Word created files with a DOC extension. New versions of the program are still able to open these, but older versions can't open the new DOCX files without a converter.

These are undesirable qualities for archiving, since it's best, whenever possible, to avoid proprietary formats. Not only do proprietary formats make it difficult to share information with patrons or other archives, but they make the files more vulnerable to becoming obsolete due to the lack of necessary software. Companies that create software programs can go out of business, making any file that used their particular format useless and unable to be opened and read. An archiving format must be able to withstand these kinds of setbacks. If you want to archive a digital text file, you may need to convert it into a format that is more general. However, documents can look different in different file formats, so if preserving the original look and feel of a document is important, then you need to choose a file format that is capable of the appropriate formatting. There are a couple of file formats for text that are more general and not proprietary and thus more appealing for archiving.

Plain Text

Plain text is a format that any word processor can open. While several types of file formats use plain text, the basic file extension for a plain text format is TXT, which is

---

TEXT FILE FORMATS FOR ARCHIVING

HTML: hypertext markup language

ODF: open document format

OTF: open text format

PDF: portable document format

RTF: rich text

TXT: plain text

XML: extensible markup language

---

easy to remember because it sounds just like the word *text*. This is a format with a lot of appeal because variety of programs can open it. This removes all the problems caused by using proprietary software and protects the file from obsolescence due to software problems. When you save your file in a word-processing program, the program usually has a "default" format that it automatically saves to. However, you typically also have several options other than the default that you can choose, including TXT files. The program Notepad, as an example, creates files with this extension as its default. The previously mentioned Microsoft Word uses the DOCX format as its default setting but can have its information saved as TXT files, too.

This file type has some serious limitations, however. There is little formatting available with plain text files, nothing beyond using simple tabs or a return to designate paragraphs. There are no variations in font style or size, no tables, and no ability for images or other multimedia elements to be inserted into the file. These kinds of files are useful for pure text but can't preserve the original look and format of a document unless that document was already in this format. There are some ways in which plain text can be used with formatting, however (discussed shortly).

Rich Text

Rich text format files, which have the extension RTF, are simple and can be opened with a variety of programs, just like TXT files. They can have some formatting, such as changes in font style, size, and color. The program WordPad makes RTF files as its default setting. However, not every program can open these types of files, and they are still somewhat limited in the formatting options available. There is another format available that is capable of much more formatting and a wider variety of information, however.

Open Document Format

The open document format, or ODF, became the International Organization for Standardization's (ISO's) international standard format in 2006. ODF actually refers to several types of useful documents. The extension ODS is for spreadsheets, ODP for presentations (a generic term for the program PowerPoint), and ODT for word-processing documents (ODT stands for "open document text").

An ODT document has formatting capabilities like the somewhat more familiar DOCX format, but it has a notable difference in that it is not proprietary. This is an open-source format, which means that it does not belong to a particular software company and is not dependent on a single company for software appropriate to open an ODT file. The open-source software Apache OpenOffice creates this file format as its default. This software is freely available online (Apache Software Foundation 2013). Many other programs are capable of creating this file format, however, including Microsoft Word. The ODT format is one preferred by the Library of Congress for text storage. If you have text files that are originally in a proprietary format and have formatting that needs to be encoded, you can convert the file to the ODT format instead, making it more suitable for archiving (Library of Congress 2013d). While ODT files are good for storing text that has formatting, it's also possible to incorporate formatting into plain text files but in a roundabout way. HTML, for instance, is written in plain text but displays formatting when viewed with browser software. Plain text, when used for this purpose, can also contain metadata.

Hypertext markup language, or HTML, is a language designed for the purpose of creating web pages and sharing information among computers online. HTML documents have a similar advantage to TXT and RTF files in that many software programs known as *web browsers* can access the information in an HTML document, and likewise, many software programs can create HTML documents. HTML is not dependent on a particular company staying in business. Internet Explorer, Google Chrome, and Firefox are some commonly used browsers, but there are many others available to use.

If you've ever browsed the Internet, you've downloaded a web page. Typical web pages have attractive visual elements, such as buttons, pictures, and background colors, or they might have unusual fonts. All of the information for those fonts and colors is encoded in an HTML document. Web designers use HTML to create, or code, web pages, and their coding is then interpreted by the browser. Web pages are created in a word-processing program, not in a browser, and HTML documents contain only text, regardless of what nice pictures might be visible in the browser. The browser is like a translator between the HTML document and the person who wants to see the information contained in the document—that is, the browser turns what would be incomprehensible text into something that makes sense for the user.

An HTML document does not show any nice colors or anything else. Outside a browser, an HTML document is just like a plain text document—no formatting or special fonts whatsoever. An HTML document viewed in a word-processing program and not in a browser can look a little odd. To see what this is like, go to a web page, right-click in an empty space, and select "view source" or "view page source" (on browsers for Macintosh computers with single-button mice, this is a little more complex and involves going through the navigation bar for the option to view the page this way). This will show the plain text file for a web page. You'll see any text that was on the page, but you'll also see all kinds of words and symbols around the text that don't necessarily make sense. These are the instructions for the browser. Figure 4.1 shows a simple web page both as it's seen in plain text and as it's seen in a browser, Firefox.

The creator of an HTML document uses different sequences of text that act as instructions to the browser and let it know how the document should be displayed. As an example, if a person creating a web document puts the characters <p> and </p> around some text, the browser will interpret all the text between the characters as a paragraph. The <p> sequence is known as a tag, in this instance, a *p* tag; </p> is a closing *p* tag. The purpose of a closing tag is to let the browser know when a certain type of formatting ends, although this is not necessary with all types of tags. As another example, the tags <i> and </i> tell the browser that the word in between should be in italics. The tag <i> is for italics. So, it's not necessary for the original HTML document to have any formatting of any kind—the browser takes the information encoded in the document and displays it in the way that the designer instructs. The text doesn't need to be in italics in the original document. The browser will convert the text to italics based on the tags. Any kind of word-processing program can make an HTML document. Because only plain text is needed, no formatting is required for proper display.

There are many ways to format a document with HTML, with a variety of tags, or instructions for the browser regarding formatting and content. As an example, the <h1> and </h1> tags designate a heading, putting the words between the tags on a line of their own and making the font large. However, tags don't apply solely to text in regard to format-

```
<html>
<head>

<title>The Title of this Web page</title>

</head>

<body>
<p>You can do all kinds of things to a web page, simply by
using text in an ordinary text editor.</p>

<h2>Like Make Headings</h2>

<h2 align="right">Or Change the Alignment of Those Headings</
h2>

<p>Though the text is plain in the editor, you can do a wide
variety of interesting things to it.</p>

<ul>
<li>Like make bulleted lists</li>
<li>Make fonts <i>italic</i>, <b>bold</b>, or <u>underlined</
u></li>
<li><font color="gray">Change the color</font></li>
<li><font size="4">Change</font> <font size="5">the</font>
<font size="2">size</font></li>
<li><font face="verdana">Or even change the font</font></li>

<p>Your patrons may be interested in images, which are easily
incorporated into an html document.</p>
<img src="roses.jpg" width="200">

</body>
</html>
```

An HTML Document in Plain Text

You can do all kinds of things to a web page, simply by using text in an ordinary text editor.

Like Make Headings

Or Change the Alignment of Those Headings

Though the text is plain in the editor, you can do a wide variety of interesting things to it.

- Like make bulleted lists
- Make fonts *italic*, **bold**, or <u>underlined</u>
- Change the color
- Change the size
- Or even change the font

Your patrons may be interested in images, which are easily incorporated into an html document.

An HTML Document in a Browser

Figure 4.1. HTML as plain text and viewed in a browser.

ting. For instance, the <img> tag tells the browser to insert a particular image at a certain location in a web page. A generic example of what this looks like is <img src="apicture.jpg"/>. The "src" in the character sequence lets the browser know how to locate the image "apicture.jpg." Other instructions within the <img> tag can tell the browser how big the picture should be or whether it needs a border.

There are a number of benefits to using this method for storing documents. Like TXT and RTF files, many programs can make and open HTML documents. Both Notepad and WordPad are capable of creating HTML documents, but there are numerous others, such as Notepad++, which is capable of editing other coding languages. Unlike the TXT and RTF formats, an HTML document can incorporate multimedia elements. A browser program is required to display this properly, however. For example, if the text in an HTML document requires an image, then the HTML file and the image file are still two separate files; opening the HTML file in a text editor won't display the image. The instructions for the browser in the HTML file tell the browser to retrieve the image and insert it in the correct location among the text information when the web page is viewed.

HTML is a format recommended for data storage by the Library of Congress (2013d). It's a good format to use if you have multiple text documents that you want to link or if you are saving information that is originally in this format. It's also handy to know about if you want to make your collection available online. HTML is also a good choice for sharing information, since most computers have a browser program for interpreting HTML documents. Files that use plain text are smaller than other types, since they have only characters and no other data. This makes information in this format ideal for transmitting over the Internet, since transmitting large files takes a long time. However, there are some difficulties with HTML. The language is continually evolving, and so some instructions do become obsolete or are interpreted differently over time. In addition, different browsers can interpret the instructions in an HTML document slightly differently, so the same information may look a little different among various browsers.

HTML is not the only format or language that can enhance plain text. There is another, similar format that can be of great use to you with your collection, and understanding HTML will help with understanding it.

Extensible Markup Language

Extensible markup language, or XML, is similar to HTML in quite a few ways. It uses the <tag> and </tag> format to communicate information, just like HTML. However, XML has a very different purpose from HTML. The main purpose of HTML is to instruct a browser program in regard to what information should be displayed and how it should be displayed, and it contains information regarding formatting and layout. XML has no impact whatsoever on the layout or appearance of a document. Instead, it contains information about the contents of a document, or metadata. For instance, if you had a book in digital format with XML tags and used the tags <title>Reading Is Easy</title>, then the tags can communicate that the title of the book is *Reading Is Easy*.

HTML has a set of tags that are universal. Everyone who codes websites must use the same set of tags. Again, it's like using a language—everyone coding with HTML is "speaking" the same language and communicating using the same pool of "words," or tags. With XML, it's possible to make up your own tags to communicate whatever information you think is relevant, like a book title or an author. However, this means that you're essentially making up your own language. There are ways around this, though. A document type definition, or DTD, has a specific set of tags that you can use. Like using HTML with its universal terms, this allows for better, more consistent communication (Combs 2011). DTDs are discussed more in-depth in chapter 12.

So, what is the point of XML? Well, if you use the appropriate software or a database, it can use a document tagged with XML tags to do all sorts of useful things. For instance, if all your documents have a tag for the book title, a software program can search for the text between the book title tags in every document that you have, then compile a list of every book title that your collection has. A patron could search for a particular book title, too. If all the chapters in a book are tagged by their titles, a program could compile a table of contents automatically (Combs 2011).

As mentioned earlier, there are a lot of DTDs, or vocabularies for XML, and these are typically designed for a specific type of information (Combs 2011). For instance, one of the preferred text formats for the Library of Congress collections is an XML-derived format known as the Open eBook Publication Structure, or OEBPS. This format uses a set of files that include not only relevant information for the document but a manifest of all the files for the document and a "spine." The spine indicates the logical reading order for the document. Software readers for this format can interpret JPEG and PNG files, so images in these formats can be included in such a document (Library of Congress 2013a).

Documents using XML have many virtues and can include a lot of useful additional information, but they are rather complicated, and learning about HTML and XML takes time. They can be important for your archive, though. XML, for instance, can be very useful for making your digital collection more easily accessible and searchable. There are still more options for storing text information that are simpler and have plenty of appeal to both you and your patrons.

Portable Document Format

The portable document format, or PDF, is a file type created by the company Adobe. The major virtue of a PDF is that it "feels" like a book to the user. Unlike an HTML document, a PDF can be separated into "pages." Like HTML, PDFs are capable of supporting text and multimedia. PDFs are also capable of other handy features, such as searchable text, bookmarks, hypertext links, and annotations and metadata (Library of Congress 2013c). PDFs are typically easier to construct than HTML or XML documents as well.

There are several variations on the PDF format. The one preferred by the Library of Congress for archiving text is the PDF/A-1. Like the ODT, this is an open format approved by the ISO, or International Organization for Standardization, and a number of companies create software that supports this file type. The ISO requires that future versions of software designed to view this file type be backward compatible, meaning that old files can be read with new software (PDF/A Competence Center 2011). This particular format doesn't allow for audio and video embedding, JavaScript or other executable files, or encryption, so it's a little more limited than a normal PDF file (Library of Congress 2013b). These limitations are to ensure that a PDF/A-1 file can always be displayed exactly like the original; features such as video or audio usually require software external to the PDF reader to function, which presents problems for display and archiving (PDF/A Competence Center 2011).

The PDF format can also use images instead of text, but this isn't really recommended as a method of image storage (Library of Congress 2013b). However, if you are digitizing books, this is something to keep in mind, as you can use an image of each page in the book as a page of the PDF. This will also keep multiple images together in the same file and, again, will feel like a book to the reader.

Image Formats

If you are storing scans or photos of text, then you need to use an image file format, even though what you are capturing is text. As discussed in the last chapter, some formats are better for some purposes than others. This is also true of images of text. For instance, JPEGs aren't good with high contrast and sharp edges, which makes them a poor choice for storing images of text in most instances.

TIFFs are a better choice, since they capture so much data and are lossless, and they are the format recommended by the Digital Library Federation Benchmark Working Group (2002). For pure black-and-white text or text with images that don't require tone, this group recommends that scans or photos be made at 600 dpi with 1-bit tone; this means that only black-and-white tones will be present in the scan, which is good for getting a clear image with the most readable text possible. If text has or is part of a grayscale image, then it recommends using 300 dpi with 8-bit grayscale. As mentioned in the previous chapter, 8 bits will create 256 different shades of gray, which is sufficient for faithfully reproducing a grayscale image with little noticeable difference between the copy and the original. For text that is part of a color image, the group recommends the same dpi but 24-bit color, or true color.

TIFFs are not suitable for display on the web, though. If you want your collection to be available online, you may want to store a JPEG in addition to the TIFF format or use a GIF or PNG, either of which is better than a JPEG with clear color boundaries, depending on how much color is needed to faithfully reproduce the image. What this means to you is that GIF and PNG files are good with crisp edges and that your text will be less blurry than it would be with a JPEG.

A good image can make it easy for your patrons to read text, just as if the text was in a born-digital format. However, your patrons will most likely want or even expect searchable text. This means that a computer is able to search through a document and match a word that the user types to one found in the document. If the document is a text file, this is a simple matter. If it's a scan or photo of a text document, however, this is more complicated.

ⓖ Searchable Text

Computers can't "read" in the sense that humans can. A computer, for instance, doesn't know that the word *computer* says "computer." Computers can't tell that the word *computer* on a screen and one in a book are the same thing either. A computer perceives the typed word *computer* as a series of eight sets of eight binary sequences, while an image of the same word is a set of binary sequences indicating colors. To a computer, these aren't the same thing at all. Although a computer can't "read," what it can do is match things.

With optical character recognition, or OCR, software, a computer can turn text in an image into text that is searchable, as if it were born-digital information. There are a few ways that this type of technology can work, but basically, the OCR software breaks down an image of a document into blocks of text, then lines of text, then words, and then letters and discards information such as images. It subsequently tries to match the letter shapes that it finds to known letter and character shapes in a dictionary of possibilities that is part of the software (Tanner 2004). OCR technology today is pretty accurate. However, there is quite a bit of variation and room for error due to the nature of computers.

While a person can make accurate guesses when it comes to reading, it's fairly easy to thwart a computer. For instance, imagine that there is an ink mark through a word on a printed page. If the line is thin enough to leave a little information about the letters' shapes, a human can still read a word that's been disrupted. A computer won't be able to guess what letters are under the line because they won't match characters in the software dictionary. A human can even, in many cases, guess what a missing word would be from context and the probable word length. This is difficult or even impossible for a computer.

A good example of the trouble that a computer can have with letters is in the technology of CAPTCHA codes. If you've spent time online and signed up for something like a free e-mail account, you've probably run across something called a CAPTCHA code. This term stands for "completely automated public Turing test to tell computers and humans apart," and it does exactly that.

What is a Turing test, though? As computers become more and more advanced, it can become more difficult to tell a human user apart from a program, and many programs are designed to mimic human responses. In the original version of a Turing test, a human judge posed questions to a human and to a computer that was attempting to emulate human responses, to distinguish which of the two was the computer. CAPTCHAs don't require a judge to tell if a computer is a computer (this is the "completely automated" part of the test). Instead, these codes present a problem that is easy for a human to solve but difficult or impossible for a computer. One of the most common types is a text-based CAPTCHA.

A text-based CAPTCHA presents a word that a human can easily read, but it has been warped or altered in some way so that it doesn't look like a tidy bit of typed text. In most instances, the human can type the correct word into a box, while a computer is unable to determine what letters are being shown because they aren't a match for its OCR program. There are some exceptions, however. Sometimes CAPTCHA codes have characters that are tricky for humans to tell apart, like the letter *O* and the number 0, and some programs are very good at decrypting CAPTCHA codes, although this is not the norm.

The point of a CAPTCHA code is to prevent malicious activity, such as spamming. People who spam others will, for example, open thousands of e-mail accounts at a time for the sole purpose of sending spam mail to other users. They can also use a program to fill out all the necessary forms for them, saving a real human time. CAPTCHA codes prevent this, since it's necessary for a human to be present to decode the CAPTCHA.

There's a program that's taking advantage of CAPTCHAs for the good of archiving, called reCAPTCHA. The reCAPTCHA program is part of an effort to scan print books and make them searchable using OCR technology. Websites that need CAPTCHA codes can participate in the program.

As an example, suppose there is a site for web-based e-mail called HandyMail.com. This site wants to prevent spammers, and so it needs CAPTCHA codes. HandyMail.com then signs up to participate in the reCAPTCHA program and puts the reCAPTCHA software on its website. When patrons want to sign up for accounts on HandyMail.com, they are presented with two words as part of the process. One is a traditional CAPTCHA code. This is the part that distinguishes that the user is a human. The other word is an image of a word from a digitized book that OCR technology can't decipher. The user types in both words. The information is then sent back to the reCAPTCHA program, which uses the word typed for the indecipherable word as the word to be used in the searchable document. For the sake of accuracy, this process is repeated a few times, with different users seeing the same word. Rather than CAPTCHA codes being a nuisance that wastes a lot of cumulative daily time, this program turns the work of millions of users faced with CAPTCHA codes into something useful—namely, helping to decode otherwise indecipherable words in digitized texts (reCAPTCHA 2013).

The accuracy of OCR software is typically represented in a percentage of accuracy, and it will guess the right character on an average of the given percentage. This accuracy varies, depending on several characteristics of the document itself. A resolution that is too low will make character recognition difficult or impossible; 300 dpi is the minimum resolution for good results (Tanner 2004).

Whether a document has been scanned with one bit, which produces pure black and white, or eight bits, which creates grayscale, can have an impact on your success with OCR technology as well. If a document is clean and tidy, with no spots, smears, watermarks, or similar flaws, or if the document text has multiple colors, then a monochromatic 1-bit color is the best choice. This will make the scan faster and more accurate, since it doesn't need to detect the threshold at which a character is a character or the background; if an image is pure black and white, then anything black can automatically be considered a character by the program, and anything white can be ignored (Lais 2002).

However, if a document has any kind of spotting, smearing, or other types of similar damage, these will show up as black spots on the scan, which may overlap or obscure letters and make it difficult for the software to distinguish letters from "noise," or things that have no relevant information. In this case, the image may be easier for both humans and computers to read if scanned in grayscale. Imagine that you made a photocopy of a document that has a faint coffee stain on it. Although you might still be able to read the original document, the photocopier will copy that coffee stain as being pure black, obscuring letters. This is what would happen in a 1-bit scan. In a grayscale scan, that coffee stain will show up as gray, making it still possible to interpret the letters under the stain.

Even if the best bit depth and resolution are chosen for a particular document, several characteristics of the text itself can cause inaccuracies for OCR software. Text that has multiple fonts and sizes, text that is skewed, or text that is unusual, such as fancy fonts or handwriting, are all struggles for OCR technology. In addition, with foreign-language texts, it's sometimes necessary to use software that has a dictionary that can recognize unusual characters (Tanner 2004).

OCR technology is improving all the time, though, and it's included with some software for creating PDFs. The convenience that it offers for you and your patrons make this technology worth exploring.

Key Points

- Today, text information is encoded in a way to offer a lot of compatibility between documents and software from multiple companies.
- Although compatibility has been improved over time, many types of file formats are proprietary and should be avoided when possible.
- TXT, RTF, and ODF files are all nonproprietary text file formats and are suitable for archiving different types of text files.

- HTML files offer a variety of formatting possibilities, and XML allows for the insertion of useful metadata into a file. PDFs allow patrons to read text information as they would a book, and they can store text and image information with equal ease.
- Patrons can benefit from the convenience that searchable text offers. However, to make image files readable by a computer, they need to be processed with OCR software. Using the correct number of bits and resolution for scanning presents the best chance for accuracy with this software.

While text and images are commonly found in archives, you may find that you have the need to store other multimedia information as well. In the following chapter, you will learn how a computer processes and stores audio and video information, and you will learn which formats are best for archiving of this kind of information.

References

Apache Software Foundation. 2013. "Reading ODF Documents (*.odt, *.ods, *.odp) with Apache OpenOffice." http://www.openoffice.org/why/why_odf.html.

Combs, Michele. 2011. "XML Indexing." *Key Words* 19 (4): 123–34.

Dale, Nell, and John Lewis. 2013. *Computer Science Illuminated*. 5th ed. Burlington, MA: Jones & Bartlett Learning.

Digital Library Federation Benchmark Working Group. 2002. "Benchmark for Faithful Digital Reproductions of Monographs and Serials." http://old.diglib.org/standards/bmarkfin.htm.

Fuller, Floyd, and Brian Larson. 2008. *Computers: Understanding Technology Comprehensive*. 3rd ed. St. Paul, MN: Paradigm.

Lais, Sami. 2002. "QuickStudy: Optical Character Recognition." *Computer World*. http://www.computerworld.com/s/article/73023/Optical_Character_Recognition?taxonomyId=11&pageNumber=1.

Library of Congress. 2013a. "OEBPS (Open Ebook Forum Publication Structure) 1.2." http://www.digitalpreservation.gov/formats/fdd/fdd000171.shtml.

———. 2013b. "PDF/A-1, PDF for Long-Term Preservation, Use of PDF 1.4." http://www.digitalpreservation.gov/formats/fdd/fdd000125.shtml.

———. 2013c. "PDF (Portable Document Format)." http://www.digitalpreservation.gov/formats/fdd/fdd000030.shtml.

———. 2013d. "Text Preferences in Summary." http://www.digitalpreservation.gov/formats/content/text_preferences.shtml.

PDF/A Competence Center. 2011. "PDF/A FAQ." http://www.pdfa.org/2011/06/pdfa-faq/.

reCAPTCHA. 2013. "What Is reCAPTCHA?" http://www.google.com/recaptcha/learnmore.

Tanner, Simon. 2004. "Deciding Whether Optical Character Recognition Is Feasible." http://www.odl.ox.ac.uk/papers/OCRFeasibility_final.pdf.

Storing Audio and Video

S O FAR, YOU'VE LEARNED ABOUT storing two types of information: images (visual information) and text (written information). These are two of the basic types of information that can be stored, and while there are many, many more, the last types of data that this book will cover are audio data and video data. Like images and text, audio and video data may already be in a digital format; for instance, an image taken with a digital camera is already in a digital format. However, your audio and video recordings may require digitization for your archiving project.

From the perspective of a computer, the data required to store and display an audio or video file isn't much different from other types of data, and so you may find much of the explanation for how this works familiar at this point, if you've read the previous chapters. However, audio and video files do have some of their own terminology as well as storage formats that are unique to them, and so you do have some new things to learn when it comes to storing this kind of data for your archive.

Because audio data is a component of a video file (unless the video has no sound), this chapter begins by explaining exactly how a computer records and stores audio information.

Audio Data

In the real world, when you hear a sound, it is continuous in nature. Imagine that you are listening to a violin player. Each time the string is drawn across the bow, it creates a continuous sound. In computer science, this is what is known as *analog data*—continuous information.

But as you know, computers don't like continuous information. They deal with information in small chunks of data, which can be stored as binary ones and zeroes. This is known as *digital information*, and the process of *digitizing* actually refers to this concept of turning analog data into digital data.

So, if you wanted to record the violinist in the earlier example using a computer, how can it be done? Whenever you record audio information with a computer, that computer doesn't record all the available information. That's impossible (at least for modern machines). Instead, what happens is that the computer takes a sample of all the frequencies that exist at a single instance in time. It keeps doing this at regular intervals so that when you listen to all these samples being played back, you hear the recording as being continuous.

You may notice that this concept is similar to how a computer records visual information, as discussed in chapter 3, but by taking samples of color rather than samples of sound. A computer can't record all of the available visual information for an image, so it instead records averages, or enough samples of color to form a full image that a person can understand. A computer can't record all sound, either, so it takes samples of this, as well. Think of pointillism in artwork—this is a technique in which an artist uses tiny dots of color rather than, say, large patches or full brushstrokes. When the artwork is seen close up, those dots are meaningless, but from a distance, they form a meaningful image. Both audio data and visual data work on a similar principle when recorded by a computer.

If a computer takes enough samples rapidly enough, then all those samples together create a good representation of the original sound. A rate of 44,000 times per second, or 44 kilohertz (kHz), is a good rate for most situations (Fuller and Larson 2008). The higher this rate gets, the more realistic the sound becomes—up to a point. Once the sampling rate exceeds a certain level, the human ear is no longer able to distinguish an increase in quality.

If a sampling rate is much lower than 44,000 times per second, then the human listener starts to notice the difference between a recording and reality and is able to tell that he or she is hearing a recording—and not a very good one (Dale and Lewis 2013). However, the optimal sampling rate also depends on what is being recorded: the sound of a single human voice speaking—which you might want to record for an archive of spoken records, accounts, or stories—doesn't need as much information for an accurate recording as, for example, a recording of a rock band would require. A human voice can be recorded with good accuracy at only 11,000 times per second, or 11 kHz (Fuller and Larson 2008).

The sampling rate also has an impact on the highest recordable frequency, or the highest pitch that a sound recording can capture. The highest frequency that can be captured is half the recording rate. For professionally recorded music, the standard recording rate is 44.1 kHz, which makes the top available frequency 22 kHz. This is good, since most people can't hear anything above 20 kHz, so essentially, this is an efficient sample rate for the recording industry (Consortium of Academic and Research Libraries in Illinois [CARLI] 2013a).

Suppose that you wanted a good recording of your violin player, so you decide to use recording industry standards and record the musician playing at a sampling rate of 44,000 times per second. If a three-minute song were played, the computer would then record 7,920,000 samples of that song in even intervals. When the samples are played back to the listener, the listener can perceive each of those little samples as being one long continuous sound, even though it's actually not.

Like image files, audio files can rapidly become quite large quite. Even if only one bit were needed for each sample, this one song would be a little less than 8 megabytes worth of information. That's around 114 times the amount of information needed to store the digital version of this chapter, and in reality, much more data is needed to store the information for each sample, since you need more than one bit per sample.

Audio files don't have to be huge, though. Like image files, audio files can be compressed to save space. The software used for this is known as a *codec*, which stands for compressor-decompressor (Lake and Bean 2008). A lot of terms used for compressing visual data also apply to audio data, such as *lossy* or *lossless*. Remember: *lossy* means that some data is lost during compression, and *lossless* means that no data is lost and the file can be restored exactly to its original. Lossy methods are typically more efficient than lossless methods and can compress files to much smaller sizes, but lossless methods are usually superior from an archiving standpoint.

CARLI (2013a) recommends a sampling rate of 44 kHz at the minimum and 96 kHz for archival-quality recording. This is a high rate that will record a lot of data. You will need to determine if a higher sampling rate is advantageous to your archive or not. This is also only applicable for digitizing music. If you are storing a recording that is already digital, you'll essentially be storing whatever rate the creator of the file used.

Although these terms are relevant to storing nearly any kind of data, several terms are relevant to audio data in particular.

Bit Depth

Along with the sampling rate, recordings have a certain bit depth—that is, how many bits are used to store the data for each sample taken during a recording. A typical sample will use between 8 and 24 bits. A bigger sample size contains more information about the recorded sound and creates a more accurate recording that is more true to reality. However, a bigger sample size also requires more space to store the data. With your recording of the violinist, the 44,000 sampling rate with a small 8-bit sampling size would create a 63,360,000-bit file (before any compression); a more robust 16-bit sampling size would create a 126,720,000-bit file (16 bits is standard for the recording industry). CARLI (2013a) recommends a recording bit depth of 24 bits, which will provide a lot of data. While you always want to be as accurate as possible, the amount of storage space that you'll need to store your collection is something that you should take into consideration for practical reasons.

TERMS FOR AUDIO DATA

Bit depth: the number of bits used for a recording

Channel: whether the recording was in mono sound (one-microphone recording) or stereo (two or more microphones recording)

Ripping: transferring audio data from a CD (a digital data storage format) to a computer (can also apply to video data)

Channels

Audio data can also be recorded in channels, either mono or stereo. Mono recordings capture a single sound using one source (there's typically only one microphone involved). Stereo recordings are more complicated and use at least two microphones during recording to capture sound from two directions.

Why would you want to do this? Well, people have two ears and hear audio information coming from different directions in the real world. Recording audio data in stereo gives a sense of realism to the recording and makes it more true to life. When you listen to a recording in stereo using headphones, for example, the exact sounds that you hear may be different on each side of the headphones, making it seem to your brain as though you're actually there, with the original source of the sound, such as a concert, opera, or a comedy monologue. To hear this effect on a computer, you need at least two speakers.

It's important to note that stereo recordings require twice as many bit captures as mono recordings and thus are much larger. Professionally produced CDs and DVDs typically have stereo sound. However, mono sound still has a number of applications, and older recordings, such as cassette tapes and vinyl records, may be in mono sound.

Ripping

Another term that might be of importance to you is *ripping*, or copying audio data from a CD onto a computer hard drive. There are some legal ramifications involved in this if the CD in question is under copyright. Ripping a CD that contains copyrighted information onto a computer is not necessarily illegal, but doing so with the intent to distribute the information is. However, you may have an agreement with the copyright holder in regard to archiving the data, and creating a copy of audio data for the sole purpose of archiving is usually perfectly legal (Lake and Bean 2008). You'll learn more about CD technology in chapter 6 and more about copyright law in chapter 13.

Audio Data Formats for Archiving

Audio data hasn't been available for computers as long as image or text data has. While sound capabilities are standard on modern computers, in the past, only the most high-end personal computers had sound cards, which are necessary computer components for playing sound. That is, only high-end computers could play sound at all.

File formats for audio data are not as well established or well known by general users as the other file formats covered so far in this book. As with other types of data, you can use a variety of audio-recording formats. However, many of these formats are proprietary or otherwise require specific software to run, so choosing one that suits your needs can be more complicated than choosing one for visual data. The software that you use may play a limited number of types of audio data, or it may not be able to convert formats easily because of these proprietary formats.

For instance, WMA is a format proprietary to the Microsoft company, and QT is proprietary to the Apple company. RA, or Real Audio, files require a Real Audio player to open. There are also some formats designed for specific operating systems, which presents an even greater obstacle to use than not having the proper software. For instance, the AIFF format is primarily used on Macintosh computers and so would not be useful for computers using Windows (Lake and Bean 2008).

AUDIO FILE FORMATS FOR ARCHIVING

AIFF: audio interchange file format

BWF: broadcast wave format

FLAC: free format lossless audio codec

MIDI: musical instrument digital interface

MP3: MPEG-1 audio layer 3

WAV: wave file

There are, fortunately, a variety of file formats considered acceptable for archival storage, and one of these will likely suit your archival needs. The wide variety can make it a little difficult to choose, though, and different types are recommended for different kinds of audio recording. Some of the many options open to you are the WAV, AIFF, MP3, and MIDI file formats.

WAV and AIFF Files

The WAV format was originally created by Microsoft and IBM, which worked jointly on the development of the format (Costello, Youngblood, and Youngblood 2012). WAV files are a commonly used file type for sound that can be suitable for archiving purposes, and WAV files can be used for storing both mono and stereo sound. To create the sound, the WAV file sends the audio information to the speakers of a computer to generate a particular amount of voltage on, which produces the correct frequency and duplicates the recorded sound (Fuller and Larson 2008). There are several variations on the WAV format, such as the broadcast wave format, which is considered particularly suitable for archiving and allows for metadata in the file header, or useful information not related to playing the audio information (metadata is discussed in chapter 12; Library of Congress 2013b). The Apple company's AIFF file is similar, and the two formats are virtually interchangeable as far as sound capability goes. Most sound-editing programs will work with both file types (Costello, Youngblood, and Youngblood 2012). Although not ideal in that they are proprietary formats, both are so commonly used that finding compatible software is not an issue.

MP3 Files

MP3 is a format considered acceptable for archiving purposes by the Library of Congress (2013c) that may be more familiar to you. MP3 is short for MPEG-1 audio layer 3. MPEG is an acronym for the Moving Pictures Experts Group, which develops standards for video compression. There are also MPEG-2 and MPEG-4 formats, which are used primarily for video data; MPEG-4 can also be used for archiving audio data. MPEG-3 was never fully developed and is not in use.

The MP3 format is a highly desirable format primarily owing to how well it compresses audio data. What happens in an MP3 file is that the file removes or reduces sounds that humans can't normally hear—cutting out irrelevant information, in a way (Andrews 2006). This greatly reduces the amount of data needed to reproduce the file, thus requiring less storage space.

The MP3 format has a lot of appeal to the general public for several reasons. These files are used with MP3 players, small personal music players like iPods. The high level of compression makes it possible to store a lot of data on one of these players; the format can also be used by a variety of other devices and software, an excellent feature to have in digital archiving. It's also popular because it makes downloading audio data from the Internet easier: the larger a file is, the longer it takes to download, and so smaller files are better from this perspective because they take less time to acquire.

MP3s may also appeal to patrons if you want your collection to be available online, since chances are good that they will already have the necessary software to play your audio files and so find this format to be comfortable and familiar. It should be noted, however, that the MP3 format is patented, which may present problems (Fuller and Larson 2008). The MP3 format also uses a lossy method of data compression, which is always less preferable for archiving then lossless methods. While you may not want an MP3 to be your main archiving format for this reason, MP3s are great for sharing, and so you may want to store multiple copies of a file: one in the WAV format, for instance, and one as an MP3.

As another consideration, the free lossless audio codec, or FLAC, is a nonproprietary file format that is similar to the MP3 but is lossless (Coalson 2009). Because these traits are appealing for archiving, you may want to examine this file format for your audio files.

MIDI Files

Musical instrument digital interface, or MIDI, files digitally simulate the sounds of real instruments, such as drums or violins. These files create synthesized music, which can be very useful. Rather than recording a performance of these sounds, MIDI files play the appropriate notes with the appropriate instrument effect. You can almost think of it as being digital sheet music that can play itself. Rather than being a recording of an actual performance, a MIDI file is instead instructions for how a synthesizer can play a piece of music or a sound. In the past, this was highly advantageous, because MIDI files are just instructions and are much smaller than actual recordings of performances. Because they use so little data, MIDI files were often used for background music and sound effects in old computer games. MIDI files are still in use today, though, and musicians can use them for music composition and other creative applications.

When you play an MP3, AIFF, or WAV file, you're playing an exact reproduction of a recording. MIDI files are instructions. While this saves a lot of space, it can be problematic in that MIDI files are somewhat dependent on the quality of the software using these instructions to reproduce the sound (Lendino 2013). For instance, imagine the difference between giving a copy of the sheet music for Beethoven's Fifth Symphony to a middle school band and giving the same music to a professional symphony orchestra. The instructions are exactly the same, but the quality of the results is quite different. MIDI files are not as commonly used today as in the past but still have some use and may be something that you want or need to archive. Again, MIDI files were common in older computer games, and so you may need to save MIDI files if you want to preserve old software as part of your project.

In many ways, storing audio data is similar to storing data for images. Video data is also similar in many ways to both these types of data as well, since it requires both kinds of data, image and audio, to create the video.

⊚ Video Data

Explaining exactly how video data is stored on a computer is a little complicated. The general principle behind it, however, is simple, and an easy way to explain it is to consider a digital video as having the same principles as an animation. As you probably know, traditional hand-drawn animation is created when an artist draws the same picture over and over with incremental degrees of change between successive drawings. When the images are shown together, one following after another in rapid succession, it creates the illusion of movement—that all those still images are moving. You may notice that this is also similar to how audio data recorded by a computer works, by playing tiny samples of sound in rapid succession.

Digital videos essentially work the same way as animation and sound recordings. They are composed of a number of still images that, when shown rapidly one after another, create the appearance of movement. If you've ever seen a reel of video film or the inside of a VHS tape, you'll notice that the film for the video is actually composed of a number of images, one after another on the tape. These are shown rapidly at a steady pace to create the look of movement. The principle used for film-based videos is exactly the same in digital format; it's just that the digital video shows digital images made from pixels.

Although there is some variation, a video typically has 30 frames per second. This means that for every second that goes by in a video, you're actually seeing 30 still images, which are going by too fast for you to even notice. For software that creates video data, it's important to keep track of how many frames there are. However, a program for video data normally does not keep track of individual frames but, rather, the seconds that go by. This is known as the *timecode*. In video editing, a timecode helps the creator of a video know when specific audio data needs to start playing, for instance.

Just like audio data, video data can be compressed with software—in this case, a video codec. You'll need to choose a codec that you find acceptable for your video data. Lossless codecs are preferable, but most video codecs are lossy. Although some codecs have the same name as a file format, they are not necessarily the same thing. For instance, you can use an MPEG-2 codec to compress a file format other than an MPEG-2. Some of the lossless options are Huffyuv, Lagarith (similar to Huffyuv), and JPEG 2000. You can also choose to simply not compress the file, but this will result in an enormous file for storage (CARLI 2013b). You can use lossy methods, but you should be aware that these are not the best choice for archiving.

Video files are typically created in a native format, similar to that for an image (as discussed in chapter 3). Remember: a native format is a file format that works specifically

TERMS FOR VIDEO DATA

Rendering: converting a video file from a native format to another format

Timecode: a method of keeping track of video data, often used for synchronizing audio data

Video codec: software used to compress video data

with a particular device or type of software. Native formats for video have the same problems (as far as archiving goes) as native formats for visual data do, in that they normally can't be opened by anything other than the software program that created the file. The video file therefore needs to be converted into a different file format, a process known as *rendering* for video data. There are quite a few data formats for videos, and as with audio file formats, you'll face a challenge in that most of them are proprietary and specific to a company.

Archiving Video

When you archive a born-digital video, you'll essentially be using the formats and specifications used by whoever created the video, just as you would for audio data (although you may need to convert the file format to something more acceptable). If you're digitizing information, however, you'll need to make some decisions.

One of these is the resolution of the video image. Resolution is measured by the number of horizontal pixels by the number of vertical pixels (see chapter 3). More is better, up to a point. A standard television today has a resolution of 640 × 480, while a high-definition television can have a resolution up to 1,920 × 1,080 pixels (CARLI 2013b).

Similarly, the aspect ratio is the width of a video image divided by the height. For example, the aspect ratio of standard cathode-ray tube televisions (before the rise of flatscreen televisions) was 4:3, meaning that videos for these televisions have images that are slightly wider than they are tall. At some time when watching a movie, you may have seen a notice that says something along the lines of "this film has been formatted to fit your screen." The reason is that films intended for movie theaters have a different aspect ratio than that of television sets, and some of the image needs to be cropped to be more easily viewed; this is a loss of information. This is also what *wide-screen* versus *full-screen* means when you purchase a copy of a movie; *wide-screen* means that the aspect ratio is true to the original and has not been cropped. Your video data will appear best at the aspect ratio at which it was originally captured.

As with audio data, you'll need to decide how large your samples will be when you capture video data. A larger sample size, or bit depth, provides more image data and is therefore superior from an archiving perspective. This does, of course, create a larger file size. CARLI (2013b) recommends a sample size of 30 bits.

Video data can also use either interlaced or progressive scanning. With interlaced scanning, each image essentially captures half the relevant data, with one image displaying information on odd-numbered lines and another on even-numbered lines. Analog video, such as a VHS tape, is usually made in this way. When film that was created in this method is digitized, sometimes the frames become blurred from small amounts of movement between one frame and the next. Progressive scanning captures all data in a single frame. This is considered the superior method as far as archiving goes, and most born-digital video uses this method (CARLI 2013b).

Video Data Formats for Archiving

Like formats for audio files, there are many formats available for video files. Most of these are not particularly suited for archiving, since they are proprietary. However, you may

COMMON VIDEO FILE FORMATS

AVI: audio video interleaved

DPX: digital moving-picture exchange

FLA: flash

MJ2: motion JPEG 2000

MOV: QuickTime movie

MPEG: file format created by the Moving Pictures Expert Group

SWF: ShockWave flash or small web format

WMV: Windows media video

want to know what kinds of video formats are available anyway so that you know what types of formats you have and what type might be suitable to display to your patrons (e.g., which formats are good for use online). This section covers some possible file types; there are many, many ways to store video data.

MPEG

As you learned earlier in this chapter, MPEG stands for the Moving Pictures Expert Group, which develops standards. There are several variations on the MPEG file format, with MPEG-1 typically being used for audio data (the MP3 format). MPEG-3 is not in use. MPEG-4 is usually used for transmitting video data online, and the MPEG-2 format is for general use with video data.

As MPEG-1 is capable of creating highly compressed audio files, the MPEG-2 format is capable of creating highly compressed video files. With this file format, frames that have no appreciable amount of change from one frame to the next are discarded (Andrews 2006). Remember, there are 30 frames per second of video in a normal capture, and so there are instances in which some of those 30 frames have no new meaningful information. Getting rid of some of those frames with no new data helps to compress the file, and the viewer won't notice the difference. However, this is a lossy method of data storage, and while you might not readily notice the difference, it's still preferable to use a lossless method of data storage. As with MP3s, though, you might want to use this format for your patrons and use a different format for actual storage.

Motion JPEG 2000

Motion JPEG 2000 is one of the file types preferred by archivists. It's an open international standard with a lossless codec. Rather than compressing the file by removing frames, as the MPEG formats do, each frame is individually compressed (Pearson and Gill 2005). This method is different from other methods of video compression in general such that very little information is lost during the compression process, making it more appealing than the MPEG formats from an archiving standpoint, for instance.

This format is commonly used for digital cinema, or movies shown digitally in a movie theater (*PC Mag* 2013).

Flash

Flash files are particularly desirable for transferring video information online (Fuller and Larson 2008). Flash files have the extension FLA or FLV. FLA files are used to create video, and an FLV file is the final product that can be shared with others. Flash animations are often used online or as components of web pages. This technology was developed by Macromedia, but the company was purchased by Adobe Systems in 2005. One of the unusual and appealing features of Flash animations is the fact that they typically use vector images rather than bitmapped or raster images for the frames (Library of Congress 2013a). Vector images are scalable, as discussed in chapter 3, which means that they look the same regardless of the size of the image, whereas bitmapped or raster images can become pixelated when resized. Shockwave Flash, or SWF, is a related format with similar features; however, it can be used for many things other than videos, such as small games or programs. These formats are both particularly useful if you want to display information online or archive information from the Internet.

Material Exchange Format

The material exchange format, or MXF, is an open standard format developed by the Society of Motion Picture and Television Engineers. This particular format is designed to work well for digital archiving. It can also work across multiple platforms and use multiple compression codecs. It works with uncompressed video data, and it works well with metadata. That is, it's designed to easily associate metadata with the video information (Pro-MPEG Forum 2013). Chapter 12 covers what metadata is and what it's useful for.

MOV, WMV, and AVI

The MOV file extension indicates a QuickTime movie. QuickTime is a format developed by the Apple computer company. Similarly, the WMV is a Windows media video file, a format developed by Microsoft. AVI is an audio video interleaved file, also created by Microsoft. These are all proprietary formats, which makes them less desirable for archiving than some of your other options. However, they're very common, and there is a lot of software available to work with these formats, which may make them appealing for sharing your archive's data online or letting your patrons interact with your archived data. CARLI (2013b) recommends AVI and QuickTime in particular as alternative options to the more desirable MXF format. Although AVI and QuickTime are less desirable for archiving, they are commonly used by the general public, so you may find it easier to find useful software and resources for the formats.

Key Points

- Audio information is stored in much the same way as other types of data for a computer and can be compressed with lossless or lossy compression.
- The realism and accuracy of audio information depends on the sampling rate and size and whether the recording is in mono or stereo sound.

- Audio information is stored in a variety of formats, but unlike other types of data, audio files tend to be proprietary, adding challenges to archiving.
- Video data is a combination of both audio and visual data and is stored as a series of still image frames played back to the viewer at a rapid rate.
- Videos can also be compressed with either lossy or lossless methods.
- Videos can be stored through a variety of formats. The original format and necessary quality level can be factors that determine what format you choose for your archive.

You've learned quite a bit about how computers store data for several types of data as well as how computers store data in general. For the purposes of archiving, though, it's never a good idea to rely on a single computer to store data, as computers can be defective or break through ordinary use. You need methods of storing digital information external to a computer as well. In the following chapter, you will learn about a method of storage that is likely very familiar to you—the CD and its variations, such as the DVD or Blu-ray disk.

References

Andrews, Jean. 2006. *A+ Guide to Managing and Maintaining Your PC.* 6th ed. Boston: Course Technology.

Consortium of Academic and Research Libraries in Illinois (CARLI). 2013a. "Guidelines for the Creation of Digital Collections: Digitization Best Practices for Audio." http://www.carli.illinois.edu/sites/files/digital_collections/documentation/guidelines_for_audio.pdf.

———. 2013b. "Guidelines for the Creation of Digital Collections: Digitization Best Practices for Moving Images." http://www.carli.illinois.edu/sites/files/digital_collections/documentation/guidelines_for_video.pdf.

Coalson, Josh. 2009. "FLAC." https://xiph.org/flac/.

Costello, Vic, Susan A. Youngblood, and Norman E. Youngblood. 2012. *Multimedia Foundations: Core Concepts for Digital Design.* Waltham, MA: Focal Press.

Dale, Nell, and John Lewis. 2013. *Computer Science Illuminated.* 5th ed. Burlington, MA: Jones & Bartlett Learning.

Fuller, Floyd, and Brian Larson. 2008. *Computers: Understanding Technology Comprehensive.* 3rd ed. St. Paul, MN: Paradigm.

Lake, Susan, and Karen Bean. 2008. *The Business of Technology: Digital Multimedia.* 2nd ed. Mason, OH: South-Western Cengage Learning.

Lendino, Jamie. 2013. "At 30, MIDI Is Still Misunderstood." http://www.pcmag.com/article2/0,2817,2418880,00.asp.

Library of Congress. 2013a. "Macromedia Flash FLA Project File Format." http://www.digitalpreservation.gov/formats/fdd/fdd000132.shtml.

———. 2013b. "MIDI Sequence Data." http://www.digitalpreservation.gov/formats/fdd/fdd000102.shtml.

———. 2013c. "Sound: Preferences in Summary." http://www.digitalpreservation.gov/formats/content/sound_preferences.shtml.

PC Mag. 2013. "Definition of: JPEG 2000." http://www.pcmag.com/encyclopedia/term/58992/jpeg-2000.

Pearson, Glenn, and Michael Gill. 2005. "An Evaluation of Motion JPEG 2000 for Video Archiving." http://archive.nlm.nih.gov/pubs/pearson/MJ2_video_archiving.pdf.

Pro-MPEG Forum. 2013. "MXF Overview." http://www.pro-mpeg.org/pages/main.php?page=0002.

CDs, DVDs, and Blu-ray

MOST PEOPLE ARE PRETTY FAMILIAR with the compact disk, or CD. It's a little thin piece of plastic, comfortably sized for the average hand to hold. The back is shiny and typically silvery, although it can be other colors, such as green, gold, or purple. Often, the disk is designed to hold information for music or a game, but it can be used for many other things. Any kind of information that can be stored on a computer's hard drive can also be stored on a CD, and the majority of modern computers (even many older computers) have a CD drive already installed into the machine.

CDs are so cheap and so common nowadays that they can be produced for the sole purpose of promotion, or made to be given away. Chances are good that you own or have seen a CD like this—maybe it has part of a music album or a mixture of songs to encourage you to buy music albums; it has a demo version of a game for you to try; or it has a partial version of a software program.

CDs are easy to use and familiar to most people, and this makes them appealing as a method of storage. However, CDs—even related methods of storage, such as the DVD—have some not inconsiderable limitations. CDs can be very useful to you, though, so it's important to learn exactly what a CD is and what it can and cannot do.

All CDs, DVDs, and Blu-ray disks are essentially the same in some key respects. They are all known as optical media (the reason why is explained in a moment). All three have the same general construction, but the differences in their construction make a big impact on the storage capacity of each type of media.

A CD is the least complex of these three types of media. A regular manufactured CD is actually composed of several layers, like a sandwich. It has a label (usually), followed by a layer of lacquer. The bottom of the CD is clear polycarbonate, which is a plastic (Byers 2003). In the middle is a layer of a reflective metallic alloy—this is the shiny silvery part that you see through the back, which is distinctive of CDs. A major function of the lacquer and the polycarbonate is to protect this layer, since the CD will not function if the metallic layer is damaged.

DVDs, or digital versatile disks, are constructed in basically the same way, but instead of a single metallic layer, DVDs have two. DVDs can store more information than a CD and can store information on both sides of the disk. Each side can have either one or two recordable layers of material, whereas a CD always has only one and is single sided (Byers 2003). Blu-ray disks have a similar construction to DVDs, but the equipment used to read a Blu-ray disk is different from that of a DVD.

So, why is it called *optical media*? You already know that, for a computer, binary signals are communicated in the form of electrical impulses. A plain plastic disk, however, is not electrical at all. You can safely handle a CD without hurting either yourself or the data on it, since there is no charge whatsoever, no pulses of electricity racing down wires as in a computer's motherboard. How is the information stored?

In chapter 2, you learned that a computer's hard drive works a lot like a record player, with an arm that seeks out a set of data while the disk spins. A CD works pretty similarly to a record as well. In fact, even though a floppy disk looks like a square of plastic, they are not actually square at all. Inside the square case is a round film disk that stores the data and works rather like a record, too. Flat spinning disks seem to be a pretty good way to store information. Although CDs and floppy disks are similar in this respect, floppy disks have largely fallen out of use, mainly due to their small amount of data storage. A typical 3.5-in. floppy holds about 1.44 MB of data, whereas a CD can hold close to 500 times that much information.

Although you can't see it, that all-important metallic layer in a manufactured CD is not smooth. It actually has many tiny little grooves, much like a record. Those grooves are called *pits*, and the spaces between them are called *lands*. They are formed around the disk in an even spiral, moving from the inner hole to the outer edge. Rather than using a needle on these grooves, though, a CD drive has a little laser inside. The laser moves along this spiral track, exactly like a record player. Like a record player, these grooves contain information, which can then be read by a computer.

When a CD (or any other kind of optical media) is manufactured, the polycarbonate bottom is the part imprinted with the little grooves, and the shiny metal layer is placed over it, kind of like how a fine layer of metal is attached to another item for gilding (Andrews 2006). You may be wondering why the metal part is important, then, if it's not actually the part imprinted with these little data-containing pits.

The little pits and lands don't do anything themselves. What they can do, though, is change how the light reflects off this metal surface. When you put a disk into the CD

OPTICAL MEDIA ACRONYMS

DA: digital audio, audio disk that can't be altered

R: writable, can be written to once by the user

ROM: read only memory, a manufactured disk that can't be altered

RW: rewritable, can be written and erased multiple times

drive of a computer, it begins to spin. As it spins, a laser inside the drive runs over these grooves along the spiral. They reflect some of the light from the laser by bouncing it off of the metallic layer. Lands reflect a lot of light, and pits reflect a little light. Another device within a CD drive that detects light reads these bursts of reflected light and converts them into ones and zeroes for the computer, thus communicating the information encoded on the disk. With optical media, a land represents a one, and a pit represents a zero (Andrews 2006). Because the encoding is in binary, exactly like a computer's hard drive, you could potentially store any kind of digital information on an optical disk. Although CDs are known for storing music or software and DVDs and Blu-ray disks for movies, digital files of any type are all suitable for storage on optical media of any kind.

There are several types of CDs and DVDs as well as Blu-ray disks, and they all have some different qualities. For instance, "burned," or writable, optical media works a little bit differently from the kind with the data imprinted during manufacturing, but the principle is the same.

CD-ROM and CD-DA

There are two types of commercially produced CDs: CD-ROMs and CD-DAs. These work exactly like the basic CD described earlier—they contain a metallic layer, which is usually aluminum, with grooves in the polycarbonate to encode the information (Byers 2003). CDs of any kind record information on one side of the disk only; that is, only the clear polycarbonate side has data.

CD-ROM stands for "compact disk–read only memory." You might notice that the ending of this is the same acronym and stands for the same words as those used to describe a ROM chip. In both instances, the device—the disk or the chip—can only be read by a computer. The computer is not able to change any of the information on the device, which is good because then it can't be accidentally erased.

CD-DA stands for "compact disk–digital audio." This is the kind of CD used for commercially produced music. It is exactly like a CD-ROM but with one major difference: CD-DAs have some additional information used for timing, which is important for music playback (Dale and Lewis 2013).

CDs are divided up into sectors that contain small amounts of information, just as hard drives encode information in small sectors for searchability. For recording music, each sector on a CD-DA has 1/75th of a second of music. For a CD-ROM, a single sector has 2 KB of data total, which can be any kind of data, such as text or photos, up to that 2-KB limit (Dale and Lewis 2013). One CD-ROM can contain around 650 to 700 MB of data total (Fuller and Larson 2008).

CD-R

A prerecorded CD-ROM is useful and can effectively store information, but for an archive, it's important to be able to record information of your own choosing to create a custom CD. This is what CD-Rs are designed for. *CD-R* stands for "CD-recordable"; these are blank CDs that have no information encoded until the user "burns" information onto the disk.

Recordable CDs also have their information encoded in a spiral in the CD; in fact, blank CD-Rs have this spiral prestamped into the CD (Byers 2003). However, they lack the pits and lands of a regular CD-ROM; the metal layer is smooth and blank, ideal for recording your own information. However, you already know that the information is encoded on a CD-ROM during the manufacturing process; it is physically embedded into the polycarbonate bottom before the other layers are put on top. To record information yourself, you don't have to make CD sandwiches in some sort of miniature factory in your computer (though that might be fun). So how do CD-Rs encode information?

The back of a CD-R is shiny and metallic, but it's not silver, like a CD-ROM. The coloration that you do see is photosensitive dye. This dye reacts to a laser in the CD drive that, while operating at a higher power than necessary for simply reading disks, is able to heat the disk and create little darkened areas of dye (Optical Storage Technology Association 2001). The prestamped spiral exists for the purpose of guiding the laser while it writes information to the CD (Byers 2003). This process is known as *burning*.

The series of dark and shiny areas is what the laser will read, rather than pits and lands (Sandstrom, Rudd, and DeMoulin 2001). They are read in essentially the same way as a manufactured pressed CD, with shiny parts reading as ones and with dark, less reflective parts reading as zeroes. To the computer, there is no difference between these two types of CDs because they work in the same way, by either reflecting a lot or a little bit of light when a laser passes over an area on the CD.

You might notice that there are several possible colors on the backs of CD-Rs, usually varying by the manufacturing company. The reason is that there are several kinds of photosensitive dyes that can be used effectively, and these dyes are different colors. All the various dyes work, but some are more stable and durable than others (discussed later in the chapter).

The basic structure of a CD-R is a lot like a CD-ROM. The bottom is a layer of polycarbonate; the middle is a layer of a metal; and the top has a layer of lacquer and some sort of label, usually designed for the user to write on. However, there is a layer of dye between the polycarbonate and the metal. The metal is typically different as well and is usually made of gold, silver, or a silver alloy. Gold is the best choice of these, as it's very stable and resistant to corrosion. Aluminum can't be used for the reflective layer like a regular CD-ROM because it reacts with the dye on the disk (Byers 2003).

CD-RW

CD-Rs are not the only type of media available that can record data. CD-RWs are rewritable, with *CD-RW* standing, rather logically, for "CD-rewritable." They are more convenient than CD-Rs in this respect; a CD-R can be used only once, and the information is permanently encoded into the photosensitive dye. A CD-RW, however, can be altered and rewritten, deleting old information and adding new information. It is not permanent. This can be a liability for an archive, however, since anyone can change the information on a rewritable disk, including patrons (if they have access) and employees (intentionally or not).

CD-RWs are pretty similar to CD-ROMs and CD-Rs in construction. They have a layer of lacquer and polycarbonate, and, as with a CD-ROM, there is a layer of aluminum in the middle. CD-RWs also have two dielectric, or insulating, layers, which are made from zinc sulfide and silicon dioxide. Rather than a dye layer, as CD-Rs have, CD-RWs instead have a layer of something known as a *phase change metal*, which is sandwiched between those two dielectric layers. This layer is made from a combination of indium, silver, tellurium, and antimony, and it is the part that contains the information on the disk (Optical Storage Technology Association 2001).

This phase-change metal is able to exist in two states—crystalline or amorphous (Sandstrom, Rudd, and DeMoulin 2001). This can be a little difficult to visualize. Imagine that you have an ice cube and a similar amount of water. The ice cube is solid because the water molecules inside it are more organized. They have a structure. The water, though made of the same material, lacks structure. The molecules are all largely independent, so they can move around easily. The phase-changing metal is like that—the crystalline state is very organized, and the same metal in the amorphous state is very disorganized at a molecular level.

Like the process of burning a CD-R, the laser inside a CD drive operates at a higher power than normal and "burns" a CD-RW. Instead of getting spots of darkened dye, however, that phase-changing layer becomes amorphous rather than crystalline under the heat of the laser (Optical Storage Technology Association 2001). The amorphous spots are dark, nonreflective zeroes, and the crystalline spots are shiny, reflective ones. What is unique about this is that the process is reversible up to about 1,000 times (Sandstrom, Rudd, and DeMoulin 2001).

OPTICAL MEDIA TYPES

CD:

- Single layer of data on a side
- Most common media type and least expensive
- Smallest data capacity

DVD:

- Can hold multiple layers of data on a single side
- Large data capacity

Blu-ray:

- Can hold multiple layers of data
- Largest data capacity, most compact data
- Most expensive
- Requires specialized reader

CD-RWs do have drawbacks, though. Older machines are not able to read these disks, and although you can record audio information, these disks can't be read by regular audio CD players. These types of CDs have significantly lower reflectivity than other CDs, which means that the reader for the laser doesn't get as much light bouncing back off the CD, and so any device that is not designed for reading CD-RWs cannot do so (Sandstrom, Rudd, and DeMoulin 2001). CD-RWs are also somewhat expensive. In comparison, CD-Rs can be read by many older machines as well as CD players and are much less expensive.

DVDs

DVD-ROMs, DVD-Rs, and DVD-RWs work in essentially the same way as their CD counterparts, with the disks being embedded with little lands and flats or having photo-sensitive dyes or phase-change metals to encode the information. They also look alike and are the same physical size. However, DVDs store a lot more information than CDs and can range from 4.7 to 17 GB of stored data, depending on how the disk is configured. Remember: a normal CD can hold about 650 to 700 MB of data. A 17-GB DVD has an equivalent amount of about 17,000 MB of data, around 24 times as much as a regular CD.

DVDs get so much information onto the disk because those little pits and lands are configured a bit differently and are more densely arranged. DVDs are also capable of having two layers of information on one side, and they can be double sided, essentially quadrupling the amount of possible storage space, whereas the information on a CD can be on only one side of the disk and in one layer. This variation in construction is what accounts for the rather wide range of DVD storage capacities (Fuller and Larson 2008). It should be noted that recordable DVDs are not capable of storing as much information as DVD-ROMs (Byers 2003).

Unlike a CD, in which the laser beam goes through the polycarbonate and reflects off the metal layer, the initial layer in a dual-layer DVD is only semireflective. It's typically made from silicon, gold, or a silver alloy, and it can allow some of the light to pass through and to a fully reflective coating on the other side, which is normally made from aluminum (Byers 2003).

Blu-ray

A Blu-ray disk is much like a DVD but has several important differences. One side of a Blu-ray disk can hold up to 27 GB of information, about one and a half times the maximum capacity of a DVD (Fuller and Larson 2008). Like DVDs, Blu-ray disks can be two-layered, having about 50 GB of storage available, and some companies are producing disks with four layers and between 100 and 128 GB of storage space. Blu-ray disks are, as mentioned, very similar to DVDs and CDs, and Blu-ray players are often capable of reading CD and DVD disks, although players or drives designed for CDs and DVDs can't read Blu-ray disks (Overton 2012).

A Blu-ray disk, as the name suggests, also uses a blue laser to read the contents of the disk, as opposed to a red laser for normal CDs and DVDs (Dale and Lewis 2013). This laser is what enables so much more information to be encoded. The red laser in a normal DVD or CD player or drive has a wavelength of 650 nanometers. A blue laser has a 405-nanometer wavelength. This finer wavelength allows the laser to be more precise.

The pits and lands on an optical disk are measured in microns, which is a unit of length about a thousandth of a millimeter, or one millionth of a meter. The diameter of the hairs on your head can also be measured in microns. The size of a single pit or land on a Blu-ray disk is .32 microns, as opposed to .74 for a DVD; so, it's less than half the size of a pit or land on a DVD. So, essentially, all the information is the same and is encoded in the same way as the other technologies but is extremely compact, putting more information in the same amount of space (Overton 2012).

Like DVDs and CDs, there are writable and rewritable Blu-ray disks. A normal manufactured Blu-ray disk is known as a BD-ROM. A writable disk is a BD-R, and a rewritable disk is a BD-RE. The capacity for these disks is the same as for manufactured Blu-ray disks (Overton 2012).

For the moment, Blu-ray technology has reached its maximum data capacity, but this may change. Other types of lasers may be available in the future that will allow for even more compact data storage than a red or blue laser. For instance, ultraviolet or x-ray lasers may be available for optical technology in the future (Overton 2012). If you choose to use optical media for your archival storage, looking to new technologies and changes in the technology is going to be an essential part of maintenance.

Optical Media for Archival Storage

Optical media has a lot to offer, but there are some serious drawbacks as well. However, this is true with any kind of storage medium (it's even true with storing information in a nondigital way; you could claim that books are heavy, difficult to store, and subject to nasty fates, such as mildew and disintegration). The size of your archive and your budget, the size and experience of your staff, and the amount of data that you need to store will all make an impact on whether the benefits of optical media outweigh the problems.

Advantages

- Familiar form of storage, easy to use
- Requires no special equipment to read
- Inexpensive and easy to obtain

Disadvantages

- Highly variable and typically short life expectancy
- Vulnerable to laser rot
- Cumbersome to store
- Somewhat small storage capacity

Advantages

CDs and other optical media disks are common and familiar. Although you may not think of it that way, this is a significant benefit to you. Chances are good that your patrons and anyone working in your archive will be familiar with this technology. This means that you won't need to train your staff in regard to what optical technology is and how it's used; they will most likely already know. If you want your archive to be easily accessible to patrons, you could offer CD copies of its contents for them to use. Again, the familiarity is convenient; most patrons will understand that to access the information, all they have to do is to put the CD into the reader of a computer; that is, you do not need to give them instructions.

Like hard drives, CDs rotate at a high speed, and the laser can essentially seek the location of the desired information. This means that accessing information on optical media is pretty quick, especially in comparison to magnetic tape (a storage medium discussed in the following chapter). Speed is a very attractive quality in information access.

Optical technology is also very convenient. Drives that can play, read, and burn CDs and DVDs are standard on modern computers, meaning that you would not need to purchase any new or specialized equipment; merely using fairly recently made computers would suffice, if your budget was limited. This technology is also inexpensive, and CD-Rs and DVD-Rs can be purchased in many stores, so you don't need equipment from a special manufacturer. However, this is true only if you purchase ordinary disks. Disks designed for the purpose of archiving in mind are more expensive, and you may or may not be interested in using these kinds of disks.

If you need to store only a relatively small amount of information, if your archive is on a tight budget, or if you need a technology that's easy to use and understand, storing your information on optical disks is an appealing option to consider. There are some problems with optical media, though, that you should be aware of before making a decision.

Disadvantages

Many manufacturers of recordable optical media claim a life span of decades for their product. However, in practical use, this is rarely true. The life span of any kind of optical media—CD, DVD, or Blue-ray, writable or not—depends on the type of disk, the quality of the disk, the disk's condition before recording information (in the case of recordable media), and the quality of the recording itself. How the disk is handled and stored also makes a significant difference in how long the disk will last (Byers 2003).

Disks may indeed last for decades under ideal conditions. CDs and DVD-RWs could have a life span of 25 years. The life span of a CD or DVD-ROM is less easy to estimate but could be between 20 and 100 years (Byers 2003). These are under ideal conditions, though. In practical use, oftentimes a recordable disk only lasts 2 to 5 years (U.S. National Archives and Records Administration 2013). This is a serious drawback to optical media because many factors determine how fast information degrades and it's difficult to determine how long your disks will last, to estimate how often they should be replaced, and to predict what the life span of a product will be when put into use. As such, optical media is vulnerable to several problems.

Laser Rot

As you know, optical disks work by reflecting or not reflecting a laser back to a sensor. When the laser shines off a metallic layer inside the disk, a computer can interpret this as a one; when this does not happen, this is interpreted as a zero. If the metallic layer becomes corrupted, however, this leads to a condition known as *laser rot*.

When a disk has laser rot, this means that the all-important shiny metallic layer has become corroded, discolored, or pitted in some way so that the information is no longer readable. The top and bottom layers of an optical disk are made from a protective lacquer and polycarbonate plastic, respectively, and part of their function is to protect the middle layer of metal. If these layers are compromised in some way, then contamination from the atmosphere can occur. If there is any discoloration of the metallic layer, then the CD no longer functions and data is lost. While the manufacturers of various optical disks have developed better, more protective coatings over time, laser rot is still a problem with poorly or cheaply manufactured disks (Iraci 2005).

Dye Stability

CD-Rs, as well as DVD-Rs and BD-Rs, are vulnerable to data loss, but they have an extra problem unique to their construction. The shiny metal layer is essential, but there are no physical pits and flats on the disk. Again, these are instead encoded depending on whether or not a laser has created a dark spot on the dye layer of the disk through heat. These dyes are therefore sensitive to heat and light, and the stability of the dyes is highly variable. Different manufacturers use different dyes. Phthalocyanine, cyanine, and azo dyes are some of the commonly found ones. Of these three, disks with phthalocyanine dye are the most stable, and azo dyes are the least stable (Iraci 2005).

In addition to physical deterioration, optical media has some other problems. If you need to preserve a lot of information, physically storing the disks can become problematic. A few dozen disks can be stored fairly easily, but if there are hundreds, then this becomes cumbersome. Storage, retrieval, and labeling of your disks will become problematic. Because the longevity of this medium is so difficult to estimate, it's a good idea to regularly move information from the old disks to the new ones to keep your data safe. Again, this will become a burden if you have hundreds of disks on your collection, but you may find it not too difficult for a few dozen.

Even if you decide that optical media is not the best choice for storing information in your archive, you may still want to store some kinds of information on disks, or you may want to preserve manufactured disks as an object, as you might for a book or journal. Storing disks correctly greatly enhances the stability and longevity of optical media.

⑥ Optical Media for Archival Storage

You can take a number of steps to preserve the life of any kind of optical media.

Temperature

Heat damages optical media and can lead to a variety of problems. Being too cold, however, is also problematic. The optimal temperature range for optical media is between 39°F and 68°F (Byers 2003). Sunlight is also damaging to optical media, particularly burned media, and so storage in an area away from windows is best (Fuller and Larson 2003). Remember: the dye on a writable or rewritable disk is sensitive to the heat and light from a laser, and so exposure to heat and light can corrupt the data written to the disk.

Humidity

The polycarbonate base of optical media can absorb moisture. This means that getting an optical media disk wet can be damaging; it also means that the humidity at which you store optical media has an impact on its longevity. A relative humidity of 20% to 50% is optimal, with even lower humidity being better for long-term storage (Byers 2003).

Storage

Most manufactured CDs come in a plastic casing known as a *jewel case*; you can also purchase jewel cases for burned CDs. However, jewel cases are not just for displaying label information for a CD or for storing a nice booklet in the front, as often happens with commercially produced CDs. That jewel case is important for protecting the disk from damage. Optical disks should always be stored inside their cases and never stacked on top of one another, inside or outside the case. Likewise, they should not be stacked on objects or have objects stacked on them (Fuller and Larson 2003). Optical disks should always be stored upright inside their cases, just as you would treat a book (Byers 2003).

There are also sleeves available for storing optical media. These will protect the disks from dirt and scratches. However, they don't offer the same amount of protection that a jewel case does. It's also difficult or impossible to get the disk out of the sleeve without touching the back, and taking a disk out of a sleeve and putting it back multiple times is likely to start deteriorating the polycarbonate, adding scratches.

Handling

Many people are not too careful with their CDs, leaving them out or dropping them, touching them excessively, even scratching them. CDs are designed with neglect from humans in mind, though, so they can withstand a bit of abuse. Careful handling greatly increases the life span of these materials, however.

Always try to pick up disks by the edges and to avoid touching the shiny side; the label side, or the top, is safer to touch. In general, touch optical disks as little as possible, only doing so to take a disk from its casing to put it into a reader and to take it back out to put it away.

Note that many patrons won't adhere to these kinds of standards. If you want them to be able to access your data on optical media, then the best solution is to have a copy in safe storage and to use a burned disk for patron use, as it will not matter if the second copy isn't properly handled. You can make a new one from the original in the event that it goes bad.

Cleaning

As mentioned earlier, an optical disk is a little like a sandwich, with two layers of plastic and either a dye or a layer of metal in the middle. The laser needs to be able to shine through to the middle layer and back again, and so the condition of the bottom layer of the disk is vital. Scratches, fingerprints, and smudges of any kind will all obscure the laser. The cleaner the disk is, the better.

If a disk needs to be cleaned, the first step should be to blow dust and dirt off without touching the shiny, nonlabeled side. Next, you can use a soft lint-free cotton cloth to wipe away dust and dirt (Fuller and Larson 2008). The direction in which you wipe off a disk is important as well, with wiping in a straight line from the middle to the outside being better than wiping in a circle around the shiny side (Byers 2003).

If the disk is still dirty, the best way to remove the dirt is to clean it with a commercial optical disk–cleaning solution or some isopropyl alcohol and a soft lint-free cotton cloth (Fuller and Larson 2008)

Labeling

Although it may seem like a harmless activity, labeling optical media is something that must be done carefully. Writing on the disk is preferable over using an adhesive label. You should never, of course, write on the shiny side, since it will interfere with reading by the laser. Always write on the label side. Felt-tip markers are safest. Markers must not be solvent based; water-based markers are best, as the solvents can deteriorate the lacquer on the label side. You should use a pen that doesn't need to be pressed hard onto the disk. Ball point pens or pencils are capable of actually distorting the information on a disk because the label is over the lacquer layer, which is much thinner and closer to the metallic layer than the polycarbonate layer is. Labeling double-sided DVDs is tricky in that both sides are the shiny, readable side; writing around the center hole is fairly safe (Byers 2003).

Maintenance

Because the life span of optical media is so variable, it's important to have a policy for checking the data on your disks regularly. Once a year or every two years is optimal. It's often impossible to tell visually whether or not a disk's data is becoming corrupted unless the damage is extreme, as in the case of a delaminated disk where the layers have simply come apart. You can purchase software that can analyze the state of the data on a disk and let you know if any has become corrupted so that you can move the information to a new disk before the corruption becomes too severe and the data is irretrievable. You may also want to simply create a policy of moving data to new disks every few years for the sake of safety (U.S. National Archives and Records Administration 2013).

IDEAL STORAGE AND HANDLING OF OPTICAL DISKS

Cleaning:

- Remove dust with air
- Wipe dirt with a soft, lint-free cotton cloth
- Remove additional dirt with an optical disk–cleaning solution or isopropyl alcohol

Handling: Touch label side or outer edges only

Humidity: 20%–50% relative humidity

Storage: Upright, in jewel cases or other hard casing

Storage temperature: 39°F–68°F (4°C–20°C)

◎ Key Points

- CDs, DVDs, and Blu-ray disks are all different kinds of optical media in which binary information is encoded with tiny spots that are either highly reflective or not.
- Optical media offers many conveniences in that it's fast and inexpensive, requires no special equipment, and is likely to be familiar to both staff and patrons.
- Optical media is vulnerable to problems such as delamination, laser rot, and corruption of dyes.

While it's a familiar and simple form of storage, optical media is only one way to store digital information for your archive. Magnetic storage is one of the oldest methods of data storage, and it continues to have many appealing qualities for an archive.

◎ References

Andrews, Jean. 2006. *A+ Guide to Managing and Maintaining Your PC*. 6th ed. Boston: Course Technology.

Byers, Fred R. 2003. "Care and Handling of CDs and DVDs: A Guide for Librarians and Archivists." http://www.itl.nist.gov/iad/894.05/docs/CDandDVDCareandHandlingGuide.pdf.

Dale, Nell, and John Lewis. 2013. *Computer Science Illuminated*. 5th ed. Burlington, MA: Jones & Bartlett Learning.

Fuller, Floyd, and Brian Larson. 2008. *Computers: Understanding Technology Comprehensive*. 3rd ed. St. Paul, MN: Paradigm.

Iraci, Joe. 2005. "The Relative Stabilities of Optical Disc Formats." *Restaurator* 2:134–50. http://www.uni-muenster.de/Forum-Bestandserhaltung/downloads/iraci.pdf.

Optical Storage Technology Association. 2001. "Understanding CD-R & CD-RW Disk Construction and Manufacturing." http://www.osta.org/technology/cdqa15.htm.

Overton, Gail. 2012. "Can New Techniques Continue to Densify Optical Data Storage Capacity?" *Laser Focus World* 48 (10): 39–42.

Sandstrom, Chad R, Gordon Rudd, and Robert DeMoulin. 2001. "How Do Rewriteable CDs Work?" *Scientific American*. http://www.scientificamerican.com/article/how-do-rewriteable-cds-wo/.

U.S. National Archives and Records Administration. 2013. "Frequently Asked Questions (FAQs) about Optical Storage Media: Storing Temporary Records on CDs and DVDs." http://www.archives.gov/records-mgmt/initiatives/temp-opmedia-faq.html.

Magnetic Tape

IN THE PREVIOUS CHAPTER, you learned about optical disks as a method of storing data. Optical disks, such as CDs and DVDs, are fairly familiar, and the majority of modern computers come installed with a drive that will read several types of optical disks, offering extra convenience to you. Optical disks do have their limits, however, one of which is how much storage capacity is available on a single disk.

Magnetic tape, in contrast, offers enormous amounts of storage space in comparison to the optical disk, and the amount of storage that a single tape can hold keeps increasing as new innovations are made to this technology. This makes magnetic tape inherently of interest to any operation that needs to store large amounts of data, including archives. Magnetic tape has many other highly desirable qualities. However, like the optical disk, magnetic tape isn't a good solution for all situations, and whether or not it's helpful to your archive will depend on your archive's needs.

Magnetic tape is one of the oldest methods of data storage, and this is another advantage to you. Although modern forms of magnetic tape are not quite like earlier versions, there are many similarities. Even if your archive does not decide to use magnetic tape as a form of storing new data, magnetic tape has been used as a method of data storage for such a long time that it's in your interest to be familiar with it should your archive ever need to deal with archival tape from other institutions.

Magnetic storage in general, including magnetic tape, is one of the earliest storage methods for computer data, and it has been in use for decades. In spite of this, magnetic tape is most likely unfamiliar to you as a storage medium because it's not commonly used with personal computers.

Early computers had several methods of storing information magnetically. The first of these was the magnetic drum, which was a cylinder coated with a magnetic material (Dale and Lewis 2013). As the drum turned, tracks of information that ran around the circumference of the cylinder moved underneath a read/write head, with one head per track (*PC Mag* 2013). If you've ever seen a music box in which a little cylinder inside turns to play the music, it's a little like that but with magnetic charges moving under electromagnets instead of little bumps that play tines. As you'll learn later, this is similar in many ways to how magnetic tape operates.

Another early storage method used a structure of magnetic rings in a grid, with each ring looped onto a metal mesh. The rings were magnetically charged to store the information. There were also disks, which were similar to records (yet another example of a round disk being used to store information) and tapes (Rusch 1969). Tapes, as you might suppose, consist of a strip of flexible material coated with another material, which is magnetizable. The tape method has been in use for some time now.

In 1888, a man named Oberlin Smith came up with the idea of using a magnetic signal to play sound. Ten years later a man named Valdemar Poulsin invented a device that did just that (IEEE Global History Network 2012). His device wouldn't look very recognizable to you, though; it consisted of a brass drum wrapped with piano wire, and it could record only a minute of sound at a time. It never really took off, since its competitor, the phonograph, was less expensive and could record sound for longer periods. It was an important invention, even if it was a commercial failure, since the technology was still innovative and useful (Gifford 1977).

It wasn't too long after this that magnetic tape, which better resembled the current version of magnetic tape than Poulsen's device, was developed for recording sound. This was invented by a man named Fritz Pfleumer in 1928, and his tape consisted of a magnetic substance bound to a substrate of paper or film (IEEE Global History Network 2012). This is much like the construction of modern magnetic tape, which means that, in essence, magnetic tape has been around since 1928.

Magnetic tape was used for recording sound during World War II and was initially used to record speeches and radio programs. Most people think of magnetic tape as something used to record sound because for decades, this was all that it was used for until its potential for recording computer data was realized (IEEE Global History Network 2012).

Why is magnetism so appealing for storing data? Magnetism still plays an important part in computers today. A hard drive, the main source of long-term memory in a typical computer, also uses magnetic memory. If you ever need to open up your computer or do anything on the inside, you must never use magnetized tools, or else you pose a serious risk to your computer's data.

Magnetism and electricity are highly interrelated, and this is advantageous when working with an electronic device such as a computer. Magnetism has some other desirable qualities when it comes to storing data. To understand why, it helps to know a bit about how magnets work.

Every method of memory storage for modern computers uses binary encoding. As stated in the previous chapter, optical disks encode the required binary ones and zeroes as strong and weak light signals, respectively. However, this is merely one of many ways in which binary information can be encoded. All that is needed to effectively encode binary data is something that can be interpreted as having an either/or condition. For instance, a light bulb is either on or off. With optical media, the either/or condition is the strength of the light: Is the light bright—yes or no? Within the computer itself, the electronic impulses are either high or low. They're never high and low, and they're never sort of high or sort of low.

Magnets are ideal for encoding binary information for just this reason, lending themselves nicely to an either/or condition, and they offer some options for either/or conditions as well. As you probably remember from basic science classes or even just playing with magnets as a child, magnets have poles (north and south, a situation referred to as *polarity*). Like poles repel each other, and opposite poles attract each other. So, a magnet can be encoded through its poles. Is the pole north, or is it south? Magnetizable materials in general can also be categorized by whether or not they are actually magnetized. Just because something is magnetizable doesn't mean that it's magnetized, and magnetizable materials have the potential for both states. For instance, when you were little, you may have run a needle across a magnet to make a compass. The needle is made of magnetizable material (probably steel) but isn't magnetized until you run it across the magnet. Since electricity can magnetize certain metals, this is perfect from the standpoint of a computer—a jolt of electricity can transform a material from one state to the other: from magnetized to nonmagnetized and vice versa.

Magnets are common in everyday life—found in toys, refrigerators, and headphones—but you may not think much about how they actually work, since their everyday function is familiar. There are two types of magnets: permanent magnets and electromagnets. Both are necessary for magnetic tape (and computers in general).

Permanent magnets are magnetic because of their physical structure. As you probably know, also from basic science, the universe is formed of materials known as *elements*. Each element has some special properties according to its form and behavior on an atomic level, or the level of a single unit of an element: the atom. Not every element is magnetizable. Elements capable of generating a magnetic field have a peculiar property that is unique to them. To think of it in simple terms, this property allows the element to generate a magnetic field, and it produces the phenomenon of magnetic poles, north and south, even at the atomic level. What this means is to you is that magnets can be exceedingly small, which is important for encoding data, since with computers, smaller is almost always better. Technically, a single atom of a magnetizable material could be considered a magnet. Iron, nickel, and cobalt are some common examples of elements with this unique property (Encyclopedia Americana 2006a).

Commercial magnets are often a combination of elements; for instance, a common alnico magnet is made from aluminum, nickel, and cobalt. In a permanent magnet, the fields of the atoms of the magnetizable elements line up according to their poles and thus have an overall magnetic field. Permanent magnets need to be orderly, even on an atomic level. If a permanent magnet becomes demagnetized, then the fields of the atoms in the magnet are randomly oriented, and the magnet has no overall pull or influence on other materials. This can happen in a number of ways, such as storing the magnet at improper temperatures or subjecting the magnet to the influence of another magnetic field, which can disrupt the field of the first magnet.

In an electromagnet, the magnetic field exists only when electricity is running through the wires that make up the magnet. Any wire conducting electricity generates a magnetic field, just like a permanent magnet, but this field is extremely weak, so you'd probably never realize that a magnet was present (it would be weird if your paper clips were attracted to your desk lamp, for instance). To make the field stronger, you can bend the wire into a loop (Encyclopedia Americana 2006a). The more loops you have in the wire, the stronger the magnetic field becomes. Electromagnets have poles, just like the permanent kind, although the poles can be reversed by reversing the flow of electricity (nothing changes the polarity of a permanent magnet like this). Both types of magnets—permanent magnets and electromagnets—are essential for both creating magnetic storage and reading it.

ⓖ Encoding Magnetic Data

A piece of magnetic tape consists of sets of data placed along tracks, kind of like the magnetic drum as previously described. You can picture the tracks as being like a racetrack in structure. Binary ones and zeroes lay along each track. They are read by a read/write head, with one head per track, similar to how there is one runner per track. So, if a tape had nine tracks, then the drive for the tape would have nine read/write heads (Wiehler 1979).

The reading and writing heads, of course, have different functions, although both are often part of the same device, rather than two separate heads (Bycer 1965). Within each head is a little device with a small electromagnet inside. This electromagnet is sensitive to magnetic fields.

A simple bar magnet has a north pole and a south pole. Imagine that within those tracks on the tape are sets of bar magnets. These magnets are all parallel to one another but can be oriented north-south or south-north. Though a simplification, this is essentially what is really happening on a piece of magnetic tape, except that these bar magnets are very, very small. Typically, a person thinks of a magnet as being a big chunk of metal or an alloy, but this isn't necessarily the case. The magnets on the tape are in fact made from powder but still have the function of a permanent magnet because the fields of the atoms in the powder are oriented to have an overall magnetic field. It's so weak and the spots of magnetism are so small, though, that you'd never have any way of noticing this yourself.

These miniscule magnets encode the binary data based on how their poles are oriented toward one another on the tape. Remember: the reader head is sensitive to magnetic fields. When it runs along a track, the electromagnet in the head is able to sense the orientation of the fields below and then converts the information about the fields that it senses into electrical signals that the computer can interpret as binary code (Wiehler 1979).

The writing head, in contrast, generates a field that can change the orientation of the poles on the tiny tape magnets. A magnetic field can influence the properties of another field, magnetizing it or demagnetizing it, which is the phenomenon in effect here. The writing head can create binary information on a new tape by magnetizing the tape below or changing the information already there by altering the orientation of the poles. In this way, the reader head encodes information onto the tape (Wiehler 1979).

◎ Magnetic Tape Construction

Magnetic tape may seem unfamiliar because it's not as commonplace as a CD or DVD. However, chances are good that you actually are familiar with magnetic tape. Though somewhat outdated, cassette tapes, used for audio recordings, are a type of magnetic tape. The less popular and less familiar 8-track is also a type of magnetic tape storage. Both these are similar in many ways to the type of tape you'd use to record computer data.

There are three basic types of magnetic tapes: reel-to-reel (which involves tape moving between two large reels), cassettes, and cartridges. The latter two are smaller than a reel-to-reel tape and are housed within a plastic casing. While cassettes and cartridges are typically aimed more at personal use rather than for use by a large company or institution, you may find them of interest for the sake of ease.

Each reel in a typical reel-to-reel setup in modern times has a diameter of about 5 or 7 inches. The reel on which the tape is stored is fitted onto a spindle for playback or recording, and the free end is threaded through the machine. An empty reel takes up the tape as the tape plays. If you've ever used a microfilm reader, the process is similar to this, with a reel of microfilm fitting onto a spindle and the loose end of the film running through the reader and onto an empty reel. This kind of a tape needs to be rewound to get back to the beginning of the tape.

A cassette, as you probably know, is like the reel-to-reel setup but contains both reels within a protective case. Cassettes are put into a tape drive, and the tape runs from one head to the other. Like a reel, it needs to be rewound to get to the data at the beginning. A cartridge works a little differently than a cassette in that it has only one reel. A cartridge is designed to play the data within an endless loop, with the tape continually being wound onto the one reel (Encyclopedia Americana 2006b). The advantage of this is that, unlike reel-to-reel or cassette tape, cartridges don't need to be rewound. Once the tape plays through, it's ready to be played once again (Gifford 1977).

Regardless of the type, all magnetic tapes have the same basic construction. A piece of magnetic tape essentially has two layers. The top is a layer of a magnetizable material. This is often some kind of iron oxide or chromium dioxide (IEEE Global History Network 2012). This is also known as the *pigment layer* or the *pigment*. This pigment is suspended within a polymer binder. While these are the only materials necessary for the top layer, the binder may contain other materials to facilitate tape reading and recording, such as a lubricant to help the tape move more easily through a device or a cleaning agent for the heads on the device (Van Bogart 1995b).

This magnetizable layer is, of course, the important part because it is all that is needed to store the data. However, magnetic tape needs to be rolled up onto a reel, and since the magnetic material is essentially a powder, it is not suitable for this kind of treatment. The bottom layer is essential for making the tape actually function.

The bottom layer is a piece of film. In the past, this part was made from cellulose acetate, but this material has several problems, including its tendency to become brittle due to moisture in the air and its susceptibility to a condition known as *vinegar syndrome*, which is also caused by moisture. Along with creating damaging acetic acid (essentially vinegar) that causes the tape to become soft or even dissolve into a powder or a slimy substance, vinegar syndrome causes the tape to smell strongly like vinegar. If you ever handle archival magnetic tapes, you may encounter this. Because of the problems created by vinegar syndrome, modern tapes are made from polyester, which is far more stable and tough. These are important qualities, as the tape must be able to withstand the mechanical stress caused by pulling it through a machine to read the magnetic coating (IEEE Global History Network 2012). There may also be a third layer on magnetic tapes, a back coat, the purpose of which is to control static or friction as the tape moves through a machine (Van Bogart 1995b).

◎ Reading Tapes

Notwithstanding the many ways to store data, you'll find that many methods are based on the same technologies or are simply evolutions from older methods and have similar principles. Magnetic tapes bear some similarity to other forms of magnetic storage, such as hard drives. In fact, floppy disks are yet another method of magnetic storage that greatly resembles tape in some ways. Floppy disks store their data on a round film, enclosed in a hard square casing, so floppy disks and magnetic tape both consist of a piece of polyester film coated with a layer of magnetizable material (Fuller and Larson 2008).

A magnetic tape basically looks like what the name implies—a long piece of plastic tape. Think about what a music cassette tape looks like. There are two reels and tape inside the case. Magnetic tape in a cassette for archiving works exactly the same way, with two reels that move the tape between them as they rotate. With a cassette tape, the reels move in one direction to play the music on one side; then, the user flips the tape to play the music on the other side. Of course, you can rewind a tape to replay a section of music before it gets to the end.

Magnetic tapes for archiving work a little differently in this respect. While a music album or audio recording has a logical sequence of information—playing from the beginning of a performance to the end—this is not necessarily the case with a magnetic tape for computer data. For example, some people use tapes to make backups of their hard drives. If you do something like this, then the software that you use will write the files on the hard drive to the tape in the order that the computer decides. A person at a music company decides the logical order for music on a musical cassette tape and makes it easy for humans to use. This may not be what happens with a data tape (although you can potentially store like data on the same tapes to improve the logic).

Magnetic tapes for music and those for data both use a method of storage known as *sequential access*. This means that the heads need to go through all the data that precedes the desired data on the tape, and the tape must also physically move to the desired location under the heads. If you had a favorite song on a music tape, for instance, you'd have to fast-forward or rewind to listen to the song again, which takes time and can be tedious.

In contrast, hard drives and floppy disks use direct access. The physical location of specific data is less important, because the head is located on an arm, which can move up and down the disk as it spins, seeking out the requested information. In contrast, the reader heads on a tape drive are fixed in place. Optical disks, such as CDs and DVDs, are another example of a method of data storage that uses direct access. Because the physical location of the data is less important and the arm can seek it out rather than go through all the preceding data, direct access is quick in comparison to sequential access.

Just like optical disks, a computer needs a device to interpret the data on the magnetic tape and to communicate with the machine. As an example, a tape cartridge requires a tape drive to both write and read the tape. Such a drive can connect to the computer in several ways, but for most purposes, a drive that connects via a USB port will likely be the most convenient. There are also drives that can be installed directly into the computer. If you don't need to be able to move the drive from one computer to another and if you have a dedicated computer that only makes tape backups, this is an appealing feature. When you purchase a drive, you need to keep the format and size of tape that you want to use in mind. A number of standard formats and sizes are available, and your drive must match these specifications. As an example, although a VHS tape and a cassette tape are similar in many ways and even look somewhat similar, you can't play a cassette tape in a VHS player. However, while a tape drive may be able to write with only one format, drives can oftentimes read several formats, which is helpful if you want to be able to read tapes from different archives (Andrews 2006).

Magnetic Tape for Archiving

As time goes on, the variety of ways to store data keeps increasing. Engineers keep striving for devices that are smaller and smaller while offering more convenience, greater data safety, and higher storage capacity. Also, as time goes on, many devices become obsolete, some very quickly. Floppy disks were once so convenient and so highly associated with external storage that a tiny image of a floppy disk in a program is practically synonymous with "save"; today, they are essentially worthless.

So, since magnetic tape is such an old method of storage, you might suppose that it's obsolete or will soon become obsolete. This is not the case at all. Like other methods of data storage, tape keeps improving, year after year. Although other methods of storage are competing with magnetic tape as the best method for data storage, tape continues to be a major contender, and tape's best features have yet to be imitated in any other storage method. Still, magnetic tapes do have drawbacks, and so it's important to know about the benefits and drawbacks before you decide if tape is the right choice for your archive's storage needs.

Advantages

- Very inexpensive per gigabyte of storage space
- Not dependent on a specific reader manufacturer
- Very large storage capacity
- Old and well-understood method of data storage
- Easily moved off-site
- Doesn't need a power source for effective storage

Disadvantages

- Magnetic tape readers are an expensive specialty item
- Storage may be expensive
- Magnetic tape is unfamiliar to many people
- Magnetic tape is somewhat delicate
- Reading and writing data to magnetic tape is slow

Advantages

One of the most appealing features of magnetic tape lies in its price. Compared to other storage methods, magnetic tape is the clear winner when it comes to storing a lot of data inexpensively, with tape costing less than a penny per gigabyte of storage space (Graham-Rowe 2010). It's the medium of choice for many companies that need to back up a lot of data, year after year, and it's appealing for archives for just the same reason. As the years go by, there will be more and more data that needs to be saved, and storing this data can become quite expensive with other storage methods.

Reels of magnetic tape come in several standard sizes, just as optical disks, such as CDs and DVDs, come in a standard size. This is extremely important, as it makes it possible to use magnetic tapes and readers that were produced by different manufacturers and it prevents your data from becoming obsolete because a particular company no longer makes tape in a certain size (Wiehler 1979). For example, all musical tape cartridges are the same size and will play in any player produced by any company, regardless of who manufactured the tape.

Typical capacities for magnetic tape cartridges are between 20 and 800 GB of compressed data (Andrews 2006). A 3.5-in. cartridge can hold about 200 GB of data (Lawrence 2003). Compare this to the common maximum data capacity of a CD-R, which is usually capable of about 700 MB of data at best, so a common 200-GB tape cartridge can hold close to 300 times as much data as a single CD.

As an example of tape's capabilities for data storage, while the 20- to 800-GB range is typical for magnetic tape, there is such a thing as a 35-terabyte tape cartridge. A terabyte, as mentioned in chapter 2, is around a trillion bytes, and so it's around 180 times as big as that typical 200-GB cartridge. In the same way that Blu-ray disks are exactly like CDs except for the fact that the data is more closely compacted, these tapes are exactly like any other kind of tape, except that the data is crammed into a staggering 29.5 billion bytes per square inch of tape (Graham-Rowe 2010). As with optical disks, the future may bring tapes that are even more densely compacted with information.

Although innovations to technology are helpful, the fact that this medium has been in use for such a long time can be an asset to you as well. Because tape has been around for decades, its limitations are well understood. For instance, researchers discovered a problem that occurs with tape during the manufacturing process. The plastic is formed in large sheets, which are cut to the correct size for a reel. If the blades for cutting the tape become dull, it can cause tiny rips in the ends of a tape, which are invisible to the naked eye but can shorten the life span of the tape or even destroy data. Information like this about tapes can be used for quality control and can improve the final product. Because tape has been studied for so long, issues like this are known and can be addressed (Lawrence 2003). Similarly, while the typical life span of a CD has not been conclusively determined yet, tape has been around for long enough that life span estimates are fairly accurate.

Along with storing a lot of data, tape offers some other benefits. For instance, tape is easy to take off-site. If you have the funds for it, you can construct a room or building designed to store tape at its optimal temperature. If this room is not part of your library or archive, then if anything should happen to your main building, such as flooding or other natural disasters, your tape backup will be safe. You could even make several backups of your data and easily store them in different locations. It's also handy if you want to share information with another archive. For instance, sending a terabyte's worth of information to someone online is a challenge and takes some time. A single 200-GB tape is also easier to send than 295 CDs. Shipping a reel of tape may be quicker, easier, and safer from the point of view of data security.

Tape doesn't need a continual source of power to store its data, in contrast to the RAM memory chips in a computer, nor does it require the Internet to access information. The fact that you can store tape away from a computer and that it needs a special machine to read the data encoded on it is an advantage to you for data security. Tape can't be accessed from the Internet, and typical computers have readers installed only for CDs or DVDs. As such, theft of magnetic tape is highly unappealing because the data is hard to access, since it requires a special reader to retrieve the information.

Disadvantages

Although tape has a lot to offer for an archive, for certain situations, it's not the ideal choice. If you don't need to store large amounts of data, then magnetic tape may not be the best choice for you. While the tape itself is inexpensive, computers don't come with readers for magnetic tape. You'll have to purchase extra equipment, such as a tape drive and software, to both read and write to the tape. However, as mentioned before, there are tape drives aimed at a typical computer user for backing up personal data. Computers using the Windows operating system often come with software that is designed to write a hard drive to a tape drive for the purpose of backup. In addition, when you purchase a tape drive, it often comes bundled with useful software, which can make things easier for your archive (Andrews 2006).

Storing the tape can be an additional expense, especially if you want a robotic or automated system of tape storage and retrieval, which is sometimes used in large facilities. These devices don't require a human user to search for and retrieve tape from your collection. Magnetic tape is also rather delicate, and maintaining a temperature- and humidity-controlled environment is another expense to your library and will be a constant expense rather than a onetime thing.

Magnetic tape is also an unfamiliar medium in comparison to others discussed in this book. A cassette tape is used as the example in this chapter often because this is the kind of magnetic tape that most people are familiar with—and cassette tapes are typically used only for audio recordings and are considered largely obsolete. Magnetic tape in general is not an obsolete form of storage, but your staff may have trouble adjusting and learning to use this less familiar medium.

Magnetic tape is not invulnerable. While the plastic substrate that the magnetic coating adheres to is tough and durable, there are limitations in the construction of tape. Dust or dirt on the tape will disrupt the data and cause problems with reading it. The plastic is vulnerable to warping, sticking, and other problems.

In addition, writing and reading data from a tape is slow, much slower than other methods of data storage and recording. A magnetic tape, as mentioned earlier, is sequential in nature. This means that every time you want to retrieve data from a magnetic tape, the head on the tape drive has to go through every bit of data that comes before the information you want, physically turning the reels and looking for the location of your requested information. Although improvements are being made, this is comparatively slow. This means that tape is best used for a long-term backup—something that you don't plan on needing again soon and that exists merely to keep information safe. If you want patrons to be able to access your information in a digital format, then this may not be the best method for it.

Although magnetic tape has been in use for decades and is one of the oldest and best-understood methods of storing data, it is not invulnerable to obsolescence. Even though tapes come in standard sizes and formats, it's possible for those sizes and formats to eventually become replaced by better versions. As a more familiar example, floppy disks originally came in 8-in. sizes, which were replaced by 5.25-in. sizes and then later by 3.5-in. sizes. All of these are floppy disks and use the same basic technology and can be read on a variety of computer brands. However, it's next to impossible to find a device that will read one of the larger floppy disks today. Likewise, the equipment necessary for recording and reading data from older tapes may eventually become unavailable. As advances are made with tape, equipment necessary to operate the old tape becomes obsolete, and companies stop making it for practical reasons. Even though there are standards with tape, once a type of tape becomes outdated, there is no guarantee that modern equipment will be able to operate old styles of tape or be backward compatible. The data on older reels of magnetic tape may be permanently lost due to an inability to retrieve it, just as the data on computer punch cards can't be retrieved because there are no more computers that can interpret it.

While some companies do make equipment that converts one tape format to another, this will be another expense for your archive and could require people to learn to use the new equipment and transfer information from one kind of tape to another (Bigourdan et al. 2006). In addition, if something cheaper and more convenient than tape is ever developed, you may have a problem on your hands, since ordinary computers don't come with a way to read tape. In contrast, if you had a collection of information on floppies before they became outdated and wanted to move them to CD, there was a large window of time in which average desktop computers had both floppy drives and CD drives, meaning that you would have needed no special equipment for the transfer. However, since so many institutions use magnetic tape for mass storage, it's unlikely that tape will be dropped from use as quickly as the floppy disk was.

◎ Storing Magnetic Tape

Like any method of data storage, keeping the item that the data is stored on safe is essential to long-term preservation. Tape has a number of enemies that must be combated, and in general, the best plan is to have a designated location for the tape that has the proper conditions.

Humidity

Magnetic tape is vulnerable to water, and high humidity is the most dangerous condition to tape. While a tape can fail in a number of ways, the polymer that binds the magnetizable substance to the substrate is the part most likely to fail on a tape, and it can degrade if exposed to moisture. This can result in tape that is brittle or soft or in tape becoming sticky and unplayable, or the magnetic powders may come off the polyester substrate. It's also possible for the magnetic coating to oxidize if exposed to moisture—that is, your tape will get rusty (Bigourdan et al. 2006). An additional and rather distasteful problem is fungal growth, which can occur on tapes exposed to humidity. High humidity for a tape is anything above 65% relative humidity (Orio et al. 2010). Storing tape at around 40% relative humidity is best (Bigourdan et al. 2006).

Temperature

Temperature is another important condition. High temperatures can cause the plastic to warp, distorting the data on the face of the tape. It can also increase the rate at which tape decays, particularly if there is high humidity present (Orio et al. 2010). Optimal storage temperature for tape is around 20°C/68°F (Bigourdan et al. 2006). Temperatures that are too low can be harmful as well; tape must be kept above freezing temperatures. In addition, if the tape and drive are not in the same area, then the tape needs to acclimate to the new temperature before playing or recording (Van Bogart 1995a). It's important to keep tape away from any sources of heat, such as radiators or heating units, and to keep it out of direct sunlight and away from windows, even ones that aren't functional, since glass doesn't insulate well.

Pollutants

Dust and dirt are enemies of magnetic tape. While a laser can sometimes read through dirt on a CD, this is a challenge for the read/write head for magnetic tape, since it is in close contact with the tape. The data on a tape is so tightly compacted that a single particle of smoke from a cigarette is enough to obscure data from the head for modern high-density tapes. Any smog or other chemicals in the air can also disturb the data or cause chemical deterioration of the tape (Orio et al. 2010). Therefore, the cleanliness of the air and the concentration of airborne pollutants is a factor to consider when choosing and maintaining a storage area for your tapes (Van Bogart 1995a).

Magnetic Fields

Since magnetism is key to both reading from the tape and writing to it, magnetic fields are another problem. Even a relatively weak magnetic field, like one on a microphone or headset, can be powerful enough to weaken the strength of data written on tape (Orio et al. 2010). Remember: magnets and electricity can influence other magnets, and if the atoms making up a magnet, like magnetic tape, become randomized, then the magnetization is lost and so is the binary code stored on the tape. Tapes should not be stored near any electronic equipment or machines that might generate a strong magnetic field (Van Bogart 1995a).

Other Problems

Although not quite within the abilities of an archive to address and combat, distortions, deformities, and other problems with the physical qualities of the tape itself constitute another issue in regard to data preservation (Orio et al. 2010). This can be avoided by storing the tapes properly. Tapes shouldn't be stored flat; the reel that holds the tape should be perpendicular to the shelf (Van Bogart 1995a). This is similar to how CDs and DVDs should be stored, since flat storage can cause warping in both mediums and lead to an inability to retrieve the data.

While all of this might sound somewhat complex, the ideal storage conditions aren't much different from ideal room temperature conditions, and they are within the capabilities of most archives to handle with minimal equipment. If you had a small building

IDEAL STORAGE AND HANDLING OF MAGNETIC TAPE

Humidity: 40%–65% relative humidity

Storage: Upright, not flat

Storage location:

- Away from windows and sunlight
- Away from airborne dust, smoke, chemicals, and general pollution
- Away from magnetic fields and electronic equipment

Temperature: 68°F (20°C), do not freeze

Transportation:

- Do not subject to harsh temperatures and moisture
- Wind tape tightly and pack well with bubble wrap
- Do not subject to handheld metal detectors

with a fairly small collection, for instance, you could simply dedicate a closet to storing your collection of tapes and just be sure that it stays cool and dry inside.

While tape can be transported, either to an off-site location for safety or to another archive, it's important to remember to maintain optimal conditions during transport. The temperature should never exceed 100°F, and the tape must not be exposed to water. It's best if the tape can be transported in the same position that it's stored, upright rather than flat. Ensuring that tapes are properly wound and protected by packing materials such as bubble wrap to absorb shocks will help protect tapes. Some detectors, like those used in airports, can erase tapes. Walk-through metal detectors and X-ray scanners aren't an issue, but handheld metal detectors generate a powerful enough magnetic field to erase a tape (Van Bogart 1995a).

When magnetic tape is stored under typical room conditions, it will last anywhere between 10 and 30 years. Cooler, drier conditions can increase this life expectancy by decades (Bigourdan et al. 2006), and the oldest tapes that are still playable are around 60 years old (UNESCO Communication and Information 2000).

As part of your routine for storing magnetic tapes, you should examine them periodically for damage. In general, there are two ways of going about this, usually at the same time. You can physically examine tape to determine the extent of decay, if any, or a computer can play through the data to determine if there is any decay.

Your recording device will also require care. Remember, the read/write heads on players are sensitive and come in close contact with tape. Be vigilant and clean them when necessary. For a tape drive designed for a personal computer, there are cleaning cartridges, which can be inserted instead of a data cartridge for the purpose of cleaning the drive. The drive will run through the tape, and the tape will help clean the heads. There is also a head-cleaning spray, which is a little like compressed air used for cleaning the insides of computers and keyboards (Andrews 2006). This gets any dust or particles that might interfere with reading the tapes out of the heads.

⊚ Key Points

- Magnetic tape is one of the oldest methods of long-term mass data storage and continues to be going strong today.
- Magnetic tape is inexpensive, and its vulnerabilities and estimated longevity are well understood, making it one of the best choices for a large archive.
- Magnetic tape does require controlled storage conditions for optimal function and longevity, and it needs specialized equipment to read and write to the tape, which adds to the overall expense. It's typically not the best choice for a small project or library.

Tape is a good choice for mass storage and is much more convenient for this than the CDs as discussed in the previous chapter, but it is not your only choice for large amounts of data storage. Hard drives are a common method of both external and internal storage, with many appealing qualities that can be used for a variety of purposes.

⊚ References

Andrews, Jean. 2006. *A+ Guide to Managing and Maintaining Your PC*. 6th ed. Boston: Course Technology.

Bigourdan, Jean-Louis, James M. Reilly, Karen Santoro, et al. 2006. "The Preservation of Magnetic Tape Collections: A Perspective." https://www.imagepermanenceinstitute.org/imaging/research/magnetic-tape.

Bycer, Bernard B. 1965. *Digital Magnetic Tape Recording: Principles and Computer Applications*. New York: Hayden Book Company.

Dale, Nell, and John Lewis. 2013. *Computer Science Illuminated*. 5th ed. Burlington, MA: Jones & Bartlett Learning.

Encyclopedia Americana. 2006a. *Magnet and Magnetism*. Danbury, CT: Scholastic Library.

———. 2006b. *Magnetic Recording*. Danbury, CT: Scholastic Library.

Fuller, Floyd, and Brian Larson. 2008. *Computers: Understanding Technology Comprehensive*. 3rd ed. St. Paul, MN: Paradigm.

Gifford, F. 1977. *Tape: A Radio News Handbook*. New York: Hastings House.

Graham-Rowe, Duncan. 2010. "New Life for Magnetic Tape." *MIT Technology Review*. http://www.technologyreview.com/news/417218/new-life-for-magnetic-tape/.

IEEE Global History Network. 2012. "Magnetic Tape." http://www.ieeeghn.org/wiki/index.php/Magnetic_Tape.

Lawrence, Ken. 2003. "Old Tape Gets New Edge." *Machine Design* 75 (11): 52.

Orio, Nicola, Lauro Snidaro, Sergio Canazza, and Gian Luca Foresti. 2010. "Methodologies and Tools for Audio Digital Archives." *International Journal on Digital Libraries* 10 (4): 201–20.

PC Mag. 2013. "Magnetic Drum." http://www.pcmag.com/encyclopedia/term/46492/magnetic-drum.

Rusch, Richard B. 1969. *Computers: Their History and How They Work*. New York: Simon & Schuster

UNESCO Communication and Information. 2000. "Typology and History." http://webworld.unesco.org/safeguarding/en/txt_magn.htm.

Van Bogart, John W.C. 1995a. "How Can You Prevent Magnetic Tape from Degrading Prematurely?" http://www.clir.org/pubs/reports/pub54/5premature_degrade.html.

———. 1995b. "What Can Go Wrong with Magnetic Media?" http://www.clir.org/pubs/reports/pub54/2what_wrong.html.

Wiehler, Gerhard. 1979. *Magnetic Peripheral Data Storage*. London: Heyden.

Hard Drives

BECAUSE THEY ARE AN INTEGRAL PART of modern personal computers, hard drives are covered somewhat in chapter 2, which discusses the basic parts of a computer. The majority of desktops and laptops produced today contain a hard drive but not all. The other current option is to have a solid-state drive, which is covered in the following chapter. For the sake of simplicity, though, just assume for now that all computers have a hard drive as a major component. This makes hard drives a little different from the other methods of data storage covered in this book. As such, you may be interested to know more about them simply for the sake of improving the efficiency of your archiving project and for enhancing the computers that you use on a daily basis and not solely for their potential use in storing data long-term.

For a bit of review, a computer operates by making many calculations very rapidly. These calculations are made by the central processing unit, or CPU. But the results of these calculations don't stay in the CPU. Imagine that you're trying to add a few numbers together in your head. Your brain is the CPU in this analogy. You can calculate the numbers just fine, but you might forget them quickly, especially if you need to be thinking about something else, like your next set of numbers. The best thing to do is to write your answer down on a piece of paper before you move on. A computer can do essentially the same thing using temporary memory, such as random access memory, or RAM chips. Once the CPU makes calculations, it can store the results on a RAM chip.

The RAM chips have a few drawbacks, and the one relevant to this discussion is the fact that they can't store information indefinitely. Once you turn off the power to the computer, RAM chips lose whatever data they had stored. This is pretty inconvenient, since you may rely on your computer to store and remember all kinds of data. Computers as people use them today would be useless if you lost every word processor file, image, song, game, or any other information that you had stored on the machine every time you turned off the power (or lost power accidentally). In any case, RAM chips wouldn't be able to handle storing the amount of data that the average user requires—RAM chips are for temporary storage only.

This is why a computer needs a hard drive, which works differently than RAM chips as a method of data storage. Hard drives don't have the rapid memory storage and retrieval that RAM chips do, but they can encode data for long-term storage. They don't lose their data once you turn off the computer, and they require no electricity whatsoever to preserve their data. All those word files, images, songs, games, and other data that you might have on a computer are all stored permanently on the hard drive. So are the programs and software that you use, as well as the operating system itself, which is essential for computer function in general. Modern hard drives are capable of storing a formidable amount of data.

If hard drives are used for regular, everyday data storage, you might be wondering—why bother with CDs or DVDs or magnetic tape for archiving? If a hard drive is perfectly serviceable, stores a significant amount of data, and is found already installed on every personal computer, then what is the point of using something else?

The truth of the matter is that you can use a hard drive disk to store your archival data. There are some perks to doing so as well. Like everything else, though, there are problems with relying on hard drives. To understand what their vulnerabilities are, it helps to understand a bit more about how hard drives function. Some of this information is covered in chapter 2; this section goes into more detail regarding the operation of a hard drive.

⊚ Hard Drive Operation

If you were to open up your computer and have a look around, you'd eventually find a box that has some small vents in the sides and is attached by a cord to your motherboard. Most likely, it would also have a sticker somewhere that says "hard drive" and gives you some helpful model information, making your search and identification of this item much easier.

This little box contains some of the few parts of a computer that actually physically move, as you'd normally expect from a machine, rather than simply creating pulses of electricity. There are quite a few things in there, such as a motor and circuits to buffer information to and from the motherboard. *Buffering*, by the way, refers to temporarily storing data so that it can be easily retrieved, processed, and so on. The important part of a hard drive, the part that holds the data, is contained on a series of disks, one stacked atop another. One to four disks is common for a hard drive. These disks are called *platters*. The disks are circular and made from aluminum, glass, or ceramic, resembling (in form and function) small records. The platters are also coated in extremely thin layers of several other substances that enable the hard drive to function, such as a layer of a magnetizable material to encode data. The entire disk is thin and fine, in spite of all the coatings.

Like magnetic tape (covered in the previous chapter), hard drives encode the binary ones and zeros using miniscule magnetic fields, with the polarity of the fields signaling either a one or a zero. This is the reason for the layer of magnetizable material. With magnetic tape, there is a read/write head that is able to use pulses of electricity to change the polarity of a binary one or zero. Hard drives have read/write heads, too, and can do the same thing to change the data.

Exactly how the read/write head works is slightly different from a magnetic tape reader, though. In a tape reader, the magnetic tape rotates, and the tape moves under the read/write head. In a hard drive, the platters with the information encoded on them are lined up on a spindle, one over another. When the spindle turns, so do the disks. The disks have to physically rotate to the right location where the data is encoded, a little like magnetic tape. Unlike magnetic tape, though, the read/write head is not fixed. It's attached to an arm, which can move up and down the face of a platter, searching for the data requested by the user (again, like a record player). This approach is much quicker than magnetic tape's method of seeking information.

The read/write head for magnetic tape is in very close contact with the tape as it turns, which is normal and desirable. On a hard drive, everything is compact and close together, so the read/write head is also close to the platters but must not touch them. The spinning of the disks creates a tiny cushion of air, which the head rests on while it reads the data. This is important because if the read/write head touches the disks, it can cause physical scratches and damage to the platter.

As you learned in the previous two chapters, the data on optical disks such as CDs and the data on magnetic tape are written in an organized way. That is, there aren't little clumps of ones and zeroes strewn all about the face of the medium. On an optical disk, the data is written in little pits and lands that are lined up along a spiral on the disk; this spiral is so important that it's physically imprinted on writable CDs to help write the information more precisely for the laser to read. On a piece of magnetic tape, the data is organized in tracks, with one track running under each read/write head, appearing just a little like the tracks on a racetrack.

The platters on a hard drive have the data physically organized as well, but it's slightly more complicated. If the disks were square, then the logical physical organization would probably be a grid pattern, but since they're circular, it's a little more like a spiderweb.

A hard drive is divided into concentric circles of data, kind of like a dartboard. Data is written along these little circles, known as *tracks*. The data is divided further, however, into sectors. Imagine the hard drive being sliced up like a pie—only, each "slice" is a sector. This is a little like how sectors actually work.

Typically, each sector can hold 512 bytes, so one sector is pretty small (a very thin slice of pie). Remember, at least eight bytes are needed to make a letter, so each sector could hold 64 letters, which is not very much data.

When a file gets written to a disk, it selects part of a track that has been divided into sectors. Again, think of it as being kind of like a dartboard—the data gets written to one of the sections on the board. The computer can write data in segments called *clusters*, which are segments of track that are adjacent to one another on the disk. Clusters are the minimum amount of space that you can use at a time.

Computers can keep track of the exact location of where the data is written, sort of like using a table of contents for a book but with data files. Most computers use something called a *file allocation table*, or FAT, although there are other ways of going about the same problem. This table "tells" the computer where to look for data; thus, the read/write head can move, and the disk can rotate to the correct physical location for the data.

Although the ideal situation is for all the data for a file to be written in one area on a disk, data can be written to different places on a disk and not stored in one location. For instance, if you were playing a game, the save files of your actual game play might be scattered about the disk and not stored alongside the data for the game itself. This phenomenon is known as *fragmentation*. As you learned in chapter 7, this would be highly inconvenient on magnetic tape, since the tape must physically rotate under the read/write head to reach the desired data. It would take even longer to access all the data that you needed if different parts of the same file were physically located on different sections of the tape.

The platter in a hard drive must rotate to the correct position as well, but this is significantly less important to access time than it would be with magnetic tape. The arm holding the read/write head moves up and down the disk as it rotates, seeking out the desired information. In combination with the quick rotation speed of the disk (7,200 rpm, or rotations per minute, on a typical hard drive today), this makes the access speed quite rapid in comparison to magnetic tape. As mentioned in the previous chapter, this method of seeking out information is known as *direct access*, as opposed to *sequential access*, the method used by tape.

This access method is not completely perfect—having parts of a file scattered about in multiple locations does reduce the speed of access in comparison to having a file in one physical location on a disk. Most of the time, a computer will allocate data to a logical spot that makes for optimal access speed, and it's possible to improve the distribution of your files. If you've ever defragmented a computer (there are programs that do this for you, and there's usually one included with your computer's software), what the computer does is move data around so that it is in a more logical configuration. It will search for files that are fragmented, or in multiple locations, and rearrange the order of the data written to the disk so that parts of files are next to one another.

All hard drives operate in the same general fashion and have the same basic parts, but there are some differences among them—for example, size (physical and amount of storage) and how they connect to the computer. You can use any hard drive and get good results, but it will be more efficient if you use a hard drive that is optimal for your situation.

Types of Hard Drives

If you want to use hard drives to store your archival data, it's important that you're aware of the typical features of a drive and how to choose the optimal one for your archive. You may also be interested in this information so that you can choose a good hard drive for your computer, for daily use rather than long-term storage, since hard drives are easily used for both functions.

Internal vs. External

Many factors are involved in choosing a hard drive, and the first of these is deciding whether you want an internal hard drive or an external one. The difference between them is pretty obvious—an internal hard drive goes inside of a computer, and an external hard drive attaches from the outside.

You may wonder what the point of getting an internal hard drive would be, since your computer already has a hard drive inside it. Your computer can, in fact, have more than

> ## QUALITIES OF A HARD DRIVE
>
> Cache memory size
>
> Connections—SATA, PATA, USB, eSATA, FireWire, Thunderbolt
>
> Installation—internal versus external
>
> Rotation speed—5,400–10,000 rpm
>
> Size—desktop versus laptop
>
> Storage capacity

one hard drive, and people who need to store a lot of data—for example, those who digitally edit video—frequently install two or more inside their computers. Many desktops even come with a space inside the case to hold additional hard drives so that this is easier to do. This applies to laptops, too—some laptops have empty space inside that is designed to accommodate an extra hard drive. If you want to be able to store more data, then an internal hard drive has appeal.

You can also have an external hard drive rather than an internal hard drive. External hard drives plug into a port on your computer. This has a couple of advantages for you. First, it requires no expertise at all to attach an external hard drive to a computer, whereas it requires some technical knowledge to correctly install a new internal hard drive. An external hard drive is also ideal if you want to store the hard drive someplace else; once installed, internal hard drives are best left inside the computer, but you can remove an external hard drive and put it elsewhere whenever you want. If you want to physically archive the object that holds your data, then an external hard drive is probably what you need.

Note that internal hard drives have some significant benefits. For one, they cost about half as much as an external hard drive, which also stores and transfers data more slowly than internal ones. They are, in essence, exactly the same thing and can be used for the same purpose, but if what you really need is an internal hard drive, you shouldn't use an external hard drive as a substitute (though you could if you wanted to).

Size

There are generally two sizes for internal hard drives—the 3.5-in. desktop version and the 2.5-in. laptop version. The number refers to the size of the platters, not the casing. Larger drives usually hold more data than small disks and typically spin more rapidly. However, it's best to just use the type of drive designed for the type of computer that you want to install it into, regardless of the pros and cons of each kind. In particular, if you are adding an extra hard drive to a laptop, you'll be limited by size and will have to use a drive specifically designed for a laptop.

External hard drives also come in multiple physical sizes and can come in portable or desktop versions. Portable hard drives are small, as you might expect from the name, and are comparable to the type of hard drives that come in a laptop. Desktop hard drives are physically larger.

Portable hard drives often hold less data and spin more slowly than desktop hard drives, which results in a slower access time. The advantage of portable hard drives is, of course, portability—they're designed to be compact and easily moved around. This may or may not be important to you, and if portability is not a factor in your situation, then the desktop version is most likely the better choice as far as usefulness to your archive.

However, portable hard drives do have a subtle advantage over desktop hard drives. The disks need a power source to spin and read the data. With a portable drive, when you connect the drive to the computer, it's usually able to draw enough power from the computer via the connection port to function. Desktop hard drives sometimes need to be plugged into an additional power source, which can be a bit inconvenient, since you'll have to be near an electric outlet and then plug and unplug the device when you want to move it.

Connections

Internal hard drives plug into your computer with a cable on the inside that connects it to the motherboard (motherboards are discussed in chapter 2). An internal hard drive can use two interfaces: a serial ATA (or SATA) and a parallel ATA (or PATA). Hard drives that use SATA connectors are easier to install and operate at faster speeds but are typically more expensive. Older computers may not have a SATA connector, which means that you'll need to install one or use a PATA. More recent computers sometimes have both kinds of connectors. Computers that are quite old might need some upgrading to recognize a new hard drive, since they are not designed to be able to access the amounts of data that a hard drive can store in modern times.

As mentioned earlier, external hard drives plug into a port on the outside of your computer. An external hard drive can connect to a few different ports—with USB ports, eSATA ports, and FireWire ports being the most common. USB and FireWire ports are covered in detail in chapter 2, since they can have many functions and connect to a variety of devices.

Hard drives that connect to a USB port are particularly common. USB ports are convenient in that they're found on nearly all modern computers and computers usually have several of these ports—that is, if you need to use multiple devices that connect to a USB port at the same time, you won't be using your only USB port for the hard drive. The convenience offered by USB ports makes them very appealing, but they're not always the fastest way to transfer data, so you might be interested in your other options as well if speed is an important feature for you.

An external hard drive can also connect via an eSATA port, which is like the connector for an internal hard drive but connects external hard drives and allows for an extremely rapid data transfer rate. However, these kinds of ports are less common than USB or FireWire ports (these two ports are more general purpose than an eSATA port), and if your computer doesn't have one, installing an additional port requires some computer expertise. However, if your computer already has such a port or if installing the necessary port and adaptor card is not an obstacle, this may be an appealing option.

If you're using Macintosh computers and you want to use an external hard drive, one that connects via FireWire could be appealing; Macintosh computers typically come with at least one FireWire port, though FireWire ports can sometimes be found on other kinds of computers. FireWire ports transfer data quickly and provide more power than a single USB port, which can eliminate the problem of needing a power cord for your hard drive since it may be able to draw sufficient power from the computer itself. However, there are a couple of disadvantages to this that you should consider.

The first of these is that FireWire is not found on all computers and USB ports are a bit more universal, which makes access to the data easier (if you're concerned about data safety, though, making access more difficult may be something that you're interested in, in which case this is a bonus). The second is that the Apple company, which makes Macintosh computers and created the FireWire port, has upgraded the FireWire port over time, so different ports manufactured at different times may not be compatible with one another. FireWire 400 (the original version) and FireWire 800 have different dimensions and configurations, so devices designed for one will not fit into the other. There are adaptor cables that can adapt a device designed for a FireWire 800 port to a FireWire 400 port, but this is a bit of an inconvenience.

Macintosh computers also have a fourth option: a Thunderbolt port. These ports are currently uncommon and are found on a limited range of Mac devices. These ports transfer data quite rapidly, and so if you have such a port on your computers, you might be interested in external hard drives that can connect in this method. There are also adapters available that can connect a FireWire device to a Thunderbolt port. It's possible that the Apple company will phase out FireWire ports for Thunderbolt ports eventually, which is something else to consider when making a purchase.

Rotation Speed

The speed at which a hard drive rotates is one of the factors that you might use in deciding which hard drive is best for your archive. The faster it rotates, the faster the data access speed. Rotation speeds of 5,400, 7,200, or 10,000 rpm are typical. If you want the hard drive for long-term storage without accessing it on a regular basis, the speed is likely to be less important to you, and slower speeds typically mean a less expensive disk, so you can save a little money by choosing a lower rotation speed. If you're looking for an extra hard drive for a computer that you'll be using for processing data, then a quicker speed may be a better choice.

Cache Memory

Like the CPU, the hard drive needs a place to temporarily store and process data before recording it. This is known as *cache memory*. The bigger the cache memory, the more efficient the hard drive is. However, if you're using the hard drive for long-term storage and don't plan on accessing the data often, this is another area in which you can save a little money, since it will matter less to you how quickly the hard drive operates. If you're adding a hard drive to a computer for function, a large cache might be something you're interested in. Similarly, the manufacturer may list the access time, which refers to how quickly it can find a file. Again, a quick access time might not matter to you for storage but might for daily function.

Storage Capacity

While you can omit some features to save money with a hard drive, by not getting the fastest, most powerful device out there, the number with which bigger is always better is the hard drive's capacity, noted in gigabytes (GB) or more recently terabytes (TB).

Remember, a terabyte is about a trillion bytes, whereas a gigabyte is about a billion bytes, so a 200-GB hard drive is a fraction of the size of a 1-TB hard drive.

⊚ Hard Drives for Archiving

Hard drives aren't really designed for the long-term data storage that an archive typically needs. They're designed to be able to change their data quickly and to be updated frequently, with the user writing new files or erasing them regularly; in fact, they can start losing their data if not used this way. However, you can certainly use them to store data long-term if you desire, and there are some advantages to using hard drives for your archive's main method of data storage.

Advantages

- Large storage capacity
- Fairly inexpensive
- Do not require special equipment to read data
- Simple to use

Disadvantages

- Short life span
- Difficult to assess condition
- Prone to reading and writing errors as well as virus attack
- Easy to break
- Needs refreshing

Advantages

In many ways, using a hard drive for storage is economical. It's not as cumbersome as using optical disks, like CDs, since it could take hundreds of CDs to store the same amount of data as a single hard drive, even a hard drive that is fairly small by today's standards. Optical disks are pretty inexpensive per gigabyte compared to hard drives, but convenience is important to the efficiency of your archive, and efficiency is always a cost saver—no one wants to take the time that it might involve to find a particular file on a particular disk among hundreds when you could find the file in seconds on a hard drive via a keyword search (it might be less convenient if your files aren't named well, though).

Hard drives aren't as inexpensive per gigabyte of data as magnetic tape, either, but if you don't need to save huge amounts of data, hard drives make for a nice compromise because you don't have to buy a reader for them the way you would with magnetic tape. In other words, hard drives are efficient if you need to store more data than what would be convenient on CDs but less than the amount that would make using magnetic tape worthwhile. This happy medium may change over time, though. Because hard drive disks are an important and cost-efficient component in most desktops and laptops, they are subject to innovation by companies hoping to profit from improving on their product and will most likely continue to have the ability to store more and more data for less money for some time to come.

Using external hard drives is pretty simple, too, which is always an advantage because your staff won't need much training to learn how to use one. As mentioned earlier, these drives simply plug into a port. Installing an internal hard drive, if you're interested in that, is a little more complex but is still something that you can often do yourself if you're careful. Using an internal hard drive, of course, requires no expertise whatsoever.

Optical disks such as CDs and DVDs have an advantage in that they're not a unique storage method—you can go into many stores, even ones that don't sell electronics specifically, and buy perfectly serviceable blank disks. This is an advantage that they share with hard drives. External hard drives are pretty common, and many stores, such as those offering office equipment, sell external hard drives that are perfectly serviceable, although you'll certainly want to get the best quality one available if your budget allows it. Magnetic tape, however, is more of a specialty item that's harder to find, and it will need to be ordered from a company specializing in the sale of magnetic tape.

If you want to make your collection available online and not simply store the data passively, data stored on hard drives lends itself pretty well for this purpose. You can use multiple hard drives and store data within a server computer by connecting these hard drives, which then can be configured to allow access to the data through a network; this network can be for your archive's computers only or the Internet, which allows for public access. Note, however, that this is also possible to do with other methods of data storage, but the access time may not be as good.

Disadvantages

Hard drives are highly mechanical. While the important parts are the platters that contain the data and the arm with the read/write head that writes and accesses the data, a hard drive consists of many parts. It has a motor, bearings, lubricants, and more. The more parts there are, the more that can go wrong. The motor can go bad; the lubricants can evaporate; the air intakes can fail, letting dust into the casing and causing damage to the platters as they spin; and many other problems can occur.

Essentially, hard drive failure is inevitable, and hard drives often have a short life span relative to other storage methods. However, this doesn't mean that you should automatically rule out hard drives as a storage medium, since all methods of storage will wear out or decay eventually—it's a matter of whether the benefits are worth the risks that are involved.

Hard drives can fail without warning. They'll be working one moment and not at all the next. Failures can happen in a number of ways. For instance, the platters, which rotate at extremely high speeds, can bump into one another. This is not supposed to happen during normal use, but, of course, accidents happen. It's also possible for the head that reads and writes to the disks to bump into the disks. Normally, there is a small cushion of air between the disks and the read/write head, which protects them from each other, but if this cushion is disrupted somehow while the disks are still spinning, it can create physical damage to the disk below, grinding away the data. These particular problems can generate audio cues indicating that something is wrong, since hard drives make almost no sound when working properly. Hearing these cues may mean that it's already too late and your data has been lost due to physical damage on the platters. It's also possible for parts of a hard drive to go bad but for the drive itself to still be functional or for sections of data to be lost but not all of them.

Assessing a hard drive's condition can be difficult in comparison to other methods of data storage discussed so far. The platters and all the mechanisms required for operation are concealed within a protective case, and opening the case exposes the drive to the environment. This can damage the drive. With a CD, for example, you can visually examine the disks for cracks or discoloration, or you can look at a magnetic tape for rust.

Hard drives are susceptible to a phenomenon known as *bit rot*. This phrase refers to the decay of the binary coding in a storage medium, and it can actually mean different things when referring to different types of storage media. All methods of media storage are vulnerable to this in some way. With hard drives, the bits of magnetic encoding are so small that they can be erased by temperature fluctuations.

Similarly, sectors on hard drives can go bad for a variety of reasons. Modern hard drives are even manufactured with this in mind and have sectors that are held in reserve for whenever sectors on the hard drive start going bad. These bad sectors can be caused by small errors in writing the data to the hard drive, which leads to an inability to read the data, or they can be caused by mechanical issues, such as dust in the hard drive. Errors with writing can be repaired by erasing the disk (filling it with binary zeroes); physical damage can't be fixed so easily. It's also possible for viruses to attack a hard drive and create false readings, making it appear as though a hard drive has bad sectors (another problem that can often be fixed).

Hard drives don't withstand physical abuse well; a fairly short drop could severely damage a hard drive. In contrast, if you were to drop a CD on a rug, for instance, it might bounce and still be readable. Trying this, however, is not recommended.

Because hard drives are quite common and have been in use for some time, they do have some of the same advantages as magnetic tape in that they are well understood. However, because they aren't really designed for archival storage and are supposed to be used for everyday data storage, their efficacy as a long-term storage device has not been explored as well as that of magnetic tape or even optical media.

Hard Drives for Archival Storage

Like magnetic tape and optical disks, the environmental conditions under which you store hard drives can make a difference in how long they last.

Temperature

One of the primary causes of bit rot is high temperatures, and so controlling the temperature is important to longevity. A temperature range of around 60°F to 69°F (16°C–20°C) is optimal (Imation 2012). Although this is a good storage temperature range, the operational range (how hot a drive is when it's actually being used) doesn't have a lot of impact on how long a drive lasts, unless it's very hot (more than 125°F/52°C). However, computers can operate at temperatures that exceed this, so what you need to do to ensure that your hard drive is safe during operation is to make sure that your computer is not overheating and that your hard drive has good ventilation and airflow to cool it adequately (Jacobi 2007).

Humidity

High humidity is bad for electronics in general, and there are a few ways that humidity can disrupt hard drive function. Low humidity will prevent many problems, with a relative humidity of 35% to 45% (or lower) being best (Imation 2012).

Location

Although you should take care with choosing your storage location, hard drives are fairly resistant to magnetic fields, unlike magnetic tapes, which are vulnerable, even though both are forms of magnetic data storage. When you store a hard drive, it's typically best to keep it flat (the disk inside should lay horizontally), as opposed to optical disks and magnetic tapes, which are best stored vertically, in book fashion. Don't stack hard drives on top of one another or put anything heavy on top of a hard drive. If you were to store multiple hard drives, for instance, you would have to put them next to one another on a shelf or have a storage setup in which each drive has its own shelf or slot.

Handling

Hard drives are designed to be used inside a computer and not moved around, and they are somewhat delicate in that respect. Handle hard drives carefully; never drop or shake a hard drive, and take precautions against static electricity. The case will help protect it, but it's always a good idea to be cautious. Don't open up the casing, as this will expose the hard drive to dust and static.

It's important that the data has finished saving to a hard drive before you remove it, in the case of an external hard drive. Failure to do so can cause damage to the drive itself, and though uncommon, it can be serious and result in permanent damage. Computers come with a wizard program designed to "eject" a drive like an external hard drive, which ensures that the data has completed writing before you remove it. This same program is useful for devices using flash memory, covered in the following chapter. When you use an external hard drive, you should always take care before removing the drive.

Use

Actively used hard drives are thought to last around 10 years. Under archival storage conditions, however, a hard drive may last longer, up to 30 years. As with magnetic tapes, this set of conditions is not much different from room temperature conditions and is within a pretty standard range for storing archival materials in general, regardless of whether they are electronic or not (Williams et al. 2008).

Hard drives are a bit different from optical disks and magnetic tape in that not only are they designed to be written and rewritten to over and over again, but they actually work best when used in this way. If left alone untouched, they will lose data or generate errors over time. With the other media covered so far (particularly with magnetic tapes), the less they are used, the better—not so with hard drives. It's in your best interest to plan for this if you use hard drives for long-term storage. Every 5 to 7 years, you should move the data on your hard drives from one drive to another. You could simply copy an external hard drive to an internal hard drive, erase the external hard drive, then rewrite the data to the external hard drive, or you could purchase a new hard drive and transfer

IDEAL STORAGE AND HANDLING OF HARD DRIVES

Handling:

- Handle carefully; do not shake or drop.
- Prevent static during transport.

Humidity: 35%–45% relative humidity

Operating temperature: Ideally, below 125°F (52°C)

Storage:

- Store with platters horizontal to storage surface.
- Do not put objects on top of hard drives.

Storage temperature: 60°F–69°F (16°C–20°C)

the data from the old drive to the new one. Rewriting a disk erases problems caused by bit rot. With hard drives, bit rot is not necessarily a problem with the disk itself; it's simply a loss of magnetization, so simply refreshing a disk is enough to help prevent problems (Imation 2012).

To be safer, though, it's a good idea to check the disk more often than this to detect errors (e.g., every year or so). Though not perfect (it's possible for software to miss problems), some software programs can alert you to errors and problems signaling that you should take action to save the recorded data. There are a few ways to do this. One is to use Self-Monitoring, Analysis, and Reporting Technology, or SMART, which is something that comes standard on modern hard drives. This feature analyzes the physical attributes of a disk and can alert you to issues and problems in the motor. Your computer may also come with programs that look for data errors or bad sectors, such as CHKDSK. If you purchase an external hard drive, it may come with diagnostic software, a feature that may have appeal to you when you're trying to make a decision.

Key Points

- Hard drives are a major component in most desktop and laptop computers and are the method for storing long-term memory in these devices.
- There are internal and external hard drives, and it's possible to install multiple hard drives in a computer to increase its storage space.
- Hard drives are not the fastest method of storing data or the most cost-effective choice, but they are a convenient middle-of-the-road option for storing a moderate amount of data and allow data to be quickly and easily accessed.

While hard drives are the storage medium of choice for many computers, it's not the only method of storing data long-term within the device itself. A growing competitor to the hard drive is flash memory, which is one of the most expensive choices for data storage but has many qualities that make it a highly desirable storage method for archiving and can be used for internal and external storage.

◉ References

Imation. 2012. "Best Practices for Archiving Removable Hard Disk Drives." http://www.imation
.com/Global/en-US/ScalableStorage/Products/RDXHDDStorage/IMN_WhitePaper_
ArchivingHDD.pdf.

Jacobi, Jon L. 2007. "Hard-Drive Failures Surprisingly Frequent." *PC World*. http://www.pcworld
.com/article/131168/article.html.

Williams, Paul, David S. H. Rosenthal, Mema Roussopoulos, and Steve Georgis. 2008. "Predicting Archival Life of Removable Hard Drive Disks." http://lockss.org/locksswiki/files/
ISandT2008.pdf.

Flash Memory

UNLIKE OPTICAL DISKS, MAGNETIC TAPE, OR HARD DRIVES, flash memory doesn't refer to a specific device or physical method of storage. While flash memory is, of course, physical in nature, it's better to think of it as a method that several different but related devices use to store electronic data.

While the term *flash memory* may seem unfamiliar to you, you are probably already aware of this technology, though possibly unknowingly. Items using flash memory storage are extremely prevalent, and this type of data storage is essential to the function of a number of everyday devices. Chances are good that you own a device (even several devices) that depends on flash memory for their operation.

An average modern computer has two methods of long-term memory storage. One of these is the ROM chips, which contain data, such as information for booting the computer. The other method is the hard drive, which is rewritable and can contain any information that you desire, such as vacation photos or videos of adorable cats.

You already know the basics of how the hard drive of a computer works, as discussed in chapters 2 and 8. It's basically composed of several spinning platters and an arm that reads the information encoded on them. The platters are delicate, though, and they can bump into one another if jostled or if something simply goes wrong during operation. If this happens while the hard drive is functioning, then the platters can scrape against one another, destroying the stored data and ultimately causing drive failure.

In a world in which people wish to access information from any location and carry their data with them, this delicacy is problematic because people routinely drop or shake their devices, purposely or by accident. There are innovations to the technology that make the platter system more portable—you can use them for the memory in a laptop, for instance—but their delicacy is still an issue. Using little platters to store data also puts a limit on how small these drives can be, presenting yet another problem, since companies want to make their devices as small and portable as possible. You may wonder then: how do small devices such as cameras and cellphones preserve their data?

Modern smartphones are like tiny computers and can even serve as a computer for users who don't need complex software programs. There isn't the space for a tiny hard drive inside, and adding one would make the phone rather heavy. It wouldn't work well anyway, since people notoriously drop cellphones, stick them into pockets, and otherwise abuse them unwittingly (or perhaps purposely) on a regular basis, which would not be good for a hard drive.

You could also use RAM chips, but those always require a little bit of electricity to preserve their data. If your computer loses electricity in the middle of a project, for instance, and you haven't saved it to the hard drive, the data from all your work will be lost because the RAM chips will lose all memory when the electricity is gone. Many people forget to charge their phones, letting the battery completely drain and leaving no electricity to preserve the data, so any data and programs would be deleted every time this happened if RAM chips were used. If your batteries were to drain in a camera that used RAM chips, all your photos would be lost.

The answer to this problem is flash memory—a technology unlike any other type of storage method—and there are a number of devices that can store data in this method. Memory cards, such as secure digital (SD) cards, and multimedia cards use flash memory. These flash memory cards are often used in digital cameras to provide extra memory storage, where the advantage of portability is essential. Along with cellphones and smartphones, flash memory is used in digital camcorders, MP3 players, and essentially anything else that requires portability and may need to endure some abuse.

In the previous chapter, you were asked to just assume, for the sake of simplicity, that a computer will have a hard drive as the major method of memory storage. This is not actually true, as computers in modern times can use either a regular hard drive or a device using flash memory. They each work equally well for this purpose (although each has some unique benefits and drawbacks), and flash memory is, as discussed, excellent when it comes to portability.

Since you're storing information in an archive, though, portability is probably not essential, and this is one of the most appealing virtues of a flash memory device. However, flash memory offers plenty of other features that may be useful to you as well and is an option that should be taken into consideration as a method of storage. As with the other methods discussed so far, flash memory is not suited to all situations, and it has some significant drawbacks, and so it's important to consider the particular needs of your archive when making a decision.

While a lot of devices use flash memory, you will most likely be interested in memory that offers a lot of storage space and can be easily removed from the computer. In actuality, there are a number of such devices, but to make things a little easier, consider flash devices as coming in three basic formats. One of these is known as the *solid-state device* or *solid-state disk*. These terms refer to the same thing and have the same acronym, SSD, which can help you when making a purchase.

The other is called the *flash drive*, also known by several other names, such as *thumb drive*, *jump drive*, *pen drive*, or *memory stick*. These are small and portable and have a connector attached that typically plugs into a USB port to transfer data (there are ones that use FireWire, but they're uncommon). They are far less delicate than optical disks and are currently popular for moving data from one computer to another.

The third type is the secure digital, or SD, card mentioned earlier, which is typically used for temporary storage in cameras and similar devices. Like flash drives, these are small and highly portable.

These three devices are slightly different and have different sizes, physically and in terms of storage. The way that these devices generally operate and how they are useful to you is the same, but there are some important differences that you should be aware of when it comes to archiving. For the moment, though, you can think of these devices as being equal or synonymous, since the way that they store data is essentially the same.

How Flash Memory Works

The way that flash memory works is much more complex and harder to visualize than any of the other methods explored so far—in part because it's not like any familiar forms of technology, such as a record or a cassette tape. The technology that it probably best resembles is that of early computers, which stored information in transistors. At the time, this revolutionized the way that computers were designed and operated. Although transistors continue to play an important part in modern electronics, chances are good that this technology doesn't seem very familiar to you.

A transistor is a device that can both conduct electricity or resist it. Because it's necessary for a transistor to be adaptive in regard to electricity, they're made of semiconductive materials that are neither good nor poor conductors of electricity; that is, they can conduct electricity but aren't very efficient at it. To contrast, think of the copper in an electrical wire, which conducts electricity very well, or of rubber, which doesn't conduct electricity at all and can instead insulate conductive material. In modern times, the semiconductive material of choice is typically silicon. The inside of a flash drive device is filled with what are essentially tiny transistors, each of which is 10,000 times finer than a human hair (Aaronson 2008).

Flash technology works by recording whether or not electrons can flow through these transistors. If it can conduct a current, then the corresponding transistor reads as a one; if it can't, then it reads as a zero. In a device using flash memory, one is the default value; erased cells have a value of one as well. When you want to save data to the device, then it has to change some of those ones to zeroes using a pulse of electricity (Aaronson 2008). This is a bit unusual, since the default value is typically zero for other storage devices. Each unit in a device using flash memory, or one of those miniscule transistors, is referred to as a *cell*.

Each cell has four basic parts: a floating gate, a control gate, a source, and a drain. The source and drain move electricity through the cell. While there are two gates, the floating gate is the one that stores electrons, which changes how conductive the cell is, thus making the entire cell read as a one or a zero based on the level of voltage detected running through the cell. The floating gate is surrounded by insulators, which help keep

FLASH MEMORY CELLS

Single-level cells: store 1 bit per cell and are the fastest, most accurate type.

Multilevel cells: store 2 bits per cell and are the most common type with median qualities.

Three-level cells: store 3 bits per cell and are the slowest but most compact type.

the electrons in place. This is necessary because, otherwise, electrons would leak out of the gate and erase the cell's binary value.

When a charge is applied to a cell, electrons are injected into the floating gate, making it a binary zero. It's erased, or changed back to a one, using another pulse of electricity. Ideally, if left alone, these electrons stay trapped in there indefinitely, and they can store information without the need for a constant power source, just as optical disks, magnetic tape, and hard drives do not need a power source.

Flash memory is more complex than other kinds of memory in that it can have more than a yes/no condition; that is, a cell can hold more than one value. To contrast, an optical disk has only two conditions: brightly reflected light or less brightly reflected light. Two conditions are typical for data storage because they mimic the two possibilities in binary, a one or a zero, and binary is the essential language of computers.

A *single-level cell*, or SLC, is like this, too. It can hold only one bit of data at a time, either a one or a zero, and the circuitry within the cell is able to detect only two thresholds for the voltage of an electrical current. However, there is such a thing as a *multilevel cell*, or MLC, which can hold two bits. The device is designed to detect four levels of voltage for a cell—a value of 00, 01, 10, or 11, depending on the level of charge stored in the cell. This gets a little complicated. In an SLC, the cell can detect either conductivity or a lack of conductivity. In an MLC, the cell can detect no conductivity, a little conductivity, more conductivity, and a lot of conductivity, and it can assign different pairs of binary values to each state rather than just one binary value (Super Talent 2013).

Though rarer, there are also such things as *three-level cells* (also known as *triple-level cells*), or TLCs, which can hold three bits per cell and have eight potential threshold values. There are some benefits and drawbacks to each method. For instance, a cell that can contain more than one value needs a more precise application of electricity to write the correct value to the cell. This results in an increase in time for writing to the cell, so while single-level cells can't store as much information per cell as multilevel cells or three-level cells, writing to them is quicker (Cornwell 2012).

You might see a couple of terms in connection with flash memory. One of these is *nonvolatile*, which refers to the fact that the memory within the cells is not lost once there is no longer electricity flowing through the cells, even though it's an electrically based method of data storage (in contrast to the optical or magnetic methods). RAM memory—used for basic computer function within the machine itself—is an example of volatile memory (explored in chapter 2). Once you turn off the computer, all the data within this type of memory is lost. For your purposes, the fact that flash memory is nonvolatile is a very good thing.

Another term that you might see is *FAT*, which stands for "file allocation table." Hard drives, as discussed in chapter 8, have a FAT, too, which is a sector on the device that records data, such as file names, sizes, and data location. Flash memory devices use either FAT-16 or FAT-32 systems (Dowler 2011).

◎ Differences among Flash Devices

Flash drives, secure digital cards, and solid-state drives all use the same technology and store information in the same general method. However, types of devices are not exactly the same, so it's important to know what those differences are.

Flash drives are probably the version of flash memory that you'll find the most familiar. They are also sometimes called *thumb drives*, and both these names are helpfully descriptive. *Flash* can refer to the storage technology as well as the speed with which it operates. These devices are, as mentioned earlier, designed to be put into the USB port of a computer, and a computer can begin reading the information encoded on the drive quite rapidly. *Thumb* refers to the size of the drive; these devices are often the size of a thumb or smaller, which makes them highly portable and convenient for transferring information.

Solid-state drives or disks (SSDs) are another type of flash memory device. The term *solid-state drive* is also descriptive, referring to the fact that these devices have no moving parts, in contrast to the other storage methods explored so far. However, flash drives don't have moving parts either, so these names don't quite describe the difference between them (although solid-state storage is far less portable than a flash drive). SSDs are physically larger than flash drives and are somewhat less portable and more delicate than flash drives.

Secure digital, or SD cards, are small, thin cards. There are actually several kinds of SD cards, such as the miniSD, microSD, miniSDHC, and more. They are all slightly different sizes, ranging between 11 and 32 mm in length (Beissel 2011a).

Again, all these devices use flash memory, but there are slight differences among them. SSDs contain a better controller for the cells within than that of flash drives or SD cards, which offers a few benefits to you. SSDs are faster than your other options. The controller also allows for better wear leveling. *Wear leveling* refers to a flash device's ability to use the cells evenly for data storage so that some cells don't wear out before the rest of the cells in the device (Beissel 2011c). However, SSDs are also more expensive than your other choices (Domingo 2013). Note that a regular SSD is designed to be a replacement for a traditional platter-style hard drive, located within the computer. For your archive, you'll probably want an external SSD, which plugs into a USB port using a connecting cord and is portable and easily removed, but there are situations in which you may find installing an internal SSD appealing.

TYPES OF FLASH MEMORY DEVICES

Flash drives: small and portable, useful for transferring data

Solid-state drives: larger with a large storage capacity, comparable to a hard drive

Secure digital cards: very small and compact, normally used for storage in devices/cameras

As far as portability, capacity, and capabilities go, SD cards and flash drives are similar to one another. However, there is one big difference that will be important to you. While some computers have a built-in SD slot, not all do; in fact, most have only one SD slot, which will not accommodate every type of SD card. Flash drives, however, plug into any USB port. As opposed to as a method of general data storage, SD cards are more commonly used in devices such as digital cameras, which then connect to a computer via a cord that plugs into a USB port. However, it is possible to buy card readers for SD cards, which can plug into the computer as a peripheral (Beissel 2011a).

SSDs are bigger and heavier than flash drives and SD cards, which makes the other two devices the optimal choices for true portability. If you want to be able to transfer files between computers, the portability and lower expense of flash drives are going to appeal to you. If you're looking at flash technology as a method of long-term information storage, then solid-state storage is more likely to be what you need.

Flash Memory for Archiving

Like any other storage technology, solid-state storage has some benefits to you, as well as some drawbacks.

Advantages

- High durability
- Works well in less-than-ideal conditions
- Does not require special equipment to read data
- Simple to use

Disadvantages

- Very difficult to assess condition and repair without a specialist
- Cells will eventually burn out
- Needs refreshing
- Very expensive
- Prone to loss or theft

Advantages

The greatest benefit of solid-state technology is the lack of moving parts. With magnetic tape, for example, simply reading the tape causes it to wear down over time and can eventually break it. Stress caused by moving the tape between reels is an issue. Regular hard drives are susceptible to a number of mechanical issues due to a high number of moving parts. Even a CD can shatter inside the reader, which spins the disk.

Solid-state storage has none of these problems. The lack of moving parts makes this technology extremely durable. You can even drop flash drives and still read the data. That's impossible with a normal hard drive and definitely inadvisable for optical disks and magnetic tape. Nothing will change the values encoded in the transistors but a change in their voltages. While it is certainly possible for devices using flash technology to fail and while they can physically break, they will withstand a lot of abuse in comparison to your other options. There are also flash memory devices specifically designed to withstand a number of extreme environmental conditions.

Along with a general physical durability, flash memory is typically very tolerant of less-than-ideal operating conditions. Even a device not designed for this can withstand some harsh conditions. As a real-life example, in 2008 a couple accidentally dropped a digital camera into the ocean from a cruise ship while on vacation. It was later retrieved by chance in a fishing net, whereupon the fisherman who found it was able to retrieve some of the images inside, posting them online so that the camera's owners could be identified, which they eventually were (BBC News 2011). This means that the device was able to withstand not only water but corrosive salt water and withstood it for some time, retaining enough information for complete files to be retrievable by an average computer—a pretty amazing feat.

While water could warp an optical disk or rust a magnetic tape or hard drive, oftentimes, flash devices will still work after exposure to water (assuming that you dry them completely before operation). These devices can sometimes operate at high humidity, 80% or higher, and at extreme temperatures, in some cases below freezing temperatures and above 150°F (Kingston Technology Corporation 2012). If you lack the ability to store devices for your data in a humidity- and temperature-regulated environment, this is a highly appealing quality of flash memory, and if your archive happens to be someplace very humid, swapping SSDs for hard drives could greatly improve your general computer function and not just be helpful for archiving.

In addition, if you are particularly concerned about the prospect of a natural disaster, such as an earthquake or a flood, the durability of flash memory devices may appeal to you, particularly that of devices designed for extreme conditions.

No moving parts also means that you don't have to wait long to access your data. Even though it may amount to only seconds in difference, you do have to wait for the platters in a hard drive or the disk in optical technology to rotate to the right location and for the arm or the laser to seek out the information that you want. Magnetic tape has to physically move to the right spot on the reel for information access. Although it doesn't offer instantaneous information access, flash memory is very quick in comparison to your other choices.

Unlike magnetic tape, which requires special equipment to access the information, it's typical for devices using flash memory to plug into a USB port (covered in chapter 2). USB ports are standard on most modern computers and provide an easy way to use external devices to communicate with the computer. In essence, all you need to do is to plug the device into the port, and the computer will automatically access the information. Flash devices are also *hot-pluggable*, which refers to any device that can be attached to the computer while the computer is running. This adds to the convenience of the devices, since you can put them into the computer at any time.

Like optical media, this technology is fairly familiar, and flash drives in particular are very common. This means that, as with optical media, your staff won't need much in the way of special training. If you store information on the familiar flash drive (as opposed to a larger SSD), many of your patrons will also understand its use and not require special instructions either. Although it may not matter to you as far as its ability to store information goes, flash memory also uses less power than your other options, since it does not physically have to move parts.

While the benefits to flash memory are numerous, it's not a foolproof method of data storage, and there are many reasons not to use it and many situations in which it's not a good choice for your archive.

Disadvantages

Flash memory does have some not insignificant drawbacks. If a device using flash memory fails, like a solid-state drive, it tends to require a specialist to retrieve the information, if the information can be retrieved at all. New drives have warnings that alert the user if the device is starting to fail, but these devices tend to fail abruptly, working perfectly one moment and not at all the next (Jacobi 2013a). There's no warning that you can use to detect whether the drive is going bad, other than any warnings that the device itself can provide you. With tape, you may be able to visually detect stress, smell funny odors, or otherwise see signs of decomposition. With optical media, you can sometimes see cracks or scratches or notice warping. Normal hard drives can give you audio cues that something is wrong (though audio cues may mean that the damage is done as well). The nature of solid-state drives conceals problems from the user, since their insides are hidden and nothing moves.

Flash memory devices do wear out. Those cells can be written to and erased only so many times before they don't work anymore. The high-voltage pulses used to erase the drive will also eventually ruin it, burning out the cells and making it impossible to keep electrons in the floating gate. Electrons can also become trapped, creating false readings or measures of resistance in the cell (Cornwell 2012). However, with technology continuing to advance, your archive may receive new devices for memory storage before this becomes an issue with a device using flash memory, especially if you don't write and rewrite to the device often; that is, while the cells do burn out, they can be erased and written to thousands of times before this happens. There may be new methods of storing data or improvements in speed, storage, and reliability that would make purchasing a new flash device appealing, replacing old ones before they start wearing out (Domingo 2013).

Similar to the problem of burnt-out cells, electrons can leak from the cells from disuse, effectively erasing the device. Flash memory doesn't need a constant source of electricity to function, but it does periodically need refreshing. While a manufacturer may state how many times a device can be written to, stating how long a device will retain data is much less common (Cornwell 2012).

Flash memory can also become pricey in comparison to other methods of storage. A simple flash drive with a few gigabytes of storage space is relatively cheap and convenient, but larger storage devices can be quite expensive. It's likely that the prices will continue to come down over time, but for the moment, the expense may be prohibitive to you.

The ease with which you can write to and read from this technology may cause you problems in that it's possible that you, staff, or patrons (if you allow them access) could accidentally erase important information. However, it's often possible to retrieve accidentally deleted files with software, so you may not find this particular issue worrisome depending on your situation. Flash memory devices are often compatible with software used for the recovery of deleted data on hard drives. Similarly, it is sometimes possible to recover corrupted data with specialized software (Dowler 2011).

If you purchase several flash devices, you may have a hard time determining how to distinguish one from another, since they may be physically identical and don't lend themselves well to labeling, as optical disks do. It is possible to name flash devices, which helps you find files once the device is connected to the computer, but you may struggle with figuring out which one you want and what information is on it. This can be particularly problematic with SD cards, which are tiny and have no room at all for labeling. However, flash drives often have a ring, hook, or similar object on one end, which enables them to be attached to a lanyard or key ring, which may help you overcome this issue.

Another issue that is a result of human error is losing the device. If you use an external SSD, then this probably won't be an issue, because the device will be too large to easily forget about. However, flash drives are well known for their portability and can be forgotten while still in the USB port, put into a pocket and carried off, or accidentally dropped and lost. If you use SD cards for photos and take them out of the camera, they are even easier to lose due to their tiny size. Many SD cards are about the size of a postage stamp or even smaller.

Similarly, because this technology is expensive and desirable, you may have a problem with theft, from patrons or staff. This is particularly true with solid-state drives, since they are expensive. Again, flash drives and SD cards are much more common and will be less appealing for theft, but it's still a possibility that you must consider. In addition, because they are so common, people could carry off a flash drive or SD card by accident, not realizing that they have the wrong device or simply forgetting that they have it.

If your archive contains information that you would prefer to restrict access to, this portability and ease of access can pose an additional problem. For example, if someone wanted to get information stored on a tape, it would be problematic for them because computers don't come with tape drives. However, the majority of computers have a USB drive that is compatible with external SSDs and flash drives. Although there are ways to protect your data, it will lack the advantage that tape has in this regard.

Flash memory as a concept has been around for quite a while, but flash memory devices as they exist today are pretty recent. This is another drawback to you. While magnetic tape's capabilities as an archiving medium are well understood and optical disk's potential and lack of potential as an archiving medium have also been explored, the archiving capabilities of flash memory are not so well known. It's difficult to say whether this type of memory will perform well for years to come or not. As another difficulty, this technology is quite popular for its convenience and quick data access speed, so new innovations are being made all the time to take advantage of a market longing for ever-better flash memory devices. The product that you purchase today could be outstripped by one that you could buy next year, even six months from now, so it's also difficult to determine how good your device is for archiving in comparison to one that is older or a newer device. Like any other method of data storage, the life span of this type of device varies and is subject to how it is handled and stored, as well as how often it is used. The typical life span of a regular flash drive, for example, is thought to be about 10 years (Fuller and Larson 2008).

So, how do you decide if flash memory is the best option for you? The expense of flash memory and its unpredictable nature typically make it a rather poor choice for your main data storage, especially if you need to store a lot of data. However, because it's so durable and withstands less-than-ideal conditions so well, it's an excellent choice as a secondary backup for your data, especially if, as mentioned earlier, you're concerned about protecting your archive against a natural disaster of some kind. It's also a good option if you can't maintain ideal archival storage conditions, since it won't degrade as readily as some of your other choices.

If you don't have a lot of data to store, then flash memory can be an attractive option. For example, a single flash drive can be more convenient than a large CD collection.

If you don't have a lot of data to store, then the expense of flash memory becomes less prohibitive as well.

Flash memory devices in general and flash drives in particular are also very good for sharing data, since these devices are noted for their rugged nature and portability, whether you need to share data with other departments, in the case of a university archive, or among archives or libraries. It can even be a great way to move information over shorter distances, from computer to computer.

⑥ Purchasing Devices

You might encounter several terms regarding the construction of a device using flash memory. As mentioned earlier in the chapter, *single-level cell* (SLC), *multilevel cell* (MLC), and *triple-level cell* (TLC) all refer to how much data can be stored in a single cell. An SLC can store one bit per cell; however, it is possible to store more than one bit per cell. MLCs store two bits and TLCs three, and they do this by having more than one possible state (other than on or off) in a single cell. Of the three, SLCs are much faster, use less power, generate less heat, last longer, and are more durable in general than the other kinds. MLCs, however, are less expensive and can store much more data in the same amount of physical space as an SLC (Super Talent 2013). TLCs are the least common and least durable of the three. MLCs are the most commonly used version in modern flash memory (Jacobi 2013b).

Typical devices can be erased 3,000 to 10,000 times; the manufacturer may have an estimate regarding how many program/erase cycles a device is good for. Check the warranty when purchasing flash memory devices as well. While 10 years is a fair estimate for a life span, the warranty can give you an idea of how long the manufacturer thinks that it will last, and products do vary in their durability from one company to another (Jacobi 2013b). In addition, you may be interested in features that alert the user about the state of the drive and whether the cells are still in good condition.

Two terms that you might see regarding flash memory are *NOR* or *NAND*. Unlike many other computer terms, these are not acronyms. What they refer to is the exact construction of the cells in flash memory, as there are several ways to construct flash memory cells. The type of cell is named after a logic gate, as the transistors resemble computer logic gates, such as AND, OR, or NOT gates (*NAND* and *NOR* mean "not AND" and "not OR," respectively, and essentially have the opposite function of those gates). Exactly what logic gates are and how they work is beyond the scope of this book, but basically, logic gates exist within the computer to make calculations.

There are four basic kinds of flash memory cells: NAND, NOR, DINOR (divided bit-line NOR), and AND. So, which type is best for you? While there are such things as DINOR and AND cells, these are less common than NAND and NOR cells, so you'll most likely be looking at NAND or NOR technology. NAND is typically optimal for personal data storage; the biggest advantages of this type of storage are that it's less expensive than your other options and the cells are compact, making the device smaller and more portable. NOR flash memory is typically used in devices in which the flash memory is embedded into the device, such as cellphones (Kingston Technology Corporation 2012). NOR technology has a quicker access time than NAND technology; both DINOR and AND cells are attempts to retain NOR's quick access time while reducing the area of the cell to one comparable to that of a NAND cell (Integrated Circuit Engineering Corporation 2002). So in essence, NAND is the cheapest, smallest type, but NOR has a quicker access time. The other varieties have mixtures of these qualities.

Using and Storing Devices

With optical disks and magnetic tape, the storage conditions make a huge impact on how long the item will last with all the data intact. This is less true with flash memory. While cool, dry conditions are best, flash media can work perfectly well when stored under far less ideal circumstances. Flash memory is not susceptible to many of the vulnerabilities of other storage mediums. As mentioned previously, it's often possible to recover data from a flash device that has gotten wet, so long as it's thoroughly dried first. Unlike tape, flash memory is not vulnerable to magnets or magnetic fields (Johnson 2010).

The major enemy of a flash device is electricity, since the cells depend on precise charges to encode the data. If you transport a flash device such as a flash drive in your pocket, as is a common practice, ordinary static electricity can be enough to cause some damage to the drive. You may want to take precautions against static with your devices. Some devices come with antistatic storage bags, or you may want to use a wrist strap that guards against static when handling devices; these straps are typically used and worn when doing computer repair and maintenance, as static is an enemy of your computer as well (Beissel 2011b).

It's possible to corrupt the data on a flash drive. One of the common ways that this happens is when the user removes the drive while the computer is still writing information to the drive (this problem is more prevalent on older machines). If the user takes the device out of the computer too soon, the computer may not have completed writing the files to the drive. To be sure that the transfer is complete, it's best to use a software wizard designed to safely remove the hardware. This wizard will stop the computer's interaction with the device and inform the user when the file transfer is complete. Removing the device too soon can result in an incomplete file transfer or in damage or data corruption to the device.

As mentioned before, if you use flash drives or SD cards to move or store information, it's possible to lose the device through simple human error. If you're concerned about the safety of the data on the device or about preventing others from accessing the information, you may be interested in encryption software, which makes it difficult to access the information on the drive. Some major companies that manufacture these devices include such software with the device.

Key Points

- Flash memory is one of the fastest, most convenient methods of data storage.
- External storage devices such as flash drives are compatible with a range of computers, new and older, and they plug into a USB port.
- Flash memory is a highly desirable technology that will withstand difficult storage conditions and harsh handling.
- Flash memory does wear out over time and is quite expensive. It's also prone to loss or theft, and data is difficult to recover from damaged devices.

In the following chapter, you will learn about a method of data storage unlike any previously explored in this book, a method that doesn't require you to use any space or storage devices or even perform checks or maintenance: cloud storage.

◎ References

Aaronson, Lauren. 2008. "How It Works: The Sturdiest Solid-State Storage." *Popular Science.* http://www.popsci.com/node/19967.

BBC News. 2011. "South African Owners of Camera Found in Sea Traced." http://news.bbc.co.uk/2/hi/uk_news/england/8510314.stm.

Beissel, Jill. 2011a. "Differences between USB Flash Drive vs. SD Card." *Premium USB Blog.* http://blog.premiumusb.com/2011/05/differences-between-usb-flash-drive-vs-sd-card/.

———. 2011b. "How ESD Affects USB, Flash Drives and Computers." *Premium USB Blog.* http://blog.premiumusb.com/2011/05/how-esd-affects-usb-flash-drives-and-computers/

———. 2011c. "USB Flash Drive Versus SSD: Revealing the Differences." *Premium USB Blog.* http://blog.premiumusb.com/2011/07/usb-flash-drive-versus-ssd-solid-state-drives/.

Cornwell, Michael. 2012. "Anatomy of a Solid-State Drive." *Queue* 10. http://queue.acm.org/detail.cfm?id=2385276.

Domingo, Joel Santo. 2013. "SSD vs. HDD: What's the Difference?" *PC Mag.* http://www.pcmag.com/article2/0,2817,2404258,00.asp.

Dowler, Mike. 2011. "Beginners Guides: Flash Memory Data Recovery and Protection." *PCStats.* http://www.pcstats.com/articleview.cfm?articleID=1869.

Fuller, Floyd, and Brian Larson. 2008. *Computers: Understanding Technology Comprehensive.* 3rd ed. St. Paul, MN: Paradigm.

Integrated Circuit Engineering Corporation. 2002. "Flash Memory Technology." http://smithsonianchips.si.edu/ice/cd/MEMORY97/SEC10.PDF.

Jacobi, Jon L. 2013a. "The Proper Care and Feeding of SSD Storage." *PC World.* http://www.pcworld.com/article/2038511/the-care-and-feeding-of-ssds-what-makes-these-speedy-drives-hum.html.

———. 2013b. "Screaming-Fast Solid-State Drives." *PC World* 31 (4): 66–71.

Johnson, Christopher. 2010. "USB Flash Drive Myths Busted!" *Premium USB Blog.* http://blog.premiumusb.com/2010/10/usb-flash-drive-myths-busted/.

Kingston Technology Corporation. 2012. "Flash Memory Guide." http://media.kingston.com/pdfs/FlashMemGuide.pdf.

Super Talent. 2013. "SLC vs. MLC: An Analysis of Flash Memory." http://www.supertalent.com/datasheets/SLC_vs_MLC%20whitepaper.pdf.

CHAPTER 10

Cloud Computing

IN THIS CHAPTER

▷ What is the Internet? How does it relate to computer networks?

▷ How does the Internet work?

▷ What is cloud computing? What are the different models for cloud computing?

▷ What are the benefits and drawbacks of using a cloud computing service for archival storage?

▷ What are some things to look for in the contract for a cloud computing service?

SO FAR, YOU'VE BEEN LEARNING about ways to keep data safe in a physical respect. CDs, magnetic tape, hard drives, and flash memory can all be considered ways of physically storing data within your archive. In this chapter, you'll learn yet another way to store data. However, this one is a little less tangible.

Cloud computing is a bit of a buzzword right now. A lot of companies claim that you can use software "in the cloud," or they encourage you to store data "in the cloud." This sounds very nice. Clouds are usually pleasant imagery, and so this phrase sounds pretty good to most people. It makes it sound as though your valuable data is hovering about the earth in a cloud, just waiting for you to pluck it back down from any computer, anywhere.

The reality is a bit less mystical and abstract. Cloud computing doesn't really have a good definition that applies to all situations. Instead, *cloud computing* refers to a couple of different but related concepts. The data doesn't exist in some cloud somewhere, either. It needs a physical method of storage, just like any other form of data, but in this case, it is stored on server computers not accessible to your archive except via the Internet.

So, to understand what cloud computing is and what it has to offer for your archive, it's therefore essential to know—what exactly is the Internet, anyway?

◎ The Internet

What is the Internet? People tend to throw the word around, sometimes incorrectly and sometimes without knowing exactly what it means. Though infamously declared to be such by an Alaskan senator, the Internet is not a series of tubes. There are no pipes draining ones and zeroes into your computer every time you check your e-mail. What actually happens is more complex than that.

Networks

Think of the Internet as way of moving information from one computer to another. This book has already covered some ways that you can do this. You can burn information from one computer to a CD-R, for instance, or put it on a thumb drive, then put the CD into the drive of another computer or put the thumb drive into the USB port of another computer. That is very easy to do.

Another fairly easy thing to do is to connect two computers so that they can directly communicate with each other, no storage medium required. If you have a couple of computers connected like this, then what you've made is a local area network, or a LAN. This is a group of computers all in one relatively small area, which are connected for the purpose of sharing information.

Suppose that you want to communicate with a computer that's farther away, though? Say, in another building? If you make a bigger network that spans a distance greater than a single room or small building, then what you've made is a wide area network, or a WAN. There's also such a thing as a metropolitan area network, or a MAN, which spans a large area, such as a city, but this is essentially just a really big WAN.

The Internet is also a WAN. Basically, the only difference between a WAN and the Internet is size. A WAN spans a few buildings or maybe a city, as in the case of a MAN. The Internet is a WAN that spans the entire earth. What this means to you is that the Internet consists of a collection of computers all around the world, connected to one another and able to directly relay information from one to another. There are several companies whose computers and connections form the major part of this relay system, known as the backbone of the Internet. Many of these companies are probably familiar to you, such as AT&T, Verizon, and Sprint. The Internet does not belong to any single entity and would still exist, at least in part, if any of these companies stopped running their part of this network. The Internet has a lot of redundancies, which is good because technical problems can occur with even the best and most well-run equipment. The Internet can still function even if part of the network isn't working. However, the major parts of the Internet exist in the United States, and the initial system that became the Internet, ARPANET, was created in the United States as well. While there are plenty of servers and other necessary components across the world, if the portion that exists in the United States were to go down, this would cause serious problems worldwide.

World Wide Web

The technology needed to create the Internet has been around for a long time, since at least the 1950s. The idea of directly connecting two computers so that they can share data or processing power is fairly simple and has been used regularly for some time. The ideas and innovations behind the World Wide Web, however, are more recent (Dale and Lewis 2013).

You learned about HTML documents in chapter 4. As a quick reminder, an HTML document is a plain text document that contains a series of commands for a browser software program. These commands tell the browser what text, images, or other items to display as well as how they should be displayed, such as location, format, and color. If you need more explanation, have a look at figure 4.1, which shows a comparison between a plain text document and a web page.

A web page is one of these translated text documents coded in HTML (a web page can use other kinds of related coding and programming languages as well, which adds to the complexity of the web page). A website is a series of related web pages that are typically interconnected by links.

If you use the Internet, you've probably been frustrated before by a slow connection or a site that just won't seem to load. Data transmission takes time to move from one computer to another, both physical time to move and processing time by your computer. Remember: image files are quite large, so it would take an extremely long time for a website to load if it were a series of static images on your screen rather than a text file being interpreted by a browser.

The innovation of HTML documents makes websites possible. They can be translated and viewed on a variety of computers and by a variety of browsers. Text documents use small amounts of data and are quicker to transmit than images, and so using text-based instructions for the browser (e.g., "make the background gray" instead of using an image of gray pixels for the background) makes transmitting information fast while still achieving attractive, usable results.

The Internet and the World Wide Web are not exactly the same thing, although people sometimes use the two terms interchangeably. The Internet is this series of connections among computers that allows them to communicate with one another. The World Wide Web is all those web pages that you can access via the Internet. So, the web pages that you browse when looking for message boards or pictures of kittens are not the Internet. They are part of the World Wide Web, sometimes shortened to "the web."

If the Internet were a series of tubes, then the World Wide Web would be more like water running through them from place to place. Without the water, the tubes are still useful (you could use them to move something else), but without the tubes, you have a lot of water all over the place, making a big mess and essentially doing nothing. Of course, you're not going to wind up with spilled binary digits all over your desk if you don't have an Internet connection (might be interesting to explain to others if that happened, though).

Without the World Wide Web, the Internet still exists and can be useful. Without the Internet, the World Wide Web is just a bunch of encoded HTML documents that sit on servers about the world with no way to share them. The web needs the Internet to function, and the Internet can do all sorts of things without the web.

Using the Internet

You most likely know how to do all sorts of things using the Internet and the web. It is, after all, designed to be somewhat intuitive. However, you may not know exactly what happens when you use the Internet or casually surf the web.

Information accessed via the Internet is not "out there" floating and intangible. It's kept on a server somewhere, the ones and zeroes physically encoded on a computer. The Internet functions using server and client computers (though these are used in smaller networks, too). When you request information—say, you want to view a website or download something—you're digitally making a request for the information to be sent to your computer through the network. When this happens, your computer (the one making the request), is the *client*. The computer that distributes the information is then known as the *server*.

The term *server* might bring up images in your mind of big rooms filled with huge, incomprehensible computers, images created due to the influence of Hollywood. There are, in fact, server computers that are like this. However, many servers are much smaller than this, similar in size and price to an ordinary desktop computer. It's also not necessary to have a special type of computer to work as a server; an ordinary desktop computer could be configured to be a server. It's better, though, to have a computer specifically designed to function as a server. If you'd like to set up a network inside your library or host your own website for public access to your archive rather than pay a company to host it, this is something that you can do.

The data needed to make the web function is stored on server computers all over the world. Sometimes people refer to the act of viewing a website as *visiting*. This makes it seem as though the web is a place that you can visit and browse around for things or that the server computers are like stalls in a market that you can go pick and choose from. Although it makes for a fun visual, the reality is actually the opposite of this situation. Remember: servers send data to the client when the client sends a request. So, what you're really doing when you "visit" a website is asking a computer somewhere to send the site to you, more like ordering a package than going to a store.

How does your computer know where to send the request, though? There are many, many servers connected to the Internet, and the web page that you want when you send a request is on one of them. Try opening up a web browser, such as Internet Explorer or Firefox (any browser will do), and visiting a site. Again, it doesn't matter which site. Look at the top of your browser—there will be a string of letters, characters, and possibly numbers. This is the uniform resource locator, or URL. Think of it like a mailing address. You send a request, and this string identifies exactly which web page you want and where it is—that is, exactly which server contains the web page. When you click a link or type an address into the search bar of your browser, you're making a request from a server computer somewhere around the world.

This URL system is a way of "addressing" computers, just like houses have addresses to avoid confusion. Remember, though, that computers like to work in numbers; it's humans who find words easy. Every URL has a corresponding IP, or Internet protocol, address. The IP address is a series of numbers that the computer uses to locate another computer. Computers have to translate one to the other, which is beneficial to people, since it's easier to remember a string of words instead of a string of numbers. Your computer has an IP address, too, if you're connected to the Internet. After all, to send information to you, the server has to know where it is going.

As you now know, the Internet is essentially a big network, and you can request information from servers attached to this network. In a LAN, computers can be directly connected to one another with cables. You don't have a direct connection to any particular computer on the Internet, though. For instance, the search engine Google has several data centers in California (and in many other locations). If you live in Maine, then there isn't a cable running from your computer all the way to a server in California. That would be pretty inefficient.

Instead, when you send a request through the Internet for a particular web page, it moves through several computers. A device called a *router* handles the requests from different computers and sends them on to other computers. It's not very precise; the router sends the request in the "general" correct direction, so your request for a web page might go through a bit of a roundabout journey on its way to the desired computer. Think of it as being a little like traveling via airplane. It would be impractical to have an airplane that goes to every place in the world at every airport, so you may need to fly between several airports before you get to one that can take you to your desired destination. Your request may need to travel through several other computers making up the network known as the Internet before it reaches the desired server computer, which can then send the information you wanted to your computer.

Ultimately, you need to have a correct URL for a server computer to get your request for a web page. A generic URL might look like this: http://www.awebpage.com. All URLs have some elements that are the same. The HTTP at the beginning stands for hypertext transfer protocol. Computers can use several different protocols. Think of it as computers using a common language. On the Internet, all computers "speak" the same language to avoid confusion and to facilitate the exchange of information; this is the hypertext transfer protocol.

The *.com* at the end of the name is a top-level domain name, or TLD; this indicates the type of organization that owns the web page. The .com TLD name is pretty generic and can belong to almost any person or organization. For instance, a business could have a .com TLD, such as the commercial website Amazon.com. It could be used for a personal website, too; your archive could also use a .com TLD if you had a website. The TLD names *.org* and *.net* are unrestricted, too. The .org is typically used for nonprofit organizations; for example, the charity organization American Red Cross has a web page with the URL http://www.redcross.org. In contrast, the TLDs *.edu* and *.gov* have restricted use. Only educational organizations in the United States, such as universities and public school systems, may use the .edu TLD, and only U.S. government websites may use .gov. Federal, state, and local governments are all allowed to use this TLD. There are many other TLDs as well, but these are the most common ones.

◎ Defining Cloud Computing

You now know what the Internet and the World Wide Web are, as well as the basics of how they work. So what exactly is cloud computing?

The concepts needed for cloud computing to work have been around for some time now. For instance, a mainframe computer contains enormous processing power and can store all types of data. Rather than everyone in a company or organization having a powerful mainframe computer, an organization may have only one. Smaller computers or workstations can then be connected to the mainframe to access its data and processing power, thus sharing resources in an efficient way. This model is typically used in a small area, such as a single building. Cloud computing is a little like this model, except that you're sharing a big, powerful computer with lots and lots of other people around the world (and you may not know who) and the distance between your computer and this more powerful computer may be quite great, rather than contained within a building or two.

The term *cloud* makes it seem as though the information stored in the cloud is nebulous, floating about in the air like the water molecules of a cloud. It drifts along, waiting for someone to pluck the information out of the air from anywhere in the world.

The reality of the situation is quite a bit less glamorous. What happens in cloud computing is that you, the user, agree to allow someone else, a company, to store your information on its server computers, typically for a fee. You can request that information in the client/server model described earlier, with whatever computer you use at the time requesting the information from the servers and with those servers sending it to you via the Internet. It really works a lot like how you get web pages. However, access to your information is typically restricted to you or to a small group that is allowed access.

Cloud computing is not easy to define in precise terms, and there isn't a pretty, tidy definition available at the moment, unfortunately. The National Institute of Standards and Technology is a part of the U.S. Department of Commerce and works to define national standards. It defines cloud computing as

> a model for enabling ubiquitous, convenient, on-demand network access to a shared pool of configurable computing resources (e.g., networks, servers, storage, applications, and services) that can be rapidly provisioned and released with minimal management effort or service provider interaction. (Mell and Grance 2011)

While this is in fact a definition—a pretty concise and accurate one, considering what it's trying to describe—it's a bit clumsy and difficult for an average person to understand. An easier way to go about this is to think of cloud computing in terms of what it can do. The National Institute of Standards and Technology also defines the features that any cloud computing service has.

Cloud computing services offer "on-demand self-service." What this means is that you don't have to interact with an actual person to access your data. This is all done automatically whenever you want to access the service, no humans involved (Mell and Grance 2011).

Cloud computing services have "broad network access." This means that they are accessed over a network and can be accessed via a range of devices (an important concept in an age of smartphones and tablets; Mell and Grance 2011).

Cloud computing services use "resource pooling" and "rapid elasticity." Both these refer to the flexibility with which a service can meet consumer demand (Mell and Grance 2011). For instance, supposing that you bought a 1-terabyte hard drive to store data, but you really need to store only 500 GB of data. The money that you spent on the rest of that terabyte could be considered wasted. With a cloud computing service, however, you pay according to exactly how much storage space you need. You can also get varying levels of computer processing power. Suppose that you had a program that you wanted to use but were storing the data for the program "in the cloud." As a simplified example, it's possible, with cloud storage, to pay for extra processing power when you want to use that program and less when you don't.

Cloud computing services offer "measured service." This refers to the ability of the service to control and meter the service, changing how much storage, processing, and bandwidth are available to users, depending on their needs and usage (Mell and Grance 2011). For instance, imagine that you and another archive are using the same service. You have a photo-editing program stored on your service, and in the mornings, you use the processing power offered by a cloud storage service to use the program more optimally than you could with your computer, since the server computer can make the necessary calculations faster than your computer. The other archive is using the service for a photo-editing program in the afternoons. The service can make more processing power available to your archive in the morning and less in the afternoon and make that extra processing power available to the other archive when it is using the photo-editing program.

⑥ Cloud Computing Models

There are several types of cloud computing systems. The first of these is a public cloud. These are clouds formed by servers available to anyone who subscribes to the service. For instance, the company Amazon offers its users cloud storage services. Because any of its users can access their information on a server and the same servers are used for many different users, this is a public cloud.

A private cloud, in contrast, is a cloud designed for one specific group or an organization. It's accessible only to members of that group or organization (ideally), making the data more secure. It also gets around many of the legal issues that can arise when using a public cloud (discussed later in this chapter). A private cloud doesn't have to be connected to the Internet to function (you could use an ordinary LAN or WAN), and so there is some debate whether a private cloud really counts as cloud computing (Corrado and Moulaison 2011). While the benefits of extra security and dodging issues with service contracts are highly appealing, a private cloud is probably going to be impractical to you unless your archive is quite large.

A community cloud is like a private cloud in some ways, but it's shared among several organizations that are similar or have similar needs. For example, suppose that you and two other archives wanted to get some of the benefits of a cloud computing service (e.g., backups in different locations). If your archive and the other two archives each had a server computer containing the data for all three archives and each was able to access any of the other servers, you'd have a community cloud. There are other ways you could go about it, as well. The organizations that operate the cloud may also manage it, or they may use a third party for this part. A community cloud can divide the operation cost among the parties involved, and unlike using a public cloud, in which you must agree to the terms of service set by the company, your archive can have a say in how the cloud is run, how resources are distributed, and how security is maintained (Corrado and Moulaison 2011).

There's a fourth option, as well, which is a hybrid cloud. This is less simple to define, as a hybrid cloud is simply any cloud service that doesn't fit neatly into the other categories and is instead some combination of the other cloud types (Dale and Lewis 2013).

Cloud computing may seem novel or possibly even daunting, and this may be the first time that you get a good definition of what it is. But like some of the other storage

FOUR MODELS OF CLOUD COMPUTING

- Public
- Private
- Community
- Hybrid

methods and concepts explored in this book, chances are good that you're already using cloud computing and just don't realize it. For example, if you have an account with Google and use its e-mail, documents, calendars, or many other services, you're using cloud computing. Other companies that provide e-mail services but don't leave a permanent copy of the e-mail on your computer, such as Yahoo Mail, are working "in the cloud." You must access your data from the company's servers, since it is not physically on your computer.

⑥ Cloud Computing for Archival Storage

Cloud computing offers benefits for archives of all sizes, but it's particularly attractive for an archive with a small staff or budget and can be quite cost-effective in some situations. As with all methods of data storage, though, there are some drawbacks, and those for cloud computing are a little more complex than those explored in the book so far. These drawbacks have less to do with physical problems or technical issues and more to do with legal and security issues, which are somewhat more abstract.

Advantages

- Multiple copies of your data (backups)
- Very cost-effective (hardware, maintenance, electricity)
- Potentially time-saving

Disadvantages

- Potential disputes with data ownership and rights
- Access is dependent on the Internet and an external company
- Potential problems with security

Advantages

One of the best things that you can do to protect your data is to keep copies of it on multiple devices and in multiple locations. This protects it from hardware obsolescence as well as any environmental issues, such as a flood or a fire in the archive. Cloud computing lends itself nicely to this. In most cases, cloud computing services offer backups of your data, which help keep the data safe (though this is something that you should investigate when choosing a company, since not all do this). In the best-case scenario, these backups are kept on different servers in different physical locations, which protects your data from a disaster occurring in one location, as there will be a backup at a completely different and unaffected area.

Cloud computing can save your archive quite a bit of money if you're on a tight budget. You don't have to buy a physical object with cloud computing. You pay for what you use, both in processing power and in storage space. While using cloud computing to store your data may be the use that first comes to mind, you can actually use cloud computing to gain a boost to the processing power of your archive. For example, in chapter 2 you learned how the CPU is a major component that controls how fast a computer can operate. Suppose that you don't have the ability to upgrade your computers right now. You could access the processing power of the server computer that you use as part of the cloud computing service to run complex programs for your archive, making the fact that your computers are kind of slow less relevant (so long as you have a good Internet connection, of course).

With a cloud service, you also don't have to pay someone to monitor a server or mainframe computer in your archive or any other equipment along those lines. Someone else does this for you. You don't need to hire someone to maintain your equipment or understand the complexities of computing. The hardware, the software, the storage space, the maintenance, the technical assistance—this is all part of what you pay for, which may make this a very economical choice for you if you have a small staff or a rather limited budget to make your archive run.

As another bonus that you might not initially consider, using your own server computer requires power. You can save money with electricity by using a cloud computing service, since providing the energy to run the server computers is the job of the company. You also save valuable space by not purchasing a physical item.

Cloud computing offers the benefits of a server or a mainframe computer, as mentioned earlier. You can keep any kind of data in a cloud, including software programs for your archive. If you do this, then you get some significant benefits. For instance, you may have a particular program installed on only one computer in your archive, and so if you want to use that program, you must use that particular computer; this is a problem if more than one person needs to use the program or if something happens to that computer. Or, you may want a certain software on every computer in the archive, and so you'll need to install the software on every computer—a time-consuming process.

If you keep your software as well as your data in the cloud, then you'll eliminate the need for tedious tasks, such as updating or installing software on every computer in your archive, and you get around such problems as software existing on a single computer. You'll need to install or update software only once, for your data in the cloud, and every other computer in your archive will be able to access the new software. The same principle can apply to your collection—you don't need to install a copy of your digital collection on every computer, since every computer can access it from the cloud. You'll need to do the tasks of updating or installing only once. This is a huge time-saver. You should be aware of the terms of service of software before doing something like this, though, since they may not legally allow software to be uploaded to a server in this manner.

For all the wonderful things that cloud computing can do for your archive, though, you should know about some drawbacks before deciding if buying this kind of service is the best choice for your archive.

Disadvantages

While the advantages that cloud computing holds for an archive are extraordinary, there are some not insignificant issues that can arise if you use a cloud computing service, largely regarding the rights and ownership of your data. Unlike the other methods of storage described in this book, in which your rights to the data that you store are undisputed (assuming you have the legal right to store it in the first place), cloud storage gets complicated.

Determining your rights with cloud computing can be a very difficult business. If the company that you choose stops offering the service for any reason, you may be unable to retrieve your information, even if you take legal action against the company. There is legal precedent for this situation as well; if you load your information to an external server as part of a cloud computing process, you may lose some or all of your rights associated with that information. That includes your rights to retrieve it and possibly your right to store it (Heaven 2013).

Some cloud computing services use programs that browse through the information stored on their servers and delete anything that may be illegal or pornographic, whether it actually is or not and, of course, without consulting the user. As an example of these issues, the cloud storage company Megaupload was taken offline by the FBI in 2012 because many of its users were using the service to store pirated films, games, software, and other illegally gained and distributed information. Anyone who was using the service to store things—legally or illegally—lost access; thus, the information was, for all practical purposes, gone (Heaven 2013). In this case, the redundancies and multiple copies of data that are such a wonderful asset to cloud computing were rendered irrelevant.

To think of this in more tangible terms, imagine that you were using a storage facility to store some old books. However, someone in the space next to yours was using it to store some illegal substance. The police find out about this and confiscate everything in the storage facility; thus, your books are now property of the police department. They are out of your control, and you no longer have access to them. This isn't equivalent to what would happen if you really were storing books in a storage facility, but it's similar to what might happen to your online data, given legal precedent.

Your legal rights in regard to who owns and has rights to your data become a sticky issue when you use a company to store your data. For example, the social media website Facebook (which you may not realize uses cloud computing to function) reserves the right to use any image or information uploaded to the site. Its property Instagram can also use the images that the users upload for the purpose of advertising (Heaven 2013). The agreement between you and a cloud storage company can even give the company ownership of the data that you store; in 2011, the online storage company Dropbox changed its terms of service, which gave the company rights of ownership over all the data its users stored. Although it reversed the policy in response to the public outcry that followed, this is something that could happen with any online storage company (Hallene 2013). Any company that you choose for such a service must be subjected to severe scrutiny to determine what exactly it reserves the right to do with your data and if this is a problem for your archive.

Cloud computing depends on the Internet to function. If you lose connection and all your archive's data and programs exist in the cloud, then your archive's work grinds to a halt for as long as it takes for the Internet connection to become restored. If your Internet connection is reliable, then this may not be a problem, but if it's shaky, then dependence on this service may not be such a good idea. Similarly, if the cloud computing service becomes unavailable due to problems with the company (e.g., technical issues), then you likewise lose your ability to access your data.

Storing information in the cloud is inherently less secure than any other storage method. Cloud computing services, of course, have security and strive to keep your data secure. However, this does not mean that hackers are completely unable to access your data if they want to. Those servers containing your data must be connected to the Internet network, which means that it is possible to get to those servers via the Internet, even for people who are not authorized to access the data. Remember: there isn't a line connecting you directly to a cloud storage server; whenever you store or retrieve your data, it will have to pass through many different lines, as described in this chapter.

Strict security may or may not be an issue for you. However, you should always be wary of someone corrupting your data maliciously or causing problems for the company from which you purchase your service. If security is indeed an issue for your archive, you can take some steps to make your data more secure. For instance, if you encrypt files before you upload them to the server and keep the key to decrypt them on only the computers at your archive, it makes it significantly more difficult to access your data illegally (Hallene 2013).

The legal issues that arise become less of a problem if you have a private or community cloud, but you may lose some of the advantages that come with a public service. For instance, you don't have to own any equipment or pay anyone to maintain that equipment with a public cloud service, but this is something that you may require if you decide to essentially create your own cloud. You may also lose the variety of locations for servers if you collaborate with local organizations; cloud storage services can have servers all over the world.

Cloud Service Contracts

Unless you decide to create a private or community cloud—in which case, you control the servers and how they are used—you will need to deal with a company that offers cloud storage as a service. This involves navigating a contract.

Cloud computing is going to be much different from your other storage options. While it's a good idea to read over warranties and other information from the manufacturer, once you buy a CD, a tape cartridge, or a flash drive, it's yours, and you can essentially do whatever you want with it. When you purchase cloud storage space, you don't own anything. Think of it more like a rental of someone else's space. What all this means to you, in practical terms, is that there will be a contractual agreement involved, and you must read this very carefully and understand all the implications that it holds for your archive. If possible, use legal counsel or someone similarly qualified to assist you in determining your archive's rights when purchasing such a service.

WHAT TO LOOK FOR IN A CONTRACT

- Does the company offer backups of your data?
- How long does the subscription last, and how is it terminated or renewed?
- How do you pay, and what happens if you miss a payment?
- What warranties or guarantees are offered by the company?
- Can the company be held liable for service or security issues?
- Does the company collect data, and what is done with the data?
- Where are the servers located?
- What kind of security is offered? Are there multiple layers of security available?
- What are your rights in regard to data ownership with the service? Does the service claim any ownership rights?

Subscriptions

It should be clear in a contract how long your subscription lasts and how, when, and under what circumstances it terminates or can be terminated by you. It should also be clear how the contract is renewed should you decide to continue using the service.

Payment

This will be an ongoing expense for your archive. Learn what it costs and what you get for what you pay, how your institution pays for this service (e.g., what methods of payment are acceptable), how often you need to pay, and what exactly happens if you don't pay, miss a payment, or are late with a payment. As an example, it would be inconvenient to you if a company deleted all your data because you were a day late with payment.

Terms of Service

Learn exactly what the terms of service are. For instance, what kinds of warranties or guarantees are offered by the company? All companies, even ones that are impeccably run, are subject to technical issues, and so you must expect that the service will be unavailable sometimes, but you should find out how often the company guarantees that the service will be up and operational. A company that doesn't run smoothly is of no use to you. You'll also want to know whether the company can be held liable for any problems that may arise in regard to your data or if it can be held responsible if something goes wrong and your stored data is lost.

Data Collection

Cloud storage companies may monitor the usage of their service, and so you should find out exactly what the company monitors and collects as far as personal data goes. You need to find out whether data that the company collects about the usage of your data stays solely within the company, how the data is protected, or, perhaps more important, if it shares or sells any data about its users.

Server Location

Although you're buying storage space "in the cloud," remember that the servers storing the data have a physical location somewhere. It's in your best interest to know where. The actual physical location of the servers determines the laws, rights, and regulations that apply to the data stored on those servers (a phenomenon of particular interests to lawyers who store data in the cloud). Your contract may specify where the servers are located, guarantee that they are located within a specific area, or have other information regarding server locations and your rights in regard to those locations (Hallene 2013).

Security

Find out what kind of security the company offers. Different companies offer different types and levels of security. Authentication, or verifying the identity of the user, is one of the most common methods of adding security. This is typically a username and password; some companies can offer multiple layers of security, though. For instance, Dropbox requires a six-digit code whenever users log in using unrecognized devices (ones they haven't used to connect to their accounts before), which helps to ensure that they are not strangers who are not supposed to be accessing the accounts (Hallene 2013).

In some services, you are able to allow different levels of authorization. For example, you can allow some users to access the data but not change it and others to both access and change it. This is perfect from the perspective of an archive, as you can permit your staff and your patrons to have different levels of access. Along the same lines, your cloud computing service should be responsible for notifying you of any security breaches, what they mean to you and your data, and any potential security breaches (that they should be working on repairing, ideally).

Data Ownership

Finally, one of the most important parts that you should look for in a contract is how the ownership of the data that you store is affected by the terms of the contract. You need to know whether agreeing to the contract gives the company you use any legal ownership over what you store and what happens to your data should you terminate your contract. The company may retain copies of your data, even if you delete the files that you have stored or if you stop using the service (Heaven 2013).

Key Points

- Cloud computing offers you an alternative to other storage methods and allows you to store data on large server computers outside your archive rather than on items within the archive.
- Cloud computing services come in several models: a public cloud service, a private service, a community service, or some combination of the three. Each has different benefits and drawbacks.
- For an archive, cloud computing's off-site storage and data backup features are very appealing, as they protect your data from local disasters or hardware issues and can provide extra processing power and other conveniences, saving your archive time and money.
- Cloud computing services do have some serious drawbacks in that they depend on an Internet connection, and if you use a company to provide the service, then you may encounter difficulties in regard to the rights and ownership of your archive's data.

While the items or services that you use to store your data are very important, you don't just need methods of data storage to create a working digital archive. You will, at the very least, require additional computers and software and, in the case of digitizing information, items such as scanners and cameras. In the following chapter, you'll learn about some of the useful equipment that your archive may need for your project.

References

Corrado, Edward M., and Heather Lea Moulaison, eds. 2011. *Getting Started with Cloud Computing: A LITA Guide*. New York: Neal-Schuman.

Dale, Nell, and John Lewis. 2013. *Computer Science Illuminated*. 5th ed. Burlington, MA: Jones & Bartlett Learning.

Hallene, Ashley. 2013. "Clearing Up the Cloud." *Gpsolo* 30 (1): 34–38.

Heaven, Douglas. 2013. "Lost in the Clouds." *New Scientist* 216 (2910): 35–37.

Mell, Peter, and Timothy Grance. 2011. "The NIST Definition of Cloud Computing." http://csrc .nist.gov/publications/nistpubs/800-145/SP800-145.pdf.

CHAPTER 11

Equipment for Digitizing and Editing Archival Materials

IN THIS CHAPTER

▷ What types of monitors are available, and what is best for my project?

▷ What are the different kinds of scanners available, and what are they best used for?

▷ How can I digitize delicate items or items that can't be scanned?

▷ What kind of software do I need to process text and image files?

▷ What equipment do I need to digitize audio and video materials?

▷ What kind of software do I need to process audio and video materials?

WHILE A COMPUTER WILL, of course, be the major hardware component necessary for your archiving project, a number of other items and software programs will be of use to you. This is especially important for a digitization project, in which you create digital copies of physical items, but much of the hardware and software discussed in this chapter can be of use to you even if you are simply storing digital objects.

The equipment that you will require will largely depend on what type of items you need to store. Are you archiving audio recordings or newspapers, for example? These will require radically different types of equipment to create a digital version of the original.

This chapter gives you an idea of what kind of equipment you might be interested in for your archive. It does not cover every possible situation or everything that you might possibly need, since it would be beyond the scope of this book to cover everything. These are just the basics that you would need to get started in most situations.

◎ Determining When to Outsource

Equipment is expensive. This chapter gives you an idea of what kind of equipment you might be interested in for your archive. Most items discussed have versions aimed at the public and those aimed at professionals. Items aimed at professionals, of course, come with a much higher price tag but typically offer more options, more control, and higher-quality results. It's up to you to decide which will best suit your needs and your budget. Sometimes, the best equipment available isn't necessary, and sometimes, it is.

After learning about your options, you may ultimately decide that you don't have the money for what you want. It is possible to outsource a digitization project to a company that does this professionally. This has some pros and cons. You won't be able to monitor what's going on or be able to control when and how quickly the digitization process happens, and you'll need to send your items away. It's also quite expensive, and you won't have made any kind of investment in equipment, which could be used again if you want to digitize more items.

However, the facility that you send your materials to will have the best equipment available. Your materials will be handled by people who have experience with digitizing materials, meaning that you and your staff don't have to learn anything to get quality reproductions and that you can spend your valuable time on something else or on some other project. While outsourcing digitization is expensive, you may discover that it's worth your while if you can't afford the necessary equipment or if you can't spare the necessary time (digitization is a lengthy, tedious process no matter what you digitize).

While you may be interested in outsourcing to save time or money, you must have some items to run a digital archive, and one of these is a good monitor.

◎ Monitors

A monitor is a type of peripheral; that is, it connects to the computer to exchange information between the computer and the outside world. The user requires a monitor or display screen of some kind for a modern computer, as it is the primary way that a computer shows data to the user.

Monitors have evolved quite a bit since their invention. In the past, monitors were often monochromatic, or had a single color. As mentioned in chapter 3, if there are only two colors, then only one bit is required to create colors and display information, which is beneficial if a computer isn't able to process a lot of information. Monochromatic screens are still in use today but not for personal computers; you would see a monochromatic computer screen displaying prices at a checkout at a store, for instance.

As computers have evolved, there has been a variety of monitors available with different numbers of colors that can be produced; for instance, along with monochromatic screens, there have been monitors that produce only shades of gray. While there are such things as grayscale monitors in use today, the most common type of monitor and the one most likely to interest you is a color monitor capable of producing a wide variety of colors.

There are two general types of monitors: cathode-ray tube (CRT) and liquid crystal display (LCD). Both types work perfectly well. However, LCD monitors have largely replaced CRT monitors, and while it is not difficult to find one, it's very difficult to get a *new* CRT monitor.

CRT monitors contain a cathode-ray tube, which is essentially a big glass tube behind the screen. The back of the screen is coated with tiny dots of red, blue, and green phosphorous material. When these dots are activated with electrons from the cathode ray tube, they glow, and these three colors—red, blue, and green—can be combined to create a variety of colors.

LCD monitors contain a substance known as liquid crystal, which is put between two layers of polarized glass (there are several other layers involved as well). It's a little more difficult to visualize how liquid crystals work, since they function on a chemical level rather than a more mechanical level, as a CRT monitor functions. In chapter 6, you learned about how lasers can change the opacity or transparency of the material in a rewritable CD. For an LCD monitor, electrical currents change the structure of the liquid crystal material in a fashion somewhat similar to that of the rewritable CD, causing it to temporarily change form and block some light waves, or certain colors, so that they aren't visible to the user (Fuller and Larson 2008).

As mentioned, CRT monitors work perfectly well. However, CRT monitors are essentially a box, which takes up a lot of room, and they are becoming obsolete. LCD monitors are much thinner, leaving more free space on a desk or workstation. LCD monitors can be much wider than CRT monitors as well, and a CRT monitor will weigh much more than an LCD monitor of comparable width. LCD monitors are also the type recommended by the Federal Agencies Digitization Initiative Still Image Working Group (2010). This group also recommends using monitors designed for use in graphic arts or photography for your project. Though having a specialized monitor like this is the ideal situation, it might be difficult to achieve, depending on the budget that you have available for your archive.

When selecting a monitor, you can look for several easy characteristics.

Resolution

A monitor's resolution is one of the important aspects to take into consideration when making a purchase. The term *resolution* means something slightly different for monitors than it does for images. With a monitor, the resolution is the maximum number of pixels that a monitor can display. For instance, a resolution of 1,024 × 768 means that a monitor can display 1,024 pixels horizontally and 768 vertically. The numbers always go in that order: horizontal, then vertical, separated by ×.

An image may actually have more information than there are pixels in your monitor. That is, you may have a monitor that is 1,024 × 786, but the photo that you want to look at is actually 2,000 × 2,000 pixels. When this happens, the monitor essentially has to take an average of the pixels and resize the image to fit your screen (Dale and Lewis 2013). Because images can be quite large, this can actually help you by allowing you to see an image at a more comfortable size. When you work with images, though, a bigger monitor with higher resolution is almost always better.

Similarly, the *dot pitch*, or the distance between the pixels, makes an impact on image quality. The smaller the distance, the closer the pixels and the better the image. The dot pitch of a monitor typically is between 0.25 and 0.31 millimeters (Fuller and Larson 2008).

Video Card

Though not part of the monitor, the *video card* (also called a *graphics card*) is the component of your computer that is responsible for controlling displayed information, and it has a significant impact on the quality of your display. It has its own memory, which is devoted to this task, known as *video RAM* (VRAM). The more VRAM, the better. A higher VRAM is also associated with a higher *bit depth*. In chapter 5, you learned about bit depth in relation to audio data. Regarding visual data, *bit depth* refers to how many bits are needed to record each color. The higher the bit depth, the more colors (which is better).

Size

As with televisions, a monitor's overall size (apart from the number of pixels that it can display) is listed not by the height or width but by the approximate diagonal measurement of the screen. Typical sizes are 15 to 21 in., but monitors can be larger than this (or much smaller). Again, bigger is usually better, since you'll be able to see images more clearly or look at multiple images at once with a large screen. However, big screens take up more room and cost more money, so you'll need to compromise.

Ports

Like a computer, a monitor can have a variety of ports. A VGA port is the most common kind, and a monitor may also have an HDMI port, DVI port, DisplayPort, and several other connectors. These are basically all ways to connect the monitor to another device. You may also find odd ports on a monitor, such as USB ports. You'll need to decide ahead of time how you'd prefer to connect your monitor to your computer, if you'd like to be able to connect any other devices, and if there are any other kinds of ports that you'd find useful.

It should be noted that there isn't a great deal of difference between LCD monitors and a flatscreen LCD television. It's not too hard to use a flatscreen LCD television as a monitor, either, and you might even find it cost-effective to do so. If you plan on using a television as a monitor, be sure that it has the appropriate ports to connect to the computer. Many televisions have VGA and HDMI ports. It should be noted that HDMI cables tend to be more expensive than cables for a VGA port.

Other Features

Some monitors are adjustable, and some are not. That is, some monitors allow you to adjust the height of the monitor on the stand, the angle, or the orientation (vertical or horizontal). These can all make work easier for whoever is using the monitor.

Some monitors come with built-in speakers, and some don't. Having the speakers built into the monitor can save space and reduce the number of cords lying around, which is convenient. However, if you are going to be working with audio or video data, you'll probably want separate speakers that are higher quality than what is typical for a monitor.

Whatever type of monitor you choose, it's important to have the monitor properly calibrated. Monitors and televisions can both have differences in how they display color from one monitor to the next. Calibration helps ensure that a monitor is displaying properly or that the colors displayed are true to real-life colors. Two basic tools can be used: a photosensor-based color calibrator, also called a *colorimeter* or a *spectrodensitometer*, and software that calibrates the monitor. However, both of these are prone to inaccuracies, so it's a good idea to double-check the results yourself, essentially "eyeballing" it. This is best done with a tool called the National Archives and Records Administration's Monitor Adjustment Target, which is an image that displays a range of grayscale values. There are other, similar tools online or tools for photography can be of assistance (Federal Agencies Digitization Initiative Still Image Working Group 2010).

⊚ Scanners

You're probably at least a little bit familiar with scanners already. These devices have the capability to capture an image of an item, such as a typed paper or a photograph. Most scanners have a couple of things in common.

Most scanners operate by using something called a *charge-coupled device* (CCD). This device is capable of recording a physical object by detecting photons emanating from the object using a light-sensitive material on a silicon chip in the CCD. The chip can then convert what it records into pixels, making the information usable by a computer. If you have ever used a flatbed scanner, which is a horizontally oriented scanner, you can see this device while it works. When you scan an item (and if you haven't closed the lid), you'll notice that there's this powerful beam of light that moves from one end of the scanner bed to the other. This light reflects off whatever object you've laid on the scanner, and the reflected light is read and recorded by the CCD (Lee 2001). However, you really shouldn't watch this happening, since it's not good for your eyes.

Instead of a CCD, a scanner may have a device called a *complementary metal oxide semiconductor* (CMOS), which is less expensive but creates a lower-quality scan. A scanner can also have a prism, which separates the light into red, green, and blue (the same colors that a monitor uses), thus enabling it to record colors (Lee 2001).

As you learned in earlier chapters, while there are differences between computers and software programs, sometimes designers and manufacturers agree to use standards to make things easier for everyone. For instance, the hypertext transfer protocol is used to make transmission of information over the Internet easier. Scanners have a standard, too, called TWAIN, which is a software standard that applies to not only scanners but also cameras, many graphics programs, and even some word-processing programs, and it facilitates communication with a computer. Any software that is marked as TWAIN compliant can work with any scanner or camera that is also TWAIN compliant.

While TWAIN is the most frequently used standard for this, it's not the only one. Windows image acquisition (WIA) is another standard that belongs to Microsoft and basically has the same function as TWAIN-compliant software. A lot of scanners have drivers that will work with both standards.

Because all scanners are similar in many respects, it can be difficult to choose which one is best. There are a couple of things that you can keep in mind when you make your purchase, though.

- What is the dpi or ppi range on the scanner? Be sure that this falls into the range that you need to scan the items that you want to digitize. Suggestions on good ranges for images and text are covered in chapters 3 and 4, respectively. Typically, the higher this number, the better the quality of the scanner is, but you may or may not require a very high dpi for your scans.
- What is the bit depth of the scanner? That is, how many bits are used to store information about each color? The higher the bit depth, the more colors are stored.

- Do you need color? Grayscale? What color range is offered by the scanner, and can it render images into two tones only (bitonal or monochrome)? Which of these best suits your needs and will scan your collection most effectively?
- How large are the items that you need to scan, and how large is the scanner bed? Bigger is better, since trying to scan an item in parts and splice it together in a photo-editing program is tedious at best.
- Is the scanner designed for the operating system on the computer that you're using? Sometimes the manufacturer will offer drivers (i.e., software that you need for the machine to communicate with your computer) for a variety of operating systems, which are available for download online, but this may present extra challenges. It's typically easier, when possible, to just purchase a device designed to be compatible with your operating system.
- How fast can the scanner operate? How important do you find the speed to be? The manufacturer may list how quickly a scanner works, but the scanning time might vary depending on what's being scanned (text versus a photo, for instance). A manufacturer will probably list the fastest scenario, which is almost certainly a monochromatic scan.
- When the scanner completes a scan, what image formats can it convert the data into? Which ones do you need? If you have to convert formats for your project, this will take time and can result in loss of data. You also don't want a scanner that generates proprietary formats only.
- What kind of a port does the scanner attach to? Does your computer have such a port available?
- How intuitive is the scanner to use? In the best-case scenario, you can hook the scanner up to a port, install the necessary driver software, and press a button to start scanning. Ease of use makes a project go faster and makes training people to do the work much simpler.
- Does the scanner offer features that you don't want or need? Unwanted features may cause confusion when you're trying to set up and learn to operate the device. Extra features may also increase the price, and the more complex an item is, the more difficult repair and maintenance are.
- How expensive is the scanner?

It can be a bit difficult to determine exactly how high the quality of a scan is based on the specifications of the manufacturer. If possible, see a sample scan from the scanner.

While the basics of how scanners work is the same from scanner to scanner, there are a few different kinds of scanners, and they each offer different benefits to you for your

TYPES OF SCANNERS

- Drum
- Flatbed
- Portable or handheld
- Sheet fed (sheet feed)
- Specialty—film, negative, microfilm scanners

archiving project. Along with deciding what features you need, you'll also need to pick out a general model of scanner.

Flatbed Scanners

Flatbed scanners are pretty common, and many people have them in their homes for scanning photos or documents. These are horizontally oriented scanners with a flat glass bed. When you use such a scanner, you place whatever object you want to scan on the bed, close the lid, and scan it. The fact that these scanners are so common can be an asset to you, particularly if your archive is on a tight budget. Most stores that sell computer equipment will have flatbed scanners available at a reasonable price. Oftentimes, they're part of an "all in one" machine that can perform multiple operations, such as printing, copying, or faxing. Typically, it's best to have a scanner that is just a scanner, since devices with more than one function tend to be a bit delicate and break down more easily, but you may find that you like the convenience that getting a device with multiple functions offers for your archive. If you need a printer, copier, and fax machine as well as the scanner, it's a nice space saver.

Flatbed scanners are good for scanning just about anything. You could lay a book flat on the scanner and get a scan of the open pages (not a suitable idea for a delicate book, though); you scan also photographs, pages, papers, or, if it's large enough, items such as newspapers or maps. Using a flatbed scanner is tedious and time-consuming, but it's certainly versatile and useful for most situations.

Sheet-Fed Scanners

Sheet-fed scanners have a vertical orientation rather than a horizontal one. These scanners are faster to use than flatbed scanners; with a flatbed scanner, you must open the lid, place the item on the scanner, straighten it, close the lid, scan the item, then remove it and replace it with the next item. Although all these tasks are very easy, it takes a long time and becomes tedious for whoever is doing the scanning.

In contrast, with a sheet-fed scanner, you place the item that you want to scan into the scanner. The scanner runs the item through the device, scanning it as it goes, and the item comes out at the bottom of the scanner. The automation involved speeds up the process. It doesn't take away the tedium of the task, but speed and efficiency are a valuable aspect to any part of a digitizing process.

Sheet-fed scanners are particularly nice for digitizing large collections of text. However, they are limited in comparison to a flatbed scanner. You can't use them to scan anything really delicate, since the item could get destroyed by the scanner when being pulled through the machine. If you want to scan a book of any kind, you'll need to take it apart, essentially destroying the original object. It's also typically not the best choice for scanning a photograph. However, if the information on the item (text) is more important that how the item looked, then this is an appealing option.

Portable or Handheld Scanners

You might not think that having a portable scanner is of use to an archive, but it could be depending on what you need to scan. Portable scanners are exactly what they sound like—scanners that you can easily move around. These contain the CCD device within the scanner, but rather than it moving automatically under an object that you place in the scanner, as in a flatbed model, you move the CCD by running it over the desired object. Software for the device corrects (in part) for human error, such as jiggling the scanner or not moving at a perfectly even pace.

This kind of scanner won't get the crisp, perfect representation that a flatbed or sheet-feed scanner will. Even the correction software and a steady hand will leave some distortions in the final image, so it won't be perfect. However, it does have some practical uses, and so you may want to consider purchasing one in addition to other scanners and software.

If, for any reason, you need to scan objects that can't be brought into the archive, a portable scanner can collect the information in a memory card (covered in chapter 8), and you can bring the data back to the archive for processing later. You don't have to bring a computer of any kind with you, just the scanner.

You may also be interested in using a portable scanner for objects that are too fragile for normal scanning, such as books that have started becoming brittle. Because you are more in control of the machine, you can be delicate with the scanning process and move it gently over the item to be scanned. There are other ways to digitize old or brittle items, though, which will get you better, more accurate results. This is covered a little later in this chapter. It should be noted that there are also such things as portable scanners with sheet-fed characteristics.

Drum Scanners

Drum scanners are typically aimed at photographers and may be of use to you if you want high-quality scans of photos, transparencies, or negatives. These scanners consist of a drum that spins rapidly during the scanning process, and the item that you want to scan is mounted within the drum. They use a device known as a *photomultiplier tube* (PMT) rather than a CCD, which a typical flatbed scanner would use; PMTs are more sensitive than CCDs. These scanners offer the highest-quality scans for photography and can generate higher resolutions than any other scanner type, capable of exceeding 10,000 dpi (*PC Mag* 2013). However, they're far less commonly found than your other choices and tend to be large and pricey.

Specialty Scanners

The scanners discussed so far are capable of scanning a decent variety of items, but you may find that you need a scanner that's designed to get a scan of something unusual. If you need to get copies of slides, for instance, then it's in the best interest of your archive to simply purchase a dedicated piece of hardware, a slide scanner. You can use a flatbed scanner to scan slides, but the quality tends to be poor, and it's time-consuming—both to scan the slides and to correct them digitally so that they result in a satisfactory image. Purchasing the correct equipment saves time and results in better-quality images for your collection.

Similarly, you can purchase scanners for regular photo film, microfilm, and microfiche. Again, it's possible to use a flatbed scanner, but a scanner designed to digitize these materials specifically will result in a better-quality result and saved time.

ⓖ Cameras

While scanners are very convenient, cameras are quite versatile and can be of great use to you in your project. For instance, suppose that you have an item that is simply too large to be scanned, like a newspaper. Instead of attempting a scan, you could instead take a photo. While you might have a hard time getting a normal film camera to capture a high-enough resolution to read text, modern digital cameras capture a very high number of pixels in a shot. When you zoom in on the image using a program, if the shot is clear, you'll be able to read the text.

If you have an item that is too delicate to scan, a camera works for digitization as well, since you can treat the item more gently than you would an item for scanning. If you want to digitize books without destroying them, a camera image is a good choice. With a scanner, you'd have to either take the book apart or lay it flat on the scanner bed, which puts strain on the spine and can ruin the book if it's delicate. For a camera, all you need to do is prop the book open to the desired pages, which is less damaging.

Cameras can also be used for recording items that don't lend themselves well to scanning, including items that you might not have considered for your collection. For example, suppose that your archive is part of a university and you want to keep a record of the art collections there, which includes a large collection of pottery. It would be pretty difficult to get a scan of a pot that contains meaningful information (you can try, of course, but only the edge touching the scanner bed will be clear). You can use your camera for something like this as well. Other kinds of artwork, such as paintings, are also well suited for digitization via camera.

The quality of your camera will have an impact on the quality of your captured images, and you should take into consideration several aspects of a camera.

- Is the camera intuitive? As with a scanner, you want your camera to be simple to use and to train others to use. You probably won't want or need a lot of special features.
- How does the camera connect to the computer to download images? Some use a USB port, and some use a FireWire port. You need one that matches your needs. If it's convenient, it is also possible to take out a memory card and put it into a computer to get the images.
- How many megapixels does the camera capture? The size of the image that a digital camera captures isn't measured in ppi or dpi (which would make your life infinitely simpler); it's measured in megapixels. Typically, more megapixels are better, but this is true only up to a point. In general, a larger sensor is more important than more megapixels for getting a better image. The sensor is the part of the camera that detects light from the subject, and a bigger sensor can detect more light and produce a more accurate image. As an example, smartphones often have cameras that are capable of the demands of an archive as far as resolution goes (the number of pixels), but you still might get better results with a dedicated camera due to sensor size (Dolcourt 2013).

If you use a camera to digitize items, you may need a few other tools, particularly if you're going to digitize fragile books. For instance, you may want to invest in a book cradle, which will safely hold the book while you capture images for digitization. You may also want something that will unobtrusively hold down pages while you capture images. There is a problem with digitizing books in that the curvature of the page may cause distortions in the image, and holding it down can help reduce this. Bone handles and vacuum plates are both often used to compensate for this, but you have other options (Lee 2001).

When you use a camera for digitizing objects, the ideal situation is to have a permanent setup, a location in your archive where a platform for the objects that you want to digitize and the camera to digitize them are permanently located. The camera can be positioned so that it's at the ideal height and orientation, and any time that you want to digitize items, the camera is ready.

The camera needs to be oriented parallel to the surface where you will place the object that you want to digitize. For instance, you could have a table to lay the items on, orienting the camera directly over them. You can also use a book cradle to hold open books for digitization. It's important that the camera maintain its distance from the item to be digitized and that it doesn't move during the digitization process. There are a number of ways that you can go about doing this; for instance, you may want an arm that holds the camera over the item. You could also use a plain photo tripod, although you'll have to ensure that it doesn't get jostled.

With a permanent setup, you may want to directly connect the camera to a computer so that it downloads images into the computer as you work; you can also potentially operate the camera directly from the computer rather than pushing a button on the camera. If this seems inconvenient, it's also possible to take the SD card out of the camera and transfer the images to a computer if you have a port for the card or if you have a device to read the card. (SD cards are discussed in chapter 8.)

You'll also need a good source of lighting. Lighting must illuminate evenly and not create any shadows. Heat can be a concern for your materials, particularly brittle or fragile ones. The bulb that you choose makes a difference; LED lights, for example, do not generate significant amounts of heat and so can be a good choice for your setup. LED bulbs can fit into regular light sockets but are rather expensive. They can last a long time, though, and so you will most likely not need to purchase more for many years.

◉ Software

To process and store the data that you create, you'll need software, but what kind depends on what you need to archive.

Images

For images, you'll need photo-editing software. Photoshop is often held up as the paragon of a photo-editing program (and for good reason), but unless you also want to digitally restore or enhance your photos, you don't really have to use a program as large and complex as Photoshop. Note that there are several version of Photoshop, including those that have limited features and a lower price than the full program, which may appeal to you. To make an image suitable for archiving, your program needs to be able to do the following:

- To control the level of black and white and the levels of different colors precisely
- To de-skew an image—that is, to rotate an image by a few degrees, should you accidentally scan a photo crookedly

- To crop an image to the meaningful data, erasing everything that isn't meaningful—such as the lid of the scanner, should the item be smaller than the scanner bed, in the case of a flatbed scanner
- To read, and possibly convert image files to, the image file format that you have decided to use for your archive (you may want to save image files in several formats for different uses, and your program's ability to convert formats can be important)

Your computer may come with software that is good enough to cover the basics. Even MS Paint, a very basic painting program that comes standard on computers with a Windows operating system, is able to convert from one file format to another. Find out what software you already have available to you and if it has any limitations that make it unusable for your archive (not only software limitations but also limitations placed by the terms of use).

Text

Deciding what kind of software you need for storing text is a little trickier, because there are many things that you can do with text. Most likely, though, you'll be interested in software that reads and creates PDF files or the archive-friendly PDF/A file formats, as PDFs are one of the most convenient ways to store text for archiving.

The Adobe company created the PDF format. It offers a program conveniently named Adobe Reader, which reads PDFs; this software is free for download from its website. It also sells software that edits and creates PDFs, called Adobe Acrobat. While Adobe is the company that created this file format, other companies offer software that will create PDFs. If you're on a tight budget, it may be in your best interest to shop around; a number of companies make software that will read or create PDFs and PDF/As. Otherwise, it's probably better to use Adobe for the sake of simplicity.

You may need word-processing software. Some software is typically included on computers when you purchase them, but you may need to buy updated software. If you're storing born-digital text, you may also be interested in software that converts one file format to another. For example, with this kind of software, you may be able to "rescue" documents with an obsolete (or unusual) file format, or you may be able to convert a proprietary format to a more archive-friendly one. Sometimes regular word-processing software is capable of this kind of reformatting as well.

If you're scanning text documents and want to convert them to searchable text, you'll need optical character recognition (OCR) software, which converts an image of text to searchable text, allowing the user to search for words within the document. This technology is discussed in chapter 4. Sometimes, OCR technology is offered as part of other software or is bundled in. For instance, Adobe Acrobat conveniently offers OCR technology as part of the software for creating PDFs. Microsoft Office, which is a set of several helpful office programs, offers OCR technology, too. You may want to purchase software specifically for converting text in this manner anyway, and you'll need specialized software if you want to attempt converting handwriting or unusual fonts, as these are beyond the capabilities of typical OCR software. However, before you do purchase OCR software, find out if you already have OCR software or if you will obtain it through another program that you'd like to purchase. You could save some money this way if you don't need to convert unusual text.

Digitizing an audio or video collection is a little more complicated and a bit less straight-forward than digitizing text or images. If you have an audio or video collection, then there are a number of ways to go about digitizing the collection and storing a digital copy, so there's a challenge in deciding how you want to do it.

If your collection is on CD, DVD, or Blu-ray, then, of course, all you need to do is to "rip" the data from the physical object onto a computer hard drive and store it in your desired method of data storage. If the data is on a tape or record or is on film, then you have a more challenging task.

Audio

Some types of audio recordings are so old that you're better off leaving it to a professional to get a digital copy, for two reasons: first, older recordings are going to be more fragile and delicate, and a professional will be able to handle the recording appropriately (E-MELD 2006). Old cylinders and early records are examples of this kind of a situation. Second, you must have a device that is capable of playing back the recording to digitize it. This means specialty equipment, which may be difficult or next to impossible to find.

More recent recording methods, such as cassette tapes and records, are probably within your capabilities of capturing digitally. The general method of getting the audio data for both these types of recordings is basically the same.

Hardware

It is possible to purchase playback devices that are designed for the purpose of recording audio data and putting it onto a computer, which is one of your options when it comes to digitizing.

Your other option is to use a regular playback device (a tape player or a record player) and connect it to the computer. For optimal results, you need a device that will play back the recording as faithfully as possible. In the case of a cassette tape, you'll need to know if the tape was recorded in mono or stereo (monophonic or stereophonic); more information on what exactly this means is in chapter 5. You'll get the best results by using a stereo deck with stereo tapes and a mono deck with mono tapes. You'll also need to know what recording speed the tape was recorded at; most tapes were created with the same recording speed, but some were recorded at a lower speed and will require a player that can compensate.

To digitize a record, you can't just use a regular record player. You need an amplified phonograph or a regular phonograph with an amplifier. This feature enables you to connect the player to the computer (Honan 2008).

Along with a player for your tapes or records, you'll need a cable to connect the audio device to a computer. Typically, you'll need a Y-cable with analog-component audio connections at one end and a stereo connection at the other. This is less complicated than it sounds. Basically, you connect the two analog-component audio connections to the player and the stereo connection to the microphone port on a computer. You can then use audio-editing software to record the sound. It's also possible to use a USB connector if a computer lacks a microphone port (Honan 2008).

While your computer probably has a sound card that will do an adequate job of converting analog sound to digital sound (what this means was also covered in chapter 5), you'll probably want an additional component for your computer—an audio analog-to-digital converter. Such devices are better at converting analog sound to digital sound than normal computer sound cards, as a regular sound card can introduce noise into the recording and the analog converter is more accurate (E-MELD 2006).

Another hardware item necessary to acquire a good sound recording is speakers and/or headphones. You need to be able to listen to your recording to see if the quality is good, and this is especially important if you need to make any adjustments for volume or clarity. Either will work, but you can listen more closely to the sound with headphones, and you won't bother others in the archive as you test the recording. The quality of the speakers and headphones is very important to determining the quality of the recording.

Software

While the hardware is an important component, you must have software to capture the sound as well as to process it afterward, just like photo-editing software with an image. If your computer has a microphone port, then it most likely already comes with software that will capture audio, but you may want something more sophisticated so that you can capture the optimal sampling rate and speed.

As with photo-editing software, you probably won't need software that does a lot to change the recording unless you are attempting to restore a damaged recording or you are making sound enhancement part of your project. You'll need to be able to control the sampling rate, recording speed, and bit depth, and you'll need to be able to make some basic changes, such as adjusting the volume on the recording and dividing it into individual tracks; for example, a cassette tape plays continuously from the start of one side to the end, even though there might be several different parts (like different songs). You'll likely want to divide your recording into these logical breaks to improve searchability and to make it easy to find exactly what your patrons are looking for. In addition, you'll need to know if the software allows you to add metadata to help your patrons find your audio files; software that allows for metadata is more helpful than software that does not. The importance of metadata is covered in the following chapter. You have quite a few options, and some of them are free; for instance, Audacity is a free software program that fulfills the basic requirements. Plenty of software is available that is capable of more sophisticated audio capture and editing as well, such as Sony Sound Forge and Adobe Audition.

Video

Like audio capture, digitizing video is essentially going to involve playing what is on the video and capturing it digitally by recording what plays. Again, it's probably better to go to a professional for very old or very delicate recordings. Video can be even more complex than audio, though, since you are attempting to capture both image and sound at the same time.

Hardware

For a video that requires a reel-to-reel projector, such as super 8 film, you'll need a projector and a digital video camera. Basically, you need to play the video using the projector, then capture it using the digital video camera. In this case, the quality of the camera is extremely important. You'll also need a screen or a surface to project the image onto, as well as something to set the camera onto and hold it steady, directly parallel to the projection (Herrman 2012). The concept behind this is rather like using a camera to capture an image when digitizing photos, paintings, or delicate materials.

The audio in such a situation can be captured either directly from the speakers, which is not the ideal situation, or from the speaker's line output, which is more optimal (Herrman 2012). As with digitizing audio, you'll need to connect the speakers to a microphone port in your video camera.

Capturing audio and video, especially in older formats, tends to be more complicated than digitizing other materials, and if you have old reels of film to digitize, this is another situation in which you may just want to outsource the project.

If you have VHS tapes that you want to digitize, you can purchase hardware to help you do this. What you require in this case is something that will play the tape, such as a VCR or a camcorder, and something called an analog-to-digital converter or ADC (Consortium of Academic and Research Libraries in Illinois 2013). This device enables you to connect your player to your computer via a USB or FireWire port.

Software

With an ADC, you need to have software that will help you adjust the recording to get the best possible results. Your ADC will most likely come with appropriate software. However, this can make your decision more difficult when making a purchase, since you'll want a quality ADC, but you'll also want it to come with software that is both intuitive and easy to learn as well as highly effective.

You'll most likely need or want video-editing software as well. Again, you don't need software that's aimed at people who edit video professionally or as a hobby. You need software that will do a few things. You'll need to be able to divide your capture into shorter segments, just as you might need to with audio, and you may need to be able to do some adjusting, such as improving color or cleaning up the capture in general, depending on how deteriorated the film was. It should be noted that the software for playback must be compatible with the codec that you use for compression if you use one (Consortium of Academic and Research Libraries in Illinois 2013). As discussed in chapter 5, video codecs are methods of compressing video files. Like software for audio data, software for video data that allows for the addition of metadata is better than software that does not.

⊚ Key Points

- A digitizing project requires equipment, and you may wish to outsource part or all of your project to a vendor, who will be able to use the optimal equipment to digitize your materials.
- Some of the equipment needed for a successful project includes digital cameras, scanners, video cameras, music players, and video projectors and players.
- A digitizing project requires software. Some equipment comes with the appropriate software, and most computers have some software that you can use, though it may not be ideal or of a high-enough quality for your project.

- Most archiving projects do not require software that is capable of a lot of editing, since the goal is typically to capture an item as is, not to change it, though quality is still important.

After a digital version of an item is created, the next step is to make it accessible. In the following chapter, you will learn about metadata and how it pertains to digital materials, and you will learn some basic information regarding patron access of your digital collection.

⑥ References

Consortium of Academic and Research Libraries in Illinois. 2013. "Guidelines for the Creation of Digital Collections: Digitization Best Practices for Moving Images." http://www.carli.illinois.edu/sites/files/digital_collections/documentation/guidelines_for_video.pdf.

Dale, Nell, and John Lewis. 2013. *Computer Science Illuminated.* 5th ed. Burlington, MA: Jones & Bartlett Learning.

Dolcourt, Jessica. 2013. "Camera Megapixels: Why More Isn't Always Better." *CNET.* http://www.cnet.com/8301-17918_1-57423240-85/camera-megapixels-why-more-isnt-always-better-smartphones-unlocked/.

E-MELD. 2006. "E-MELD School of Best Practice: How to Digitize Analog Audio Recordings." http://emeld.org/school/classroom/audio/howto.html.

Federal Agencies Digitization Initiative Still Image Working Group. 2010. "Technical Guidelines for Digitizing Cultural Heritage Materials: Creation of Raster Image Master Files." http://www.digitizationguidelines.gov/guidelines/FADGI_Still_Image-Tech_Guidelines_2010-08-24.pdf.

Fuller, Floyd, and Brian Larson. 2008. *Computers: Understanding Technology Comprehensive.* 3rd ed. St. Paul, MN: Paradigm.

Herrman, John. 2012. "Digitize Your Home Movies Before They're Gone Forever." *Popular Mechanics.* http://www.popularmechanics.com/technology/how-to/tips/digitize-your-home-movies-before-theyre-gone-forever.

Honan, Mat. 2008. "Digitize Your Cassettes and LPs." *Macworld.* http://www.macworld.com/article/1131449/feb08playlist.html.

Lee, Stuart D. 2001. *Digital Imaging: A Practical Handbook.* New York: Neal-Schuman.

PC *Mag.* 2013. "Definition of: Drum Scanner." http://www.pcmag.com/encyclopedia/term/42020/drum-scanner.

Metadata and Accessing Information

S O FAR, YOU'VE LEARNED a lot about how to create your digital collection. You've learned what formats are best and why, what mediums you can use to store your data, and even what equipment and software can help you with creating your collection.

None of that does anyone any good if no one knows what you've digitized or how to access it. You need to go a step further by organizing the files that you create. You may already know much of the information in this chapter, particularly if you do a lot of cataloging. Otherwise, it can serve as a refresher.

What you need to do after creating your digital files is to add metadata, extra information about those files and what they contain. Not only will doing so help your patrons, but you will help yourself when you try to locate items or evaluate your collection. There are several standard metadata schemas, which are covered briefly as well.

Metadata

So, what is metadata? It's sometimes a tough concept to get your mind around because the common way to explain it is that it's data about data. But what does that mean?

As you learned in chapter 2, a file on a computer is simply a mass of electrical impulses that can be interpreted as ones and zeroes. The computer itself doesn't know what these are; it simply retrieves or stores or makes calculations based on what you, the user, tell it to do. It can't really tell one series of ones and zeroes from another in a way that's meaningful.

That's where metadata comes in. Metadata can be information such as whether a file is a music file or an image; how many pages or how large it is, in the case of a book with a physical format; and who created the item, such as an author or an artist. All this provides information about the item, which is useful to the user.

Your files will contain some metadata upon their creation. Your computer will be able to detect a few things about the file, such as how large it is, how old it is, and what the file extension is, indicating which programs are appropriate to open the file.

Metadata in Everyday Use

People who use the World Wide Web often use metadata without even realizing it. For example, suppose that you have an account with a website that allows its users to share and store images, such as Photobucket or Flickr. You load an image to your account of an adorable brown and white beagle puppy chasing a tennis ball. The site may then prompt you to use tags, or words that accurately describe the image for users who might also want to see the image. You decide to oblige (you don't *have* to add tags in most sites like this), and you type "puppy" (the subject), "beagle" (the breed), "brown, white" (the colors), "tennis ball" (an object in the picture), "chasing" (what's happening), and "adorable" (an opinion but, in this case, still a helpful descriptor). Now, if another user comes along and decides to do a search on this site and types "adorable brown puppy" into the search box, your photo will be one of the ones that show up because you used those words as tags.

This puppy photo, for a computer, is just a series of information regarding the colors of pixels to display. Detecting a subject in an image is a complicated task for a computer, so it can't determine what the image is itself. Your tags are a type of metadata that helps human users find the photo by describing it in a meaningful way, because the computer can't do it for you.

On the social media site Twitter, people can communicate to others using short messages known as "tweets." People using this site use words known as "hashtags," which are words or series of words preceded by a "#" symbol, to describe what their tweets are about or who their tweets are designed to communicate with. This can create "trending topics" when many people use the same hashtag descriptor. Sometimes people use the hashtag for humorous intent; for instance, they might describe a situation in which they made a social blunder and use a hashtag like "#awkward." Though not exactly used in an efficient or professional manner, these hashtags provide useful metadata and can assist users of the site. These hashtags are metadata describing the general contents of a message, helping users find desired and relevant information.

Why Is Metadata Necessary?

As mentioned earlier, at the moment, computers right now aren't very good at interpreting what they're looking at. They can't "know" that a picture of a puppy is a picture of a puppy or that a book about architecture is a book about architecture. They need you to do that part. They need you to be able to tell them "this is a book about raising orchids" or "this is a Norman Rockwell painting." The best way to communicate this is through words and numbers, which are easy for a computer to interpret—thus, the concept of tags.

Tags are a type of metadata; they describe the data. In the case of the image site, the tags tell users what is in an image so that they can search for images of specific subjects. Your main purpose with adding metadata to your digital information is to make it possible (and, ideally, simple) to interpret what is in your collection, as well as to make it possible to locate relevant items. Without metadata, you'll have a lot of files, but you won't necessarily be able to do anything useful with them.

Metadata in Libraries

Cataloging and adding metadata are overlapping concepts. Creating a catalog entry is a type of metadata, and it's basically all that you need to do with tangible items in a collection, such as books or CDs. The catalog entry will have all the information that you need about the item. Digital items can be a little more complex.

Traditional metadata is separate from the item that it describes. Think of an old-fashioned card catalog in which the information about the books and so forth in your collection is written on cards; you may even still be using one for your archive, since they work perfectly well. The cards describe the items in your collection, giving, at the minimum, the title, the creator, terms that describe the item (e.g., what a book is about), and information to help a patron find the item, such as a Dewey Decimal number. This is essentially metadata.

You could absolutely do the same thing with digital materials. For example, you could enter them into a digital card catalog, with all the same data that a normal holding would have, and then add a hypertext link to the item in your collection (assuming that the collection is online), which a patron can click and then be taken to a copy of the item, just like a link to a web page online. If your collection is not online, then the entry could instruct the patrons that the item they seek must be retrieved by you or however you want patrons to be able to access your data. You could even add cards for digital items in a traditional, physical card catalog.

Now, with a physical card catalog, you don't keep the cards with the items; that would impractical. But although keeping cards with the item makes no sense for tangible items, it can work just fine for digital ones. It's possible for computers to attach data to an item but have it remain "invisible," just like the tags in the earlier example of the photo of a puppy. The tags aren't written over the image, labeling it "a picture of a puppy"; they're simply attached to the file so that a computer knows that it's relevant information to anyone searching for the keyword "puppy."

As an example of this phenomenon, many people who create web pages add metadata content to them. It serves no purpose whatsoever to the usability of the web page and does not change the layout in the slightest, but it adds information that search engines can use to decide if the web page is relevant to a person's search. For example, suppose that a person named Robert Smith discovered an amazing way to make pancakes and wanted to share it with the world, so he created a web page to show how to make his pancakes. His web page doesn't have much text, but it does have a lot of pictures, and as discussed earlier, computers have a difficult time telling what's in a picture. Normally, a search engine would look for words within a site to help make it searchable.

So to make his web page easier for people to find, he adds metadata using the following HTML code:

```
<meta name="description" content="Amazing Pancakes">

<meta name="keywords" content="pancakes, breakfast food">

<meta name="author" content="Robert Smith">
```

You don't have to be an expert in HTML code to get the idea of what this means. The "description" here indicates to the search engines that the page is about amazing pancakes. The "keywords"—"pancakes" and "breakfast food"—are helpful, too, and might match keywords that a person puts into a search engine. The "author" code says that the author of the page is Robert Smith. Again, this is all invisible to the user unless one looks at the page source; if you're curious, instructions on how you can do this are described in chapter 4. It is extremely useful.

Metadata for Digital Items

Many digital cameras automatically add metadata, unbeknownst to you, to whatever photos you take. This can include information such as the camera model, when the image was taken, or even where the image was taken (many smartphones have GPS capabilities that can add this type of data to an image). Digital video can record much of the same type of information—again, invisibly. To make things simpler, many programs add at least some relevant metadata to a digital item.

But in many instances, you'll need to add the meaningful information yourself. This can be a daunting task, especially if what you have in mind is a large project. How can you decide what the meaningful subjects of a photo are? How can you determine what the best keywords of a book should be? What if you don't have much information about the item at all?

You can take a few shortcuts regarding digital materials that are impossible to use with tangible ones. For example, if a text item is searchable—that is, a person can search for specific words on the page (enabling computers to search for text on an image of text is discussed in chapter 4)—you can use the computer to help you determine what some good keywords are. For example, you could use a program that counts the frequency of the words in an item such as a book. Words that are unique nouns or are otherwise meaningful, such as "Appalachian Mountains," could be good keywords to help your patrons find the item. Programs that help you automatically generate metadata such as this are known as extraction tools (National Information Standards Organization [NISO] 2004).

Using and creating metadata does not have to be difficult. Remember, while there is a lot of useful information that you can attach to a data item, your main goal should be making it possible to search for relevant data and to organize your collection in a meaningful way. If you were very limited on your time and resources, you could simply add some relevant keywords to the file name or use a highly descriptive title. For example, if you had a photo on your computer of an elm tree that was hit by lightning in the summer of 1937 and taken by a person whose last name was Smith, you could name it "photograph elm tree lightning strike summer 1937 Smith.jpg," and it would come up if you did a search on your computer for any of those words in the name, such as "photograph," "elm tree," and "lightning." Computers can pick out individual words from a file name, and while typing in "elm" would bring up every other image of an elm tree on your computer, it's an easy way to get your collection organized and useful to users.

Some photo-editing software allows you to add metadata to photographs. Photoshop is one of them (discussed in chapters 3 and 11), but there are other programs. When you add metadata to a photograph, your image will become more searchable. For example, in the aforementioned scenario, in which you use the file name to make the image more meaningful, you're limited by what you can put into the name. Computers don't like it when file names get too long, and early computer files were very limited on the allowed number of characters, which would make this particular method difficult or confusing. If you can add metadata to a photo, then the name of the file becomes less important. You could add all the same information—that the image is a tree hit by lightning in 1937 and the photographer was Smith—but have a shorter file name, such as "image37.jpg." Searching for the keywords in the associated metadata on your computer will still bring up the image that you wanted, regardless of the file name. This can help you name your files more efficiently, as the actual name of the file will be less important.

When using photo-editing software in this manner, be sure that the metadata is embedded into the photo—that is, it's permanently attached to the image file. If software merely associates metadata, then the metadata and the item are separate, and you can't access the metadata with programs other than the one that you used in the first place. The program that you used will merely associate certain metadata with a file name; the metadata is stored in the program, not with the data file (Ashenfelder 2013).

Using more descriptors is usually better. You can have metadata that helps your archive in particular, rather than your patrons, such as letting you know if something is part of a series, if an item has been damaged, if an item has been only partially digitized, and so on. You may want a more in-depth method of describing your data than simply a descriptive file name, in which chase, you'll be interested in some of the metadata schemas that are in use today.

◎ Metadata Types

There are many ways to categorize metadata, and some people break down metadata into many different types. There isn't a standard of terminology in this respect either (Taylor 2004). Although it's not a formal way of dividing things, an easy way to think about metadata is to break it into three categories: descriptive, structural, and administrative (NISO 2004).

Descriptive metadata: This is the easiest type to understand. It is anything that simply describes the item that you've archived for the purpose of making it easy to find. Titles, authors/artists, and keywords are all types of descriptive metadata.

Structural metadata: This describes the structure of the item, or how it's put together. For example, it could describe the order of pages or chapters in a book. It could also note what versions are available (both a JPEG and a PNG, for instance) or aspects such as scan resolutions (Taylor 2004). If it describes what the file is and how it can be displayed, it's probably structural metadata.

Administrative metadata: This is typically information that's really only useful to your archive. This can include information about when your file was created, who is allowed to access it, and other information along those lines. For you, it might also include information about how to preserve the item for archival purposes. If it's useful information but doesn't describe the item and doesn't help with defining how it goes together, generally it's administrative metadata.

It's up to you to decide what information is relevant or not and how much data you want to include. For instance, you might have a collection of photos that go together, but you want to create only one catalog entry or describe them as a set, not as each individual photograph. You could include the dimensions or even the weight of a book that you want to digitize, or you could omit that information. You do require a balance with metadata—the more information you have, the better, but the more information you have, the more time-consuming it will be to enter all that metadata and to describe the item you are attempting to save. Whatever you do, be consistent. The importance of consistency in your project is further discussed in chapter 15.

⑥ Metadata Schemas

There is no reason whatsoever that you can't use your own system for organizing your data. If you have a small archive, are limited on funds and the available software and resources, or have an unusual collection, then you might even benefit from coming up with your own system tailored to your needs.

If you want to be able to communicate with and share your data with other archives or libraries, then you're probably better off using an already established metadata schema (or at least being aware of the different options available today). A metadata schema is basically a method of organizing and describing an item in a consistent manner. Sometimes a schema will be designed to describe something specific (e.g., images). Consistency is important for making metadata easy to use and compatible with software, and so format and vocabulary may be controlled as part of a metadata schema.

Using an already established metadata schema can make it easier to search for and process your metadata, too, since you can purchase software from a vendor that is designed to work with the standard you choose, to organize and search for your information. For example, many types of software make it easier to create the metadata to begin with. Software that offers templates will create fields that the user can simply type relevant information into, and then the software will generate the formatted metadata for you.

If your archive already uses a particular metadata schema but you'd like to try a different one or if you are collaborating with another library or archive that uses a different metadata schema from the one that you want to use, you can convert one metadata schema to another using software. Software programs that do this are known as conversion tools, and they consist of software that can alter the format of a metadata schema by locating matching relevant fields. You'll most likely need a person to guide the process, though, since it's possible for schemas to be slightly incompatible, or you may want more or less metadata than what is available in the metadata that you want to convert (NISO 2004).

Many metadata schemas are aimed at a variety of items that you might want to describe. For example, there are metadata schemas designed specifically for government documents. It would require an entire book to explore all your different options, and so this chapter discusses only a few of the common, general ones, which are most likely the ones that you'd look at for an archive, anyway.

MARC

MARC stands for "machine-readable cataloging" (not a perfect acronym but easier to say than MRC). This kind of cataloging has been around since the 1960s. It was remarkable at the time of its invention because it didn't require a standardized field length (Taylor 2004). To understand the problem of using a standardized field length, imagine that you wanted to use a cataloging program to enter the title of a book. The software programmer decided that you'd need only 40 spaces, or room for 40 characters at the most. But your book has a long title with a subtitle, and you need more space than this. You'll have to decide what to do and to compromise on accuracy. Or, suppose that you have a book with a short title. All the extra room for characters could be considered wasted space.

But why would a programmer set things up that way? If a computer "knows" that there are going to be only 40 characters for the title, then it can process the data you submit and know that after 40 characters (even if those spaces are blank), it's reached the end of the title and that the next set of data is new information, such as the author or the publisher. It knows what data is what, by *where* it is in a series of binary ones and zeroes.

What you might want to catalog is not so tidy, though. You might want to catalog a photograph, not a book. A book might be part of a series. You might want to make all kinds of notations or enter a variety of data about an item. If you have a series of standard fields, or areas in a form that can be filled out but with a limited amount of space, then you're limited in what useful information you can add about an item.

With MARC records, you can add data that signals to a computer what the information is. You use sets of numbers and characters that can signal to the computer "this is the author," and everything that comes after that set of symbols is then interpreted as the author of the book. In this instance, the MARC record would look like this: "100 Mark Twain." The "100" part signals to the computer that this is the author and that the author is Mark Twain. The specialized series of numbers or characters signals to the computer that a new field has started; for instance, after "100 Mark Twain," it might read "245 The Adventures of Huckleberry Finn," and the "245" part signals that this is no longer the author but rather the title of the book. You can do this for the publisher, the call number, even the retail price of the item (Library of Congress 2009). There are many options with MARC records, and this is good because, as discussed earlier, more information is better toward helping your patrons find what they need.

There are several variations on the MARC system. Currently, librarians in the United States typically use the MARC 21 standard, which is essentially an agreement among librarians in the United States, Canada, and Great Britain to use the same method of cataloging. Previously, each country used its own version of MARC records.

MARC has some advantages. It's well established, which can be a good thing. Many libraries use the format, and so there are many items already cataloged with this format. This can help you if you want to communicate easily with other facilities, and it can save you time and money if someone else has already created a MARC record for an item that you want to archive and digitize.

There are some drawbacks, though. It's not intuitive. The MARC standard was designed at a point in time when computers were huge and slow. An average modern cellphone can probably do more than one of the computers in use at the time of design of MARC records. MARC records are easy for computers to handle and process. Computers like using a short set of numbers or unique characters to label information—people, not so much. Humans like words. For a human, staring at a MARC record doesn't immediately make sense. MARC records also don't lend themselves well to some things that a modern archivist might want as part of the metadata for an item, such as a book's table of contents, thumbnails of images, or pictures of book jackets (Tennant 2002).

Since computers today are much more capable of accommodating human preferences, such as words and pictures, some librarians look to other methods of encoding metadata. MARC records were generally designed to describe items such as books. Standardized generalized markup language is more flexible in many ways and can include more information, which is good for a digital collection that may include some unusual items that need to be described in a way tailored to the item.

Standard Generalized Markup Language

Standard generalized markup language, or SGML, isn't in itself a method of organizing metadata. It's a general term that describes how to construct and use "markup languages," which include information or instructions inserted into text that are not actually part of the text information itself. That is, it could include metadata, or general information about the item, information about how the item should be formatted and displayed to the user, and information about how the item relates to other items (e.g., the item could be part of a set or a series).

All markup languages are similar to one another, since they all follow the same general format and rules of SGML. When you understand one, the others make more sense because they are all similar in some respects. HTML, or hypertext markup language, is described in chapter 4; look at figure 4.1 for a general idea of what a document using markup language looks like.

You can use specific markup languages to describe specific items. For example, a document type definition, or DTD, is a set of markup declarations for a document. Basically, it's a set of rules to follow when you add the markup language information to a document. There are many, many DTDs, some of them extremely specific. For example, there is a DTD that is designed just for describing comic books.

You can create a DTD yourself, and many DTDs have already been created for a variety of applications. The Library of Congress has some preferred DTDs that it uses for its digital items as well. A few of the ones that might interest you follow:

TEI: TEI stands for *text encoding initiative.* This DTD is designed specifically for encoding text, as you might infer from the name. It not only adds metadata information into a document but helps to define how a digital document should be structured and displayed. This is important for making things consistent; an item will look the same regardless of the type of computer that it's being displayed on or what software is being used to display it. If you work with another archive, this might be particularly important to you. This DTD is pretty complicated, since it was designed to accommodate a variety of text documents, and it isn't necessarily for libraries. It was originally designed to help people conducting research in the humanities. There's a simpler version called *TEI lite*, which is aimed at librarians. This DTD is commonly used for adding metadata to full-text documents that are encoded using SGML. If you have documents with this metadata encoding, the metadata can be used to generate a MARC record and vice versa (NISO 2004).

EAT: EAT stands for *encoded archival description*, and it's designed to describe and locate items in an archive. Using this DTD could help you better communicate with other archives. What makes this DTD a little different from the others is that it allows for detailed explanations regarding a single item or your collection as a whole, such as its historical significance and who was involved in creating the original item or who was involved in creating the digital one. If you had a collection of letters by a notable author, for example, the metadata in this schema could describe how you acquired the letters, who they were written to, where they are now and how they are organized, how the digital versions are organized, and it could include a biography of the author (NISO 2004).

MARC: This schema was designed to add MARC 21 cataloging to a digital item (Taylor 2004). If you're already using MARC 21 cataloging and/or want to digitize items that have already been cataloged, using this schema could save you some time because you already have the relevant data. In addition, the MODS DTD, or metadata object description schema, works on a similar concept and is designed to add MARC 21 records to digital objects or to create a MARC 21 record from the object's metadata (NISO 2004).

Options that use markup language may seem complex, and it does require you to learn some new skills if you have no experience with it. However, you can purchase software that will make this easier. Markup tools are designed to help you format your metadata correctly so that it will be readable and "make sense" to software programs designed to read that metadata (NISO 2004).

Dublin Core

The Dublin core metadata element set started at a workshop held in Dublin, Ohio. The metadata schema that arose from this workshop is simply known as "Dublin core." This method of adding metadata has only 15 categories of information for an item, but it is designed to be flexible and to be able to describe a variety of items. The original object of this schema was to address the problem of adding metadata to and cataloging web pages.

The people who created Dublin core recognized that the number of web pages is growing at an enormous rate, and if anyone wants to store information about these pages or study them in a meaningful way, they require metadata that will help with this process. As discussed earlier in the chapter, there are already ways for web authors to add data to their web pages with the purpose of making them easier to locate with search engines. Dublin core may therefore seem like a redundant concept, but it's really not.

Because the number of web pages greatly exceeds the number of catalogers who can handle all of them, Dublin core was created for the purpose of attempting to get the creators of web pages to catalog their own web pages, removing all the work from librarians. Dublin core is therefore very simple and easy to follow because the people for whom its use was intended aren't catalogers and don't have the time to create a comprehensive catalog entry, since this isn't what they are paid to do. There are 15 elements in the Dublin core schema, most of which are self-explanatory, such as "title," "creator," "subject," and "publisher."

Dublin core is simple, and that can be a good thing. It's also capable of describing more than just web pages, so if you decide that Dublin core is a good choice for your archive, you can use it to add metadata or catalog a variety of items. It can also be made more complex; qualifiers are used with the main elements to refine them or make them more specific. The basic version is unqualified Dublin core, and the more complex version is qualified Dublin core (referring to the qualifiers, not who can use this particular schema).

If you're working with a small staff or working with a staff that doesn't include many (or any) catalogers or you're relying on student workers, Dublin core's simplicity and the fact that it's aimed for general users could be a bonus to you. Even if you aren't interested in this schema, knowing what it is can help you if you want to store web pages as part of your archive.

Creating a Good Schema

Regardless of what you do, a good metadata schema should always accomplish a few things. NISO (2004) offers the following guidelines:

- The schema should be appropriate to the things that you want to archive, so only use schemas designed for adding metadata appropriate to your collection.
- In the best-case scenario, the metadata schema is compatible with other schemas and makes it easier to share information, not more difficult.
- The metadata should help you with preserving and managing the items in your archive, or ongoing maintenance. It's also a benefit if the metadata can specify the rights and terms of use for the item that it describes.
- Metadata should be consistent, which typically means controlled vocabularies.

⊚ Other Considerations with Digital Metadata

As you know, digital materials are vulnerable to obsolescence, with the file format, the software, or the equipment required to read the file becoming impossible to locate. Metadata can help you protect your digital items.

This is another advantage to keeping the metadata with the item—no matter what happens to your card catalog, physical or digital, the data that you need is safe with the item, as part of the same file as the item. You can keep adding metadata over time if needed, as well.

But why would you need to do this? Suppose that you are working with two other archives to digitize books and that you have an entry for a 100-year-old book on botany with many illustrations. Suppose that it's many years from now and that you now have software that is easily able to determine what the image is (e.g., a flower). You now want to rescan your images using this software so that your patrons can better find what they are looking for, but you're working with two other archives. Where is the original physical item? You're collaborating, so who owned the book that you digitized? You can, of course, go through the records of your collections, but this will take time, and what do you do if there are multiple copies among the three archives? Logically, you would have digitized the best copy, but who held it? What if the clearest copy had missing pages, so you digitized two different books to get a whole copy? How will you remember?

If you added metadata about when and how the digital item was created and who made it, then this isn't a problem. The metadata for the item will indicate who made the scans and, therefore, who holds the book in a collection and, possibly, even where it is. If you needed two or more copies to get a good digital copy, you can leave some notes for yourself with the digitized item. If you ever move to a different archive, whoever takes your place will have invaluable information with the collections that you created and won't struggle to continue your project.

There are all kinds of useful information that you can add to born-digital collections, too. For example, suppose that you want to archive a kind of software. Software becomes obsolete over time for many reasons, one of which is that it is no longer compatible with a new operating system. You can indicate to future users which operating system it was most compatible with, which will help them determine how they can make the software run, if desired.

As you know, file formats can become obsolete as well. Imagine that someone created a better format for images—say that it had all the benefits of a JPEG but took up even less space digitally. All the new software companies want to use this new file format instead of the old clunky JPEG. The JPEGs that you have are in danger of becoming obsolete, so you want to save them in this new file format. If you used metadata to indicate the fact that your JPEGs are, in fact, JPEGs and perhaps which program or programs you used to create them, you can start locating those files and either converting them or making notes in their metadata that they require conversion. Knowing which programs that you used can help you determine how you can view the JPEGs again, or it can help you start to determine the most efficient way to convert your files.

You could also use metadata to indicate that a file is not optimal. For example, suppose that you had an image of a mayor that you think is important for local history. This photo, though, has a big crease down the middle. You'd really like a better copy, but it's the only one that your archive has. Someone from the community might have a better copy, if you ever locate one. You can indicate that your copy is not optimal and could be better in the metadata, too.

Metadata helps your patrons locate relevant items. As part of the process of creating a digital archive, you need to decide how your patrons will access your items and how much they will be allowed to do with your digital materials once they have located their desired items. You have many options and many possible levels of access for your patrons.

Accessing Digital Materials

Once you've created your digital materials, you need to think about how you want your data to be accessed and who you want to be able to access your data. You'll need to consider this even further if you happen to be archiving anything that shouldn't be accessible to the general public, information that is sensitive in any way, or data that you are simply archiving for the sake of archiving and are not legally capable of making accessible to the public (situations in which this might happen are discussed in the following chapter).

Information that is available via the Internet is always less secure than information that is not available online. No matter how much security you use or how many promises a cloud computing company makes, data that is accessible through a network is always less secure than information that is not. If you have information that is particularly desirable and valuable, hackers will attempt to access it. Even if you don't have sensitive information, hackers will occasionally hack systems solely to see if it can be done or for their own amusement. While an archive isn't a particularly brag-worthy target in this respect, it's always best to be prepared. If your archive is part of a university, for instance, your local bored computer science majors may see even your databases as a worthwhile target.

If you do have information that is sensitive, the best thing to do is to store it offline. You would archive the item storing your data as an object, keeping it away from a computer or a reader, in the case of magnetic tape. If there is no online access, then there is no way for someone to access your data remotely.

If you'd like patrons to be able to access your data but want them to be able to do it only locally—that is, only when they are within your building—then you could load your data onto a computer that is not connected to a network. This would involve saving it on a computer's hard drive. While it's possible for the data to be copied via items such as CDs or flash drives, you can take steps against this, too, such as physically blocking or removing ports and CD drives (if you don't want patrons to be able to take the data with them) or limiting access to relevant folders or programs on the computer. You could also have a local network, or a series of computers that are connected to only one another and not the Internet, which is similar but allows patrons to access your data from several computers.

You may not have any security issues and want the general public to be able to freely access your collection as well. In this case, you'll likely want to load the data either to a server connected to the Internet or to a web-hosting service. This will involve creating a website for your archive.

You may also want only authorized users to access your data—for example, your archive is part of a larger library system, and you want only registered patrons of the library to access the data. This is also possible but is a little more complex to set up. It is, of course, definitely possible to do—otherwise, it would be impossible to have security on the Internet for making purchases from online shops, and it would be possible for anyone to access your e-mail. It may also be a feature of a cloud computing service, should you decide to use one. Cloud computing services are described in detail in chapter 10.

What you should also keep in mind is what you want to do if you want patrons to have access to your data but only as a physical object. For example, suppose that you have a collection of audio interviews and decided that it was best to put them on an external solid-state drive. A patron could request to use the drive, treating the data item more as you would a tangible item in your library. However, solid-state drives are easily altered. The patron could erase your data or write in his or her own, whether accidentally or maliciously.

It's possible to make files *read only*, which means that the file cannot be altered (for Macs, the option "Stationery Pad" is the equivalent of a Windows "read-only" file). The file can be deleted, however, or moved to different folders and copied, so this isn't a perfect solution to the problem. You can change the permissions on files, which limits access and alterations by unauthorized users (your patrons, in this instance). This is part of the security options for a file. You need to be sure that patrons who know something about computers aren't able to simply switch the options back. This means that you require more than one account on a computer: one for you and your staff and one for patrons. This will allow you to use your account to deny some things to anyone on the other account. The account for your archive and staff needs to be password protected to limit access like this.

Key Points

- Metadata is information about a digital item, and it is a necessary part of creating and maintaining a digital collection.

- Adding metadata and cataloging are similar processes with similar goals, and someone trained in cataloging has the skills needed to create good metadata. However, there are ways for amateurs to create useful metadata and even for computers to automatically generate some metadata.
- A number of metadata schemas are used in modern times, which are similar to one another in many ways but are sometimes tailored to achieve a specific goal or are designed to be used for a certain type of collection.
- Along with requiring special cataloging considerations, accessing digital information poses some security issues that must be addressed.

Digital collections work differently than do paper collections in many ways, and the legal aspects of creating and maintaining a digital collection are not always readily evident or intuitive. In the following chapter, you will be given an overview of copyright law—in general and as it pertains to digital materials in particular.

⊚ References

Ashenfelder, Michael. 2013. "Personal Digital Archiving: Adding Descriptions to Digital Photos." http://publiclibrariesonline.org/2013/09/personal-digital-archiving-adding-descriptions-to-digital-photos/.

Library of Congress. 2009. "What Is a MARC Record, and Why Is It Important?" http://www.loc.gov/marc/umb/um01to06.html.

National Information Standards Organization (NISO). 2004. "Understanding Metadata." http://www.niso.org/publications/press/UnderstandingMetadata.pdf.

Taylor, Arlene G. 2004. *The Organization of Information*. 2nd ed. Westport, CT: Libraries Unlimited.

Tennant, Roy. 2002. "MARC Must Die." *Library Journal*. http://lj.libraryjournal.com/2002/10/ljarchives/marc-must-die/.

Copyright Law

COPYRIGHT ISSUES ARE A COMMON PROBLEM for all libraries, but digital archiving presents some unique challenges. Part of your archiving process will most likely involve determining whether or not you actually have the right to create a digital copy of information and, if you do, whether or not you can offer it to your patrons or make it available online.

It is the aim of this chapter to refresh your memory on the current copyright laws regarding tangible materials, then to discuss how these laws are similar to those for digital materials. Digital materials are easily copied and shared, which is good in many ways but also makes it very easy to violate copyright law. Therefore, more laws were created that are specifically designed to help copyright holders protect their digital materials. This is also discussed. You'll need to understand your archive's rights as well as the rights of copyright holders when it comes to dealing with both types of items, digital as well as tangible.

This chapter can't cover every aspect of copyright law that you would ever need to know. It's always a good idea to learn more if you have doubts about an item that you are archiving and since the laws keep changing, you'll need to keep updating your knowledge to ensure that your archive is working within the law. If you have any doubts about the legality of your project and what you want to digitize or store, consult an attorney or other legal counsel.

So, what exactly is copyright law? It's important enough that it's part of the U.S. Constitution—specifically, article I, section 8, gives Congress the power to promote the arts and sciences by giving creators the exclusive right to their works—in other words, copyright protection. Several branches of government are involved in creating and overseeing copyright laws. Congress can enact new copyright laws, while the Copyright Office of the Library of Congress is in charge of the administrative aspects of copyright laws, and the federal courts interpret these laws and enforce them.

Copyright law, as it's used in America today, originates from the British legal system, and the concept of copyright is fairly old. Prior to the invention of the printing press, works of art, writing, and similar creations were essentially all done by commission. Someone from the aristocracy or the church who had the available funds could pay someone, such as a writer or an artist, to create a specific item, and in the past, this was how artists and writers made their money (Hoffmann 2001). Works of this type were considered more as a craft than an art—the concept of "art" in general is fairly new.

The ability to mass produce works of art and writing changed all of that; for example, prints of woodcuts or etchings were a way to mass-produce art, as opposed to having a single work of art, such as a painting. Although copyright laws did protect the creators somewhat, the purpose of copyright law was actually to prevent commoners from gaining materials that might incite either political or religious rebellion, thus upsetting the church or monarchy's power. It wasn't until the early 18th century that copyright began taking on the sentiments of modern copyright law (Hoffmann 2001).

Copyright law is important. In essence, it gives people the right to make a profit from their own creations. America would be a very different place if anyone could use the works of any other person for any purpose. For instance, the Disney company is well known for creating animated movies for children. If its movies were not protected by copyright, then anyone could copy its movies and sell them, which would make creating animated movies unprofitable for this company. It would also make it very difficult to control the use of their characters, such as Mickey Mouse, or to control the company image. Without copyright, there would be no monetary reason to make anything creative in nature, because you couldn't make a significant profit from it. The protection that is offered by copyright law motivates people to create intellectual properties, such as stories or song lyrics, motivation that would be lost in many ways without this protection. America would be without many works of art, writing, music, inventions, and other works created in the hope of making a profit.

Copyright law is also designed to protect the general public by *not* giving the creators of copyrighted works absolute control over those works. There are exceptions to copyright law, instances in which people who do not hold the copyright to a work are permitted to use the work. The concepts of "fair use" and the "public domain" are part of this. These concepts are explained in detail later in the chapter.

An archive's aim is to preserve the past and, sometimes, the present for the sake of the future. Trying to adhere to copyright law can therefore seem to be a burden, even irritating, since archival preservation is done with good intentions. However, it's essential to keep within the rules of copyright law for several reasons. The most practical of these, of course, is to avoid a lawsuit from an unhappy copyright holder. Violating copyright law can carry some steep fines on top of legal fees, and no one wants to have to deal with this when you could be using your time and resources to do more archiving. At the minimum, a person who violates a copyright can be fined for damages up to $30,000 per work or up to $150,000 if the violator did it intentionally. For instance, if someone created prints of another person's artwork with the intention of selling them without the artist's permission, this would be an intentional violation of copyright. A person winning such a suit is also subject to recovering attorneys' fees. There can be other problems or penalties arising from a violation of copyright law, whether it was intentional or unintentional or whether it was for a benign or malicious purpose.

But the other important reason is to keep protecting the people who make things worth preserving for the future. With the Internet, the transmission of information is extremely easy, and you may wish to put your digitized collection online to help people all over the world who want information. If you put something online that you do not have the rights to or that someone doesn't want put online, then this harms the person who created the item, most likely by making it difficult or impossible to profit from their work or making it possible for less scrupulous people to steal and profit from the work. This also discourages people from creating and sharing things. It's essential that, in the rush to preserve things for the future, people are not harmed in the present. Even a project that may seem noble, such as sharing information with the world, is not noble if someone gets hurt by it in the process.

Copyright law is simultaneously simple and complex. You're probably already familiar with copyright law, but to understand the additions to copyright law that address digital materials in particular, it's helpful to remember the basics of copyright law in general, without the complications that digital materials add to it.

Works That Are Protected by Copyright

While the types of things that can be copyrighted vary greatly, most copyrightable works can be sorted into a few basic categories.

- Music is copyrighted, but it must be recorded in a tangible format, such as a tape or a CD, to be copyrighted.
- Movies, television shows, and other audiovisual works are copyrighted. A DVD of a movie, for instance, is a copyrighted work. Like music, these performances must be recorded.
- Performed works, such as dances, public performances, and pantomimes, are under copyright protection.
- Written works, such as books, news articles, poems, sheet music, and plays, are copyrighted.
- Artwork such as paintings, sculptures, and photographs are copyrighted.
- Computer programs are copyrighted. This may be of interest to you if you want to preserve software—that is, the software that you preserve may be under copyright law.
- Architectural works such as building plans are under copyright protection.
- Derivative works or compilations of works are under copyright protection.

In general, works must be "fixed" in some manner to be under copyright, and thinking of works in this manner is a good way to help you figure out if something is potentially copyrightable. You cannot copyright a mere idea. For instance, suppose that you came up with an idea for a fictional story. Unless you actually write the story down, it's not copyrighted, and if you were to tell your idea to someone else and that person actually did write the story, you would not be able to claim a copyright violation. If you were to perform an original piece of music for an audience, but (a) it was never recorded, (b) you never wrote down how to play it, and (c) someone else did, you would also have difficulty claiming a copyright violation.

Works are under copyright upon creation. There is no need to register a work for it to be copyrighted; this is simply helpful for identifying the owner of a work and is useful should there be any issues regarding rights and ownership. When a work is registered, the creator can easily prove that he or she holds the copyright should there ever be a legal dispute or a violation. A work doesn't have to have any kind of notice for it to be under copyright either; this is essentially assumed. Though necessary in the past, a copyrighted work doesn't have to have the copyright symbol, which is the symbol ©; this has not been needed since March 1, 1989.

Anyone owning a copyright on a work has six exclusive rights in regard to the work:

- The owner can reproduce the work. As an example, suppose that an artist creates a painting. The artist has the exclusive right to create prints of the painting and sell them.
- The owner of an audio recording, if he or she holds the copyright to the recording, can publicly play it.
- The owner can publicly display a work, such as a sculpture or a photograph. This particular right can get tricky when it comes to digital copyright law and is be discussed later in the chapter.
- The owner can create derivative works, or works that are based in some way on the original.
- The owner can publicly perform a work. This would apply to someone who writes and performs music, for example. It would also apply for a choreographer and others as well.
- The owner has the right to distribute the work. For instance, if someone wrote a book, he or she has the right to distribute and sell copies of that book.

But it is possible for someone other than the original creator to hold the copyright for a work. The creator of a work can sell his or her copyright to someone else, giving that person all the rights regarding the work. Creative works can also be commissioned with the intent that the copyright will belong to the person who requested the commission. For example, suppose that a company wanted a new logo. It hires a graphic designer to create the logo. While the graphic designer created the logo, the company who hired the graphic designer owns the copyright on it. In copyright law, this is considered a "work for hire" situation (Butler 2011).

In general, the rights that a copyright holder has are designed to help him or her profit from the work. It is therefore not too difficult determining what works are subject to copyright and figuring out what rights a copyright holder has: works that are original and creative in nature and have been recorded in some manner are usually subject to copyright law, and anything that interferes with a copyright holder's ability to profit from the work is probably a violation of one's rights. However, the protections offered by copyright are not indefinite. Because the laws keep changing regarding how long a copyright lasts, figuring out whether something is still under copyright or not is challenging.

Works No Longer under Copyright Protection

Copyright doesn't last forever. Works eventually fall into what is known as the "public domain." What this means is that after a certain period, a work that has been created becomes free for anyone to use for any purpose whatsoever. For instance, there is a parody book titled *Pride and Prejudice and Zombies*, by Seth Grahame-Smith, which is simply the book *Pride and Prejudice* by Jane Austen, but Grahame-Smith has altered the text to include zombies, largely for the purpose of comedy. While there are special rules regarding parody and copyright, using large amounts of text straight from the original is possible and lawful owing to the fact that *Pride and Prejudice* is no longer under copyright, although it should be noted that *Pride and Prejudice* was written in England and laws in other countries are often different from those in the United States.

Essentially, anyone can do whatever one likes with works that have fallen into the public domain, including profit from publication. However, *Pride and Prejudice and Zombies* itself is under copyright—remember, derivative works are protected by copyright law.

Knowing how long copyright law is in effect is not simple. The laws keep changing to extend the length of copyright. Recall that Mickey Mouse is an example of what might be a consequence of not having copyright laws. To prevent early Mickey Mouse movies from falling into the public domain, the Disney company has been a major force behind extending the time that a copyright is in effect for a work.

Because the laws keep changing to extend the length of copyright ownership, whether or not a work has fallen into the public domain is becoming increasingly difficult to determine. In addition, laws vary depending on what type of work was copyrighted and whether or not a work was published and when. The following are some general guidelines regarding U.S. copyright law:

- Any work published in the United States before 1923 is in the public domain.
- If a work was published between 1923 and 1963 and there is a copyright notice attached, the copyright on such a work at the time could be renewed for another 67 years. If the copyright wasn't renewed, it's in the public domain.
- If a work was published between 1923 and 1963 and it has no copyright notice, it's in the public domain.
- If a work was published between 1964 and 1977 and has a copyright notice attached, then the copyright was automatically renewed on the work for a total of 95 years of copyright protection.
- If a work was published on or after January 1, 1978, then it's under copyright for the life of the owner plus 50 years. If more than one person was involved in creation or holds ownership, then the lifetime of the longest-living holder is used to determine how long copyright is in effect. January 1, 1978, is the date in which the 1976 Copyright Act came into effect, which is why the rules change after this date.
- If a work was published on or after January 1, 1978, and has a corporate author or is a work for hire (as in the example with the company hiring a graphic designer for a logo), then the work is under copyright for either 120 years after creation or 95 years after publication, whichever one is shortest.

Again, the length of the effect of copyright law keeps changing. Current copyright laws apply to works for the life of the creator plus 75 years after his or her death. This is an extension from the previous life plus 50 years. In 1998, the Sonny Bono Term Extension

Act was created in an effort to preserve the rights of musicians during the rock-and-roll era who died young so that the copyrights would not run out while their music was still popular (Wherry 2002). While these musicians can no longer benefit from the work, their families benefit from this law and the resulting income generated by copyrighted works.

If a work is anonymous, then copyright law becomes a little more difficult to follow. The work is still under copyright. It must be emphasized that because a creator cannot be found or is not associated with a work, that does not mean that the work isn't under copyright. If a work is anonymous, is a corporate work, or is created by a person for a company (work for hire, as mentioned earlier), then the copyright lasts 95 years from the date the work was published or 120 years after the date that it was created, whichever span is shorter. Remember, a work does not need to be registered to be copyrighted. Again, this is an increase in time, also due to the Sonny Bono Term Extension Act (Hoffmann 2001).

Determining whether something has fallen into the public domain is not easy, and neither is determining whether a copyright holder renewed his or her copyright. If you need to find out whether a copyright was renewed, there are basically two ways to do it. The U.S. Copyright Office will find out for you but for a rather steep fee. You can also browse its online records and try to find out for yourself if an item is still under copyright. There are a couple of other online databases that can help you search for copyrights as well, such as the Copyright Renewal Database or the Catalog of Copyright Entries (Butler 2011).

You may wonder what happens if you can't find the copyright holder to determine if you are free to archive something. If finding out who holds the copyright or whether copyright is still in effect is difficult or even impossible, then the item in question is known as an *orphan work*. Orphan works are problematic, since you may want to use an orphan work in your archive, but it may still be under copyright. You could search for an owner and then determine that you've given it a sufficient amount of effort and use the work anyway, believing that it is no longer under copyright protection or that the owner has abandoned rights to the work, but this has problems, too.

For example, a group of research libraries and universities known as HathiTrust digitizes materials and has over 9.5 million works on its servers. Some of these are orphan works. To determine if a work has been orphaned, this group puts lists online of works that it wants to digitize that it believes are orphaned; then, it waits for a certain amount of time for a copyright holder to claim ownership and prove that it is not orphaned. The group probably uses this method because it is digitizing a large number of items, and this method is a fast, cheap, and easy way to deal with the problem of orphaned works. However, the group was sued for this practice in 2011 by three author groups and eight individual authors, who were concerned about copyright infringement issues and the security of the digitized files (Bosman 2011). While what you do in the event of an orphaned work is up to you and your organization, it's best to be safe and to ensure that you do in fact have the right to digitally archive all the items in your collection to avoid problems like this.

Works That Aren't Copyrighted

So far, this chapter has discussed what types of tangible works can be copyrighted, what rights a copyright holder has, and how to find out if something has fallen into the public domain, making it free for you to use. Copyright does not apply to all works, and so there are many items that cannot be copyrighted at all. Any item that falls into this category is free for you to digitize, regardless of when it was made and by whom. The following are some of the kinds of works or creations that can't be copyrighted:

- Slogans, titles, names, and other short phrases cannot be copyrighted. It should be noted, though, that company slogans can be protected by other laws, such as trademark laws (Wherry 2002).
- Lists of ingredients, processes, and methods can't be copyrighted. For instance, you can't copyright the list of ingredients on a recipe for chocolate chip cookies.
- Phone books aren't copyrighted. This is an item that might interest genealogists in particular.
- As discussed earlier, ideas can't be copyrighted. They must have some tangible format, such as a book or a music CD.
- Any facts or news can't be copyrighted, such as the kind of data you'd find in an almanac or an encyclopedia, although the text itself could be copyrighted.
- Familiar symbols can't be copyrighted, such as a flag.
- Common-property works can't be copyrighted—for example, height and weight charts. Calendars can't be copyrighted, either, although artwork on a calendar might be.
- Any work that falls into the public domain upon creation is not under copyright. There are some works like this—almost anything created by U.S. government employees automatically falls into the public domain if it was created as part of their job.

It's possible for a person to voluntarily give up the rights to his or her copyright, in which case a work is free for anyone to use. There are also alternative licenses to copyright that a person may use to make their work more freely available for others to use; this is discussed later in the chapter.

Once again, works that aren't fixed in a tangible medium are generally considered not under copyright. A photo or a book would be an example of a tangible medium. If someone gave a speech and it wasn't recorded in any manner, though, then the speech wouldn't be under copyright.

In the past, this distinction—whether something was recorded in a tangible way—made it pretty clear whether something was under copyright in most instances. If someone paints a picture, she or he holds the copyright. One's idea, the image, is fixed in a tangible medium: the painted image. But in modern times, this distinction is not so clear, and the general rule of thumb leads to some obvious complications. For example, is a website tangible? It's ephemeral in some ways and can change radically and without notice. It is composed of electronic signals. Are websites tangible, or aren't they?

Problems with Digital Copyright

It should be obvious that, yes, a person who creates a website controls the copyright of the site and all the data on it, assuming that he or she is not violating copyright. The website is a creative work, and there would be chaos if website designers and people who post their works online had no protection; it is also possible that there would instead be very little to see online without copyright protections, since creative people would not want to share their works.

Each time that something new is invented that makes it easier to share information or to profit from someone else's work, copyright laws need to change to protect people who create intellectual works. The problems that are arising from digital information today are not new. For example, in 1909, copyright law needed to adapt to protect composers and publishers, since they feared that the new invention at the time, the piano roll, would represent a serious cut into their profits. The phonograph was a similar cause for worry, and so the laws were again changed to protect people's rights (Wherry 2002). Photocopiers, VCRs, and many other inventions that make the distribution of information faster, easier, and cheaper all required the laws to adapt.

The Internet and the rise of digital information is really no different, except for the fact that some of the things that have been used to make judgment calls about whether copyright law has been violated with tangible materials don't transfer well to digital materials. For example, you learned in chapter 10 that when you "visit" a web page, what actually happens is that a server sends you a copy of the necessary data to re-create the web page via a browser program, and all that data is temporarily stored on your computer. Technically, you've just made a copy of copyrighted material. Is that a violation, or isn't it? If you were to put a link on your web page to an article on someone else's page, does it count as distribution? Since translations are normally considered derivative works, are you violating a creator's exclusive right to derivative works if you use an online language translator, such as BabelFish (Hoffmann 2001)? What happens on wiki pages, in which the authors of the content may be numerous and anonymous?

Links and copies of digital items are common online and are necessary for web function. However, linking doesn't have a clear tangible equivalent, and making copies is clearly a copyright violation for tangible materials. Current laws are designed to help address this kind of confusion and to protect, not only people whose rights can be violated by the easy transmission of information, but also people who have no ill intentions from an erroneous lawsuit.

Digital Materials and Copyright Law

If you are digitizing tangible materials, the laws regarding their use will be somewhat more important to you. However, you may be interested in archiving born-digital materials. In this case, you'll need to know about the laws pertaining specifically to born-digital media.

Digital Materials under Copyright

So far, this chapter has discussed what kinds of tangible materials are under copyright. But what kinds of *digital* materials are under copyright? Some digital materials have a "tangible" equivalent, so sometimes determining what digital materials are under copyright is somewhat intuitive. The following are some digital items that are under copyright protection:

- Blogs, vlogs (or video blogs), and podcasts (just like books, video recordings, and audio recordings)
- Web pages and wikis, or sites that allow for user collaboration (e.g., Wikipedia)

- Images in a digital format (just like regular photos, paintings, or other images). This is important, considering that many artists are able to create works of art using computer software; art created in this way will have no original tangible medium. Digital cameras also create images with no original tangible format.
- Digital movies or other videos (just like film videos or movies). Again, this may not have an original format that is tangible in the way that film has a tangible format.
- Digital advertisements (just like printed ads)
- Software programs

Although most of this is intuitive, something that is copyrighted that you may not know is protected under copyright law is e-mail. If you use e-mail to send messages, every time you create a new e-mail, it's under copyright. If you reply to an e-mail and it contains the contents of the original e-mail, you're technically in violation of copyright law by using the original sender's material without permission. This is not typically something that people go to court over, however.

Something that could be problematic, though, is an attachment to an e-mail, or additional files sent with the e-mail (Butler 2011). For example, suppose a friend of yours sends you an image of a kitten. For the sake of simplicity, say that it's a picture that the person took of his or her kitten. You now have a copy of that image, but you don't necessarily have the right to use that image. Forwarding it to someone else who appreciates cute kittens could technically be a violation of copyright law. If the picture that your friend sent was taken from somewhere online and doesn't belong to that person at all, then things start becoming quite murky.

It's often easy for people who create born-digital materials to specify certain conditions under which their materials can be used as well, which makes following the law even more difficult. This is a situation that is common with software in particular. When you install software, typically you must agree to a license before the software will install. Oftentimes, people skip reading the license because it's long and technical. However, if you want to archive materials such as software, then reading the license is something that you need to do. Many times, software companies limit your rights, but companies also often allow for "backups" to be made of their software, which would allow your archive to make extra copies for the purpose of archiving.

It's also possible for the creators of born-digital works to specifically give up some or all of their rights to a work, just as they can with tangible materials, which allows you to freely archive an item, just as with tangible materials. Laws regarding digital works in the public domain are similar to those for tangible materials.

Digital Materials in the Public Domain

It may have occurred to you that most born-digital items won't have lost their copyright and fallen into the public domain yet, since the length of time needed for the copyright to expire won't have passed. There *are* digital items that are in the public domain, though, since, as mentioned earlier, copyright holders can give up their rights. However, figuring out which is which is just as difficult, if not more so, than determining what is and what is not under copyright with tangible materials. There are a lot of misconceptions when it comes to materials found online, which should be cleared up.

Misconceptions with Copyright Online

A lot of people treat everything online as being in the public domain, and a lot of people feel that materials offered via the Internet should be free to use while ignoring copyright law. That is more of a philosophy than a reality.

Some people assume that because an item is freely available to use or view online, this means that it can be used for any purpose. For example, suppose that a blogger or someone who writes for a blog wants a picture of a sunset to illustrate a post. This blogger does a search online to look for a picture and finds one. The blogger then makes a copy and posts it on his or her blog.

This image may be freely available to use, since many sites online offer images that anyone can use for any purpose (further muddying the distinction between what is and what is not under copyright with digital materials), but it's more likely that the image is under copyright and the blogger does not have the right to use it, even if he or she really wants to. Just like tangible materials, digital materials don't have to have a notice of copyright to be under copyright protection. Creators do not have to register with the copyright office either. Digital materials are under copyright upon creation, just like tangible ones, including computer software and websites.

Orphan works are extremely common online, and all the same rules apply to digital orphan works as tangible ones. Even if the copyright holder cannot be located, this does not mean that one's work is available to use. Sometimes, it's possible to contact the copyright holder, for instance, via e-mail. If the copyright holder doesn't respond, this also does not mean that the item can be freely used.

The ease with which people can create and post online material creates some problems for you. While you will most likely find the copyright information for a professionally published book with the copyright office, you're unlikely to find legal information regarding the copyright of the material on a blog or other online resource.

It's important to keep within the law for many reasons. However, your archive will have some special rules that are designed to make things more fair; again, copyright law is not only for protecting copyright holders but for helping the general public as well.

Laws for Archives

Seventy years after the death of a creator is a very long time for an item to be under copyright, and since the creator can't benefit from the work any longer, many libraries feel that such a long extension of copyright law has no benefit to anyone—not the creator and not society in general (though corporations certainly benefit from the extension). It can be argued that because the creator can't benefit, such extensions get away from the purpose of copyright laws (Hoffmann 2001).

There's a provision in copyright law aimed at archives to address this issue. This provision gives your archive, as well as libraries and nonprofit educational institutions, the right "to reproduce, distribute, display, or perform in facsimile or digital form a copy . . . for the purposes of preservation, scholarship, or research" (Hoffmann 2001) so long as one of the following provisions are met:

- The work is no longer "subject to normal commercial exploitation." This condition is not defined by the law (Hoffmann 2001).
- The work can't be obtained at what the archive considers a reasonable price.
- The copyright holder gives permission.

These conditions, while helpful, are unfortunately not defined very well. You may decide that a creator can't benefit from a work any longer, but he or she (or his or her family) may have a different opinion on the matter. You still need to make a decision whether something falls into one of these categories.

In addition, archives oftentimes have the right to make a digital copy of an item for the purpose of preservation only. However, there is a difference between preservation and dissemination. That is, if you make a copy and store it but don't make it available to the public until the copyright has run out, this may be within your rights according to the Digital Millennium Copyright Act.

Ⓖ Digital Millennium Copyright Act

In 1998, Congress passed two bills that are essentially additions and amendments to the 1976 Copyright Act. One of these is the Sonny Bono Copyright Term Extension Act, mentioned previously. The other is the Digital Millennium Copyright Act (DMCA), which is designed to address copyright issues that are specific to digital works and the Internet.

Many of the rules of the DMCA simply make it illegal to circumvent or ignore security that is already in place on digital items. For instance, many sites online exist solely to distribute files such as music, PDFs, games, or movies, most likely in the belief that online information should be freely available. Oftentimes, these are items that are actually under copyright. As an example, you might be able to go onto one of these sites and find a copy of a movie that was recently released on DVD and download it. This, of course, is illegal and is known as online piracy.

To prevent products from winding up on such a site, many companies embed software code into their products that protects them from piracy, or they require a password of some kind for their products to function. The DMCA includes a law making it illegal to do anything to circumvent this, to remove the antipiracy software, or to copy something that is protected in this manner (Wherry 2002).

It's also illegal to do this for online websites. While much of the World Wide Web is open for anyone to browse, there's a significant portion of it that is kept hidden from access, for commercial purposes or for security reasons. It's illegal to try to get around any software or security that limits access to something via the Internet (Hoffmann 2001).

Similarly, it's illegal to attempt to make items available for the public to access that should otherwise be under password protection. For example, let's say that an item was part of a digital course reserve at a university and it was limited to student access via password protection. If you knew the password and made it freely available, this is in violation of the DMCA laws (Wherry 2002).

Along with these restrictions, the DMCA provides extra rules that pertain to archives and other nonprofit institutions, giving these organizations extra rights, which is helpful to you. Under some circumstances, it's legal to circumvent software and web page protections (Wherry 2002). You may be able to copy DVDs or CDs, for instance, for the purpose of archiving. As mentioned earlier, in the terms of service of many kinds of software, there is a clause stating that it's legal to make a backup copy, and so it would be legal for your archive to store a backup copy of the software so long as you (a) owned an original copy and (b) did not distribute your backup copies.

It would therefore not cause any problem if you were to, say, make backup copies of a copyrighted audio collection and put them into archival storage. If you were to make your copies available as part of your online collection, though, then this might be illegal. When trying to determine whether something is legal or illegal under copyright law, a good place to start is to consider whether or not what you want to do could interfere with a creator's profiting from his or her work. If it could, then it's probably a violation of copyright law.

If you make your collection available online, it's essential that you are sure that you have the right to display everything in the collection, not just to protect copyright holders, but to protect your organization. There is a rule in the DMCA that is designed to protect the rights of copyright holders by removing material from the web that is being used without permission. Many people who use the web will, as an example, look for nice photos to illustrate profile pages, blog posts, or personal websites, without being aware of who actually owns the rights to the photos. If the owner of the photo catches the person who is using it, the former can make a complaint to whoever is hosting the website. The host is required by law to take down the offending web page and to notify the owner of the violation. The owner of the website must then either notify the host that the photo was in fact legal to use or remove it from the site if it was not legal to use. The response must be sent to the owner of the photograph, who must then indicate whether court action will be taken. If the owner doesn't send a notice, then the host needs to put the web page back online between 10 and 14 days (Wherry 2002).

This particular part of the DMCA is helpful to copyright holders and gives them quite a bit of power, which is highly beneficial to them, since it's very easy to "steal" material from others online and claim it as one's own. The problem with this law is that anyone could falsely accuse any site of using copyrighted material without permission (Wherry 2002). What this means to you is that it's important to check and double-check to ensure that you have the right to post any material that you might want to display online, since having a web page down for 10 to 14 days could wreak havoc with your archive's website. You can protect yourself by taking the proper steps to ensure that you have the right to use everything in your collection and that you can prove it, too.

As an additional consideration, you might suppose that if it turns out that you don't have permission to display something after all and someone complains, you can simply remove the offending item and this will resolve the problem. However, because it's so easy to copy and distribute materials, if you put something online that should not be there, other people can create copies of your files and put them elsewhere online, out of your control, which means that the damage is already done from the perspective of a copyright holder. Remember: there are sites devoted exclusively to distributing copyrighted material illegally. It's important to be careful, not just for your archive, but for anyone holding a copyright on an item.

⌗ Fair Use

Sometimes, you can use an item that has a copyright without asking permission or paying a fee. This is known as *fair use*. The government decided that, while it's important for people who create works to be able to profit from their work, it's also important for people to be able to learn and exchange ideas without worrying about violating copyright law; thus, it created the fair use rules. A few kinds of activities fall under fair use. Most of this will not pertain to your archive, but it's good to be aware of the rules of fair use anyway, if for no other reason than to know what you can't claim as being covered under it.

In copyright law (section 107), four factors determine if a work falls under fair use:

1. What is the item being used for, and is it for nonprofit or educational purposes?
2. What kind of a work is being used?
3. How much of the work is being used (e.g., a certain percentage of the total work)?
4. What is the effect of using this item on the item's market value? In other words, will using this item affect the profit that the copyright holder can make?

There are many situations in which using part of a copyrighted work can count as fair use and is therefore legal. For example, quoting a passage from a book or a few lines from a song for the purpose of criticism or critique counts as fair use (although the creator may think otherwise). Parodies are also under fair use. Summaries of works count as fair use, and teachers and students are able to reproduce portions of works for the purpose of education (U.S. Copyright Office 2012).

Something that may be of use to you is the fact that reproducing part of a damaged work owned by an organization such a library can fall under fair use practices. If you're preserving a collection that is deteriorating and you can't get new copies of your items, then these laws may enable you to legally save your collection without the difficulty and expense of replacing it (U.S. Copyright Office 2012).

The legal precedent for fair use and infringements of copyright law has been to determine whether the offending party infringed on copyright deliberately, without determining whether it was legal, or if it attempted to use material under the rules of fair use.

Like all other aspects of copyright law upon the rise of computers in everyday life and the use of digital materials, new rules regarding fair use with digital copyright needed to be created, and in 1994, a group called the Conference on Fair Use attempted to create a fairly extensive set of guidelines that would address fair use with digital materials. Unfortunately, these guidelines are an agreement among the organizations that created the guidelines, and they are not actual law. No major library organizations endorse these guidelines (remember: the Library of Congress is heavily involved in copyright law). However, if you're interested in whether using something digital or transmitting information online counts as fair use, then these guidelines can give you an idea of what you could do and what may not be legal (Wherry 2002).

⊚ Other Types of Licenses

In modern times, there are people who feel that copyright law is too restrictive or doesn't benefit society as a whole. For instance, some people feel that all software should be freely available to use. With this mind-set, some people have put their works under alternative licenses that allow for others to freely use their works (often software) so long as certain conditions are met. Items under these licenses are typically available for archiving or even making them available online, regardless of other laws or when they were created, because the creators have forfeited part or all of their rights under copyright law, either on moral grounds or for the purpose of helping others.

Free Software Foundation

As mentioned previously, some people feel that all software should be free to use. The Free Software Foundation has therefore created its own license, the general public license, or GPL. This license states that the user of software has the ability to use it for any purpose, make and share changes, and share the software with anyone (Butler 2011). This enables other programmers to use and change software without worrying that they are in violation of copyright law, and sometimes it encourages collaborative efforts on complex software.

Open-Source Software

Open-source software is software that is not only free but may be modified by its users, something that is usually forbidden in commercial software. The term "open source" refers to the fact that the code for the software is available to view and change. Coding for software programs is often kept hidden from the user to discourage others from modifying it or discovering how it works, in which case, other programmers could make similar programs and profit from them, cutting into the profits of the original programmer.

If the coding source is open, then programmers can easily see how the code works and make their own changes. Sometimes, people who create open-source software will request that others share their modifications in the interest of adding new and improved features to a program or fixing errors, or "bugs."

Open-source software licenses require that the distribution of the software is free and that it is freely available via the Internet. While the license can restrict some forms of modification, it must allow for derivatives and modifications. Open-source licenses must also not discriminate against a particular person or group, and they must be technology neutral; that is, the software doesn't work on a single proprietary device (Butler 2011). In most cases, open-source software can be archived.

Creative Commons

Creative Commons (http://creativecommons.org) is a nonprofit organization that essentially provides alternatives to copyright. It has a similar sentiment and function to the GPL but can apply to a range of works, not just software. Under a Creative Commons license, a person could create a work and allow for others to use and modify it to suit their needs (Butler 2011). There are several variations on this type of license, and so you need to read exactly what your rights are with a certain work; typically, these works are free to use so long as the intent is not for profit, the works are not modified, and the original creator is attributed to the work.

Key Points

- Copyright law has adapted to address the issues that arise from progress in technology, with the rise of the Internet radically changing how easily copyright law can be violated as well as what works can be considered under copyright.
- Changes in copyright make it difficult to determine what works are under copyright and which are not, although there are guidelines that can be followed and online databases that can make the process easier.
- Copyright laws for digital materials are very similar to those for tangible materials, with the addition of specific rules designed to help the copyright holders of digital materials.
- The rights of an archive can vary depending on what items are to be archived and how these items are to be used. Making copies of digital materials and archiving items for the sake of preservation is often treated differently from archiving for the purpose of distributing information.
- The rise of the Internet and computers as tools for everyday life has also led to the invention of some alternatives to copyright as a license for use, since there is a philosophy among some people that information distributed via the Internet should be free for everyone to use.

Digital materials present many obstacles to archiving—both legal obstacles and moral ones. In the following chapter, you will learn more about the issues presented by digital items—not problems arising from the costs of archiving, as discussed in previous chapters, or problems arising from user access, organizing, legal problems, or moral issues. The issues discussed in the next chapter concern the problems arising from archiving digital media due to the fact that it is digital in nature.

References

Bosman, Julie. 2011. "Lawsuit Seeks the Removal of a Digital Book Collection." *New York Times.* http://www.nytimes.com/2011/09/13/business/media/authors-sue-to-remove-books-from-digital-archive.html?_r=0.

Butler, Rebecca P. 2011. *Copyright for Teachers and Librarians in the 21st Century.* New York: Neal-Schuman.

Hoffmann, Gretchen McCord. 2001. *Copyright in Cyberspace: Questions and Answers for Librarians.* New York: Neal-Schuman.

U.S. Copyright Office. 2012. "Fair Use." http://www.copyright.gov/fls/fl102.html.

Wherry, Timothy Lee. 2002. *The Librarian's Guide to Intellectual Property in the Digital Age.* Chicago: American Library Association.

Problems with Digital Archiving

THE ADVANTAGES TO USING A COMPUTER to search for information are numerous, and really, this book has covered only a few of them. Computers can look for digital information more quickly than a human researcher can with tangible materials. Computers can search for specific words or phrases in a written work, making it possible to find exactly what information you are looking for in seconds, as opposed to thumbing through a book and hoping that you notice something appropriate or going through an index and hoping that someone indexed the word you want. Although the technology is not very refined at the moment, computers can search for images that are similar to one another, making matches. Computers can sort through the massive amounts of data created by humans and show you the most likely matches to the information that you want, reducing the time-consuming process of searching and deciding.

Computers don't create miracles, though. Many of the problems that you will face with digital preservation have been discussed in previous chapters. This chapter discusses them more in-depth. This chapter is a bit different from the others in this book in that it doesn't tell you specifically how to do anything for your archive. Instead, its aim is to discuss the limitations of computers and digital files so that you can be prepared to deal with these issues in a logical way that is suitable to your archive.

⊚ Issues with Digital Information

In general, you will encounter four issues with a collection of digital information:

Mutability: the changeable nature of digital information.

Binary data encoding: the nature of how computers encode their data.

Obsolescence: the problems that arise when technology is outdated.

Data decay: the tendency for digital data to degrade.

Mutability

The word "mutable" is an adjective. It means that something is easily changed or subject to change, such as the weather, and so it's a perfect word to describe how digital information works. Data is mutable in nature, in many different ways.

The purpose of an archive is to preserve information and to keep it safe. This can mean different things, but for the most part, an archive aims to make sure that all its information is accessible and that it stays exactly as it was when it was first created. Trying to do this with something that is mutable in nature, then, presents some obvious difficulties.

People have found a lot of different ways of effectively storing information over millennia, by making symbols on clay or stone tablets, leaves, papyrus, or parchment, for instance. The method of information sharing that people are probably most familiar with, though, is the book, which is one of the more efficient ways of storing and displaying information. Books are also not particularly mutable in nature, which is good from a preservation standpoint.

Historians have a pretty good idea about the development of the book and writing over time, and they have information about this from countries all over the world. The concept of making symbols that represent words, numbers, or ideas is very old and has been reproduced in many civilizations. The ability to record information, even something as mundane as how many cows someone has, has a drastic impact on all aspects of a society.

Since writing is so valuable to society, people are constantly working on ways to make writing easier to access and distribute. For example, movable type revolutionized the way that books were produced. Before movable type and the printing press were invented, all books had to be painstakingly handwritten, an enormously time-consuming task. This meant that books were available solely to the church and very wealthy and that there might be only a handful of copies of a work. An individual book might be the only one in existence, which is a terrible thing from the perspective of an archivist.

Mass-printed books using movable type made books available for lower classes, which also meant that there might be many copies of a work. Information and the exchange of ideas became open to more and more people as the years went by, making the transmission of information and ideas far easier than before. Further innovations only made printing books easier, cheaper, and faster, making books more and more easily accessible.

Historians can mark the point in time at which movable type was created, since information about this historic event is still available, even hundreds of years later. The Gutenberg Bible was the first book printed this way, sometime in the 1450s. Although the first copies were printed centuries ago, copies of it still survive today, and these copies are still readable.

The printing press produced a physical object that has historical value. A lot of events in history do, and that makes it easier to study the past, since historians have actual items that they can look at for their studies. A problem with tracing the history of events with computers, then, is that oftentimes, the revolutionary object is not physical in nature and can be changed as well.

The year 1989 marked another historic occasion in the transmission of information—work on creating the World Wide Web began, and in 1990, the first web page was designed, an item that may be considered by future generations to be as revolutionary to human society as the Gutenberg Bible. However, unlike the Gutenberg Bible, there are no copies of this pioneer web page. Nobody saved one. The original was overwritten by other files (Ward 2013).

The World Wide Web (discussed in detail in chapter 10) was developed at CERN, the European Organization for Nuclear Research. When CERN began searching for early files and web pages decades after its creation, it soon discovered that, while the first web page was created in 1990, it did not have any copies of web pages created before 1992. So, the earliest web page available to study is from 1991 (Ward 2013). When the World Wide Web was being developed, its creators wanted to promote their idea and created demonstration materials to show the benefits of their idea to others. This early web page is available because someone decided to keep a copy of those demonstration materials. The person who saved the materials has a computer that may hold other digital files that are historically relevant to the development of the World Wide Web, but at the moment, these are hidden and unavailable because no one remembers the password to access the relevant computer. This particular obstacle may be overcome in time, however (Ward 2013).

No one thought to save the first web page because no one really knew what a revolutionary thing the World Wide Web would be. Probably, no one thought this about the Gutenberg Bible either, beyond thinking about how much profit could be made from printing books this way. Unlike a computer file, though, printing a book leaves behind a physical, tangible object. You can't simply erase it out of existence with the ease that you can a collection of electronic impulses. You can burn it or do other things to destroy a book, of course, but you can't accidentally forget to save your book or suddenly not be able to access your book due to a hardware failure. Destruction of books is typically done deliberately. The fact that digital information is so easily prone to being lost in this way is one of the many ways in which it is mutable but not the only one.

You learned a little bit in chapter 12 about how problematic it would be if patrons were allowed total access to your archive. What if they started saving their own files on your storage materials, or what if they started altering the data that you do have? The integrity of your digital materials would be compromised, and one of the major goals of an archive is to keep things exactly the same. While there are things that you can do and ways to save things in a more permanent, unchanging way, all the information using the storage methods discussed in this book can be changed and are designed to be changed (with the exception of some optical disks). Most people appreciate this, since they can, for example, rid of old photos and make room for new ones or delete an old report that they don't need anymore and make a new one. This is all a good thing—unless you don't want anything to change.

This makes your digital materials vulnerable in a way that tangible ones are not. If someone goes into an art museum and attempts to vandalize a work of art, for example, there are people trained to restore damaged artwork. The changes will be noticed, and people can attempt to restore the work to its original condition. If someone attempts to change the words in a book, the alterations will be completely obvious by the scratched-out or omitted words.

Although the type on the printing press was movable to make it possible to reuse letters for many books, once printed, the words are always in the same place on the page. They might fade, but they'll never be completely erased, change positions, or be replaced with other words. For digital information, this might not be true.

If someone gets into a word-processing file and deletes a paragraph, no one might ever notice that something is wrong, since the program will simply reformat itself around the changes. Someone could use a photo-editing program and add all kinds of things to a digital image. If the person changing the photo is good at it, someone looking at the image might never know that something has been changed. After all, the point of sophisticated photo-editing programs is exactly this: so that you do not know that the altered image is not exactly like the original.

As another example, suppose that you don't want to save items that have an originally tangible form. You want to save web pages, for instance. But web pages change, too. Say that you're saving a web page that helps students find open-source texts for study on the web. The website updates monthly, adding new texts. Recently, it underwent a layout redesign—the navigation buttons are now along the top, and the background is blue. Do you keep updating your copy? Do you save a complete copy of the website every time it updates? And if you're saving a great number of websites, then how do you know that something has changed in one of them? If you're trying to keep track of a forum or other media in which many people are able to contribute, what do you do if someone changes the text of a comment that he or she made? How can you preserve the integrity of history like this?

Digital information is easily changed, erased, and written over. It can even be done by accident, not maliciously. This presents a problem for you as an archivist. If you put a book someplace, you expect that you'll have exactly the same item when you retrieve it (assuming that it isn't attacked by mildew or insects, of course). The illustrations will be the same, and the words will be the same. Digital materials are different. They are capable of changing. They can change even if no one interacts with the item, altering spontaneously. For example, in chapter 8, you learned that hard drives function best if they are used often so that the data gets refreshed. In essence, digital materials and tangible ones tend to be opposites. Many digital materials are safer the more they are used, and tangible ones are more prone to damage the more that they are used.

For your archive, this means that you need to consider a few things with your archiving plan:

- How can you make sure that your digital materials can't be erased or written over?
- How can you ensure that your digital materials are true to the original and are unaltered?
- How will you deal with preserving materials that are inherently prone to change?

Finally, you need to think about digital materials differently than you do tangible ones. Archiving traditionally involves repairing or maintaining an object and storing it someplace safe, where it won't be harmed or touched unnecessarily. Although it depends on how you store your data, you should probably think instead about how your data can be interacted with to keep it safe and to monitor it for degradation and change.

Binary Data Encoding

So far in this book, the concept of binary has been presented in a positive manner. Computers work efficiently with the binary system of numbers. It's a numerical system that works very well for computers and will probably continue to work well for some time. (Some people are trying to come up with ways to make other systems work efficiently, however, which has wonderful implications when it comes to storage space; in chapter 9, you learned how the ability to store multiple charges makes flash memory efficient.) Although there are only two numbers to work with, you can store all kinds of information using the system. Binary is also a problem, though.

The biggest issue with digital media is that you require a tool to use it—and not just any tool, either. Computers are capable of detecting fluctuations in a magnetic field, electrical impulses, or changes in light (in the case of optical media) that are far smaller and more minute than what anything a human can sense, even with tools such as magnets or magnifying glasses to assist. This is also what makes computers so helpful: the fact that they are capable of storing so much information in a tiny amount of space.

As mentioned at the beginning of this book, computers are glorified calculators. Everything is numbers to them. Even though programmers use coding, or sets of words that act as instructions to the computer, what actually happens is more complicated. Those words are all for the benefit of human programmers, working with human language. When a programmer has completed a program, that program needs to be "translated" into numbers so that the computer can understand the instructions. Programmers are actually working several levels away from what a computer can understand. And while humans are capable of using *machine code*—the term for languages that don't need translation and are directly accessible by the computer—such code is extremely difficult and tedious to write. When it comes to programming, very few people work this way or are even capable of it.

Humans don't work well in binary. Not only is it removed from the comfortable decimal method, but humans generally like words, not numbers. Even if it were possible for someone to, say, detect the dark and light spots on a burned CD without the aid of a computer, the majority of people would not be able to translate what was on the CD, because it's simply too difficult.

If every computer suddenly went down today, all the digital data saved everywhere would be completely lost. It would simply not be worth the time and effort to get the information without a computer to do it. Everything that was written down in books or other materials, however, would be perfectly accessible. Books are tangible items that are large enough for people to see without any sort of aid. The characters or letters in a book represent concepts or sounds that are easily translated for most people, since humans are language-based creatures and easily connect a symbol with a word.

The scenario of every computer everywhere suddenly breaking all at once is pretty unlikely, but it serves a point. Your data is useful only if a computer can read it. So, apart from your major archival goal of digitizing tangible materials or saving born-digital materials, your primary goal must be to ensure that a computer somewhere is able to read your data. Without the calculator (i.e., computer), your sets of electronic numbers are completely useless, and all of that hard work creating your archive would have been for nothing.

Unlike the idea of every computer in the world breaking simultaneously, the scenario of having data that no computer in the world can read is not implausible at all and has in fact already happened.

Obsolescence

Even though people tend to think of computers as being fairly modern, it's really only the personal computer that's new and innovative. Starting in the 1940s, there were plenty of computers available that were similar to the modern concept of a computer. They just weren't as common as computers today, and people did not have them in their homes.

People didn't have computers in their homes for a couple of reasons. First, computers were incredibly slow compared to computers today, so they had fewer capabilities; basically, they were only used as calculators. You couldn't use one to write up reports or keep track of accounts, for instance. There was no World Wide Web, so you couldn't do banking or shopping or search for information. Computers also lacked the capability for games, movies, or music, and they didn't have monitors capable of showing you the relevant information for games or movies, anyway. All these activities simply wouldn't be practical. So, only large companies or universities would have wanted or needed one or would have been able to afford it.

Second, they required quite a bit of maintenance. You probably do very little to maintain your computer. Maybe you run some antivirus software or a defrag program to clean up the hard drive, or you might use some compressed air to blow dust out of the circuits and the fan. But computers used between the 1940s and 1960s needed constant maintenance. Fuses and transistors had to be replaced on a regular basis—"regular" meaning daily or more often. Third—and the one reason that may be most relevant to the discussion—is the fact that the original computers were huge. Anyone owning a computer would need an entire room to hold it, not just a desk, since each computer weighed more than 30 tons.

Early computers had several ways of storing data, but one of the most prominent was through the use of punch cards: heavy pieces of paper with holes to encode the necessary numbers. A program could consist of hundreds and hundreds of these punch cards, which needed to be inserted into the computer in a specific order for the program to function.

Punch cards work nicely as a data storage method. They were even used before computers were created. Some punch cards were designed for mechanized looms, with the holes being used to designate fabric patterns. It's easy to tell when a punch card has gone bad, too, unlike modern methods of data storage. A bad punch card will be torn, folded, or otherwise mangled.

People keep innovating, however, and although modern storage methods are troublesome in some ways, they store a lot more data and are much more convenient than those punch cards, if for no other reason than they take up less space. The humble punch card was replaced by storage methods that offered easier access and stored more data, such as magnetic tape.

There are many punch cards around today, and their data is still good. Unfortunately, though, all those cards are completely useless. The computers that used them aren't around anymore. It's simply not practical to keep a massive, energy-devouring machine for the sole purpose of reading programs that are decades out of date. As mentioned earlier, data without a computer to interpret it is useless. Punch cards are so worthless today that people use them for art or craft projects, and there are suggestions available through the web for interesting things that can be done with these otherwise useless items.

It's somewhat of a tragedy for archiving, though. There won't be any equivalent Gutenberg Bible for computer programs, really. Even though there's information available about the development of programming over the years, it's not the same as a tangible object, and it's impossible to tell what people in the future will wish that the people of today had preserved. Will it be those early punch card programs?

In some ways, it's simply not practical to keep everything. You probably don't want your archive filled with boxes and boxes of cards that no one will be able to use, taking up precious space in your facility. But the phenomenon illustrates a point—technology becomes obsolete. This has been mentioned over and over throughout this book, but it really requires repeating. Even though punch cards were in use for decades, the speed at which technology becomes useless today is really quite alarming.

Floppy disks, for instance, had around 20 or so years of common use by everyday computer users. Once recordable CDs and other methods that could store more data became available, the use of floppies rapidly declined, and they are rarely used today. During the time in which floppy disks were the major method of external storage, there were three sizes in production, starting with 8-in. disks, moving on to 5.25-in. disks, and finally ending with 3.5-in. disks. The larger the disk, the older the technology, in this case. Each type required a completely different drive designed to accommodate that specific type.

Twenty or so years probably sounds like a pretty long time, but it's really not. Twenty years is a fraction of the amount of time that you could expect a book to be useful. Remember, the Gutenberg Bible is more than 500 years old. There's writing available that is much, much older as well. Consider the Dead Sea scrolls, for instance, or the Rosetta stone. The technology needed to use these is still available, since humans have not evolved anything better than eyeballs in the past few thousand years.

Even the coding languages used to create software programs can become obsolete or change over time. For example, HTML, which is used to create web pages, keeps updating. Some instructions are added to make it easier to create web pages, and some are deleted, being categorized as obsolete. So, any web pages that you might want to archive might no longer work with future browsers; they won't display the way that they should.

It's difficult to determine if a technology is becoming obsolete. Technically, punch cards have been in use since the 1700s, but they went out of use in the 1970s and are now totally useless. Magnetic tape, covered in chapter 7, has been around in varying forms for close to a hundred years and is still in use today, although those early forms are probably no longer readable by any device. Paper tape, a sort of combination between the principles of magnetic tape and punch cards, is even older than magnetic tape, it but stopped being used in the 1990s and is now exactly as useful as a punch card.

As another consideration, oftentimes, someone will create a new technology that is an improvement in some way or is novel, but it won't catch on with general users. It may have a fatal flaw or be too expensive or inconvenient to use. It's difficult to predict if something is merely a fad or a technology that will be around for decades to come. As an example, there was a need in the 1990s to create a technology that held more data than a floppy disk. The one that ultimately proved to be the best at the time was the optical disk (CDs and DVDs), but there were quite a few other technologies developed for the same purpose. The MiniDisc was one such invention of the time, along with Zip drives, Jaz drives, and the SuperDisk, which was essentially a glorified floppy. But it was impossible to know that these technologies would not have the practical value of an optical disk, since the other technologies all did what was desired—that is, they created something that had a greater storage capacity than a floppy disk (Lilly 2009).

It's very difficult to predict what will work out when it comes to technology. For example, the Blu-ray disk is exactly like a CD or DVD, but it has an enormous storage capacity in comparison to these other two technologies. Movies on Blu-ray are available for purchase and do pretty well, but they haven't completely replaced DVDs by a long shot. Why not? Probably for a variety of reasons—Blu-ray disks are more expensive and Blu-ray players, less convenient, and when it comes to viewing quality with movies, the difference between a DVD and a Blu-ray disk may not be enough to entice people to buy (as opposed to the difference in convenience and quality between a VHS and a DVD). It may be that the ability to stream content online is a factor as well. There isn't really a clear, tidy answer for it, so all that you can really do is to monitor developing technologies and be sure that you don't get caught with something useless and that you move your data before it's too late.

Part of the appeal of digitizing materials is to save space. It would be pretty inconvenient to be storing stone tablets in your archive just because they have an excellent longevity and are generally fire and water resistant. But the fact that the technology changes so rapidly should influence how you think about your archiving project. Here are a few questions to think about:

- How will you keep an eye on developing technologies so that you can plan for the future of your collection?
- How will you determine whether a data storage method is becoming obsolete and that your data needs to be moved to something new?
- How will you determine if a new storage technology is simply a fad or if it's a revolutionary innovation that will replace the current technologies?
- How will you migrate your collection from one technology to another in an efficient and logical manner?

Obsolescence is a definite problem and one that you will unquestionably need to address when you create a plan for your archive and determine which technologies you want to start with. However, digital materials face an even bigger problem, touched on in the chapters so far.

Data Decay

On January 10, 1921, an infamous event occurred, which causes great frustrations for genealogists and historians in the United States today. A fire broke out in the Department of Commerce building in Washington, DC. The ultimate result of this is that most of the 1890 census was completely destroyed (National Archives 2005). There is absolutely no way of getting that data back. It became irretrievable ash, and anyone who needed that data is simply out of luck.

It may be alarming to you to realize that vast amounts of data are just as completely destroyed on a daily basis. You possibly know someone who has lost years and years' worth of photos (or maybe it's happened to you) due to a hard drive crash or because the rewritable CDs that were supposed to be so revolutionary didn't hold up as well as they were supposed to. Maybe you or someone you know was writing an important letter or paper and suffered computer failure. Because the file was not saved on the hard drive but was being stored temporarily in the RAM, the data is gone. Or maybe you have tax records on floppy disks and didn't realize that your new computer doesn't have a floppy drive, so now they sit in a drawer somewhere, slowly deteriorating.

Humans make mistakes and forget things. While some programs automatically save information periodically to help with this, it doesn't completely solve the problem, and computers are rather unforgiving. Even computer professionals make mistakes. Remember: that first web page was overwritten with other files.

A book can easily be burned by a fire. Fire is also bad for digital materials, melting magnetic tape, CDs, and so on (some types of flash drives are designed to be fire-resistant, though). Other disasters are also bad for your archived materials, tangible and digital, such as floods and earthquakes, although restoring a waterlogged book is a much easier prospect than dealing with a soaked hard drive, for instance.

Digital materials have an extra vulnerability, though. When you put a book away, you'll expect that when you take it out again, you'll have exactly the same book. None of the words will have randomly disappeared; the illustrations will all be there in the same place. While the pages may become brittle over time or the words faded, they never completely vanish. You'll never open up a book and suddenly get a notice between the pages that you can't read it due to an error.

This is not the case with digital materials. You've already learned a little about bit rot and data decay. These phenomena refer to the fact that digital materials can change over time, with the data on them vanishing. Magnetic tapes can lose their magnetization, and so can hard drives. Flash drives can lose their charge, and writable CDs fade.

How fast this happens is open to debate. No one really knows just how long data will be safe on any item, since none of it has been around long enough to truly test digital materials in real time and under normal storage conditions. Some methods of data storage become obsolete before a test like this can even happen. Many tests and experiments have been conducted on digital materials in an attempt to simulate an accelerated aging process. These experiments are quite useful and can help with predicting how to best preserve digital materials, but they cannot truly predict the future qualities and life span of these items.

Some companies will claim that their digital storage materials last for a hundred years or more. A hundred years is a long time. A human being might not even last a hundred years. Yet, it still pales in comparison to the capability of a book for surviving through time. The capability of artwork surviving is possibly even greater—consider the prehistoric cave paintings in France, still visible and, to some extent, understandable after more than 30,000 years. And so, here is what you need to think about in regard to the longevity of your project:

- How will you ensure that your digital materials are not deteriorating?
- How will you ensure that your digital materials are safe in the event of a disaster?
- How will you ensure that your archive is not ruined by a storage device going bad?

Digital materials are inherently difficult to archive. That makes your work as an archivist even more important. In modern times, people are embracing the advantages of digital materials. Digital images take up less physical space than paper ones. A music collection on a smartphone or computer is less cumbersome than a collection of CDs or tapes or records. The same goes for movies. Many people's thoughts and ideas are in the form of blogs, not newsletters or pamphlets or books. It's highly possible that the creations of today will be lost due to the mutable nature of digital materials, just as surely—and just as frustratingly—as that 1890 census.

What this means is that it's important to keep track of the creations of today. As an example, the Library of Congress has been saving "tweets" from the popular social media website Twitter (Gross 2013). Twitter is briefly discussed in chapter 12; tweets are sentences or phrases that are short and have a limited word count. They can be "tagged" with words to indicate the content of the tweet, and they can be directed toward a person's online account. Many tweets are lacking in content and simply link to another location online, or they are responses to the tweets of others. Some are venomous in nature or exist solely to promote something outside of Twitter. Some are completely indecipherable without context. However, tweets are a way that people in modern times communicate. Will they have any value or relevance hundreds of years from now? Maybe not, but they will exist for study if needed, since the Library of Congress has decided to preserve them.

Tweets are digital in nature and have no physical form. This presents an extra obstacle to archiving. However, if you are digitizing tangible objects, you'll have the advantages offered by both a tangible object and a digital one.

⊚ Tangible Materials and Longevity

If you plan on digitizing a collection, you should not eliminate the original physical copies of your items unless it's really necessary or you're attempting to preserve something that is deteriorating to a state beyond practical use. As mentioned before, tangible items have a much greater life span than digital ones. Not only is their predicted life span longer, but it's been proven to be longer through trial and error over thousands of years.

Many archiving projects that are designed to preserve digital materials turn to tangible items to truly preserve their information. For example, the Internet Archive is a nonprofit group that has many goals, including keeping copies of online web pages. However, it has another project that is more physical in nature: collecting a copy of every book published—ever. These books are not being digitized. They're being stored in a cool, dry warehouse inside of large shipping containers. Along with books, the Internet Archive is collecting music and movies to store (Stokes 2011).

E-books are cheaper and more convenient than paper ones. But the object of this vault is not to distribute information. Should digital versions of these items vanish, as so many digital items have, there's still a copy available because of this project. If someone thinks that a digital version has been tampered with, which is so easy to do, then there's a copy available that is not so easily changed and can be used for comparison (Stokes 2011).

Miniature items, or tangible items that are extremely small, may be a technology to look into in the future. For example, the Rosetta Project is designed to archive the languages of the world. The creators of this project fear that a huge number of the languages in use today will simply vanish over the next century, and so they are attempting to document them now. The method by which these languages are being preserved is via an item that they call the "Rosetta Disk." The disk has a 3-in. diameter and is made from nickel, and it is stored in a spherical casing made from stainless steel and glass. On the face of the disk are approximately 14,000 pages of information about languages. Rather than using binary data encoding, the pages are actually microscopic images that can be read by a person (using magnification, of course). This disk, should it be kept safely in the casing, could last for thousands of years (Rosetta Project 2013). Even if every computer in the world was destroyed tomorrow and humans were never able to re-create computers as people think of them today, these disks would still be serviceable and useful.

Oddly enough, it seems to be a trend that older technologies do better than new technologies as far as archiving goes, as though things are working backward. Consider the huge longevity of stone or clay tablets, for instance. The company Hitachi is working on a method of storing data that will be similar in principle: etching binary code onto pieces of quartz glass. It's a little like working with pressed optical disks, but the glass is much more resistant to extreme temperatures and won't degrade over time (Clark 2012). Scientists are even working on encoding data using the oldest method on the planet: DNA (Richards 2013).

The conveniences offered by digital information and the rapid speed at which information can be created, shared, and stored are changing human society, and people can benefit greatly from digital technology. You will be benefiting others by making the information that your archive holds part of this easily transmitted data. However, the point that must be made here is that, while technology is wonderful and helpful and a great way to make your collection available to patrons, it has limitations and problems that have not yet been fully addressed. You should never expect technology to solve all your problems, and you must always be on the watch for better, more stable methods of storing data.

⊚ Key Points

- Digital media is not as stable as traditional tangible materials. As such, the normal methods of archiving don't address the problems facing digital media very well.
- For your archive, you will need to develop policies that are specific to the difficulties of digital media, and you will need to monitor developments in technology to avoid obsolescence. It is the instability of digital media that makes traditional media still relevant today.

In this chapter, you learned a little about what kinds of questions you should be asking about technology and your collection to develop good policies. In the next chapter, you will review the information covered in the book so that you can start developing a coherent plan for creating a digital archive.

⊚ References

Clark, Liat. 2012. "Laser-Etched Quartz Will Store Data for Hundreds of Millions of Years." *Wired*. http://www.wired.co.uk/news/archive/2012-09/25/hitachi-quartz-data-storage.

Gross, Doug. 2013. "Library of Congress Digs into 170 Billion Tweets." http://www.cnn.com/2013/01/07/tech/social-media/library-congress-twitter/.

Lilly, Paul. 2009. "Computer Data Storage through the Ages: From Punch Cards to Blu-Ray." http://www.maximumpc.com/article/news/computer_data_storage_through_ages?page=0,0.

National Archives. 2005. "The 1890 Census." http://www.archives.gov/research/census/1890/1890.html.

Richards, Sabrina. 2013. "DNA-Based Data Storage Here to Stay." *Scientist*. http://www.the
-scientist.com/?articles.view/articleNo/34109/title/DNA-based-Data-Storage-Here-to
-Stay/.

Rosetta Project. 2013. "Concept." http://rosettaproject.org/disk/concept/.

Stokes, Jon. 2011. "Internet Archive Starts Backing Up Digital Books . . . on Paper." *Wired*. http://
www.wired.com/business/2011/06/digital-books-on-paper/.

Ward, Mark. 2013. "Online Appeal Unearths Historic Web Page." http://www.bbc.co.uk/news/
technology-22652675.

Putting It All Together

SO FAR, THIS BOOK HAS COVERED quite a bit of information about computers. If you read all previous 14 chapters, you know what computers can and cannot do, what file formats are and what the differences are among them, how computer data is stored on a physical object, what kind of equipment is necessary for digitization, how to access digital information, and how laws differ regarding copyright protection for digital information.

Now you're probably wondering how you can practically apply what you've learned toward your collection. This chapter outlines the general steps to take when creating a digital archive; it reviews important information from the previous chapters; and it asks you questions to consider when creating plans for your own digital archiving project.

There is not a single correct way to go about making your archive, and so you may decide to take a different approach from the one outlined in this chapter. You will also certainly have questions that are not covered in this chapter. As you read, think about the questions provided by this chapter and any others that you may have.

◎ Setting Goals

Although it may seem unimportant or obvious, consider what your goals are before you start. Why are you creating a digital archive? There are a lot of good reasons to make one:

- You want to make it easier for patrons to obtain information or for your archive to share information.
- You want to be part of the effort to archive a digital culture.
- You want to work with other institutions that are digitizing their collections.
- You have a special collection that needs to be protected.
- You want to make information available to your patrons while protecting the original object; that is, patrons can use the digital version without ever handling the tangible object, which keeps the original object safe.

Or, you might have another motivation that doesn't fit into one of these categories. Write down your basic reasons for making an archive and what your goals are. These might influence how you go about creating your collection and what you need to consider your project a success. Writing down these reasons might also help if you need to talk about your project to groups or communities that might be willing to provide funding or other kinds of assistance to help your project reach its goals. Some of the benefits of creating a digital archive are discussed in chapter 1.

When you create a plan for your project, be as consistent as possible. Consistency is vital for digital archiving. Should you leave the archive, having a comprehensive, consistent plan will make it possible for other workers to carry on without you and make decisions on their own without needing to consult you. A consistent plan will also make it easier for you to share your work with other archives if desired.

After determining what your goals are, you should next decide what you want to archive.

◎ Your Collection

Regardless of what you want to store, the first thing that you must consider is the size and scope of your collection. If you have a small collection, if you want to archive only a few things, or if you want to archive a specific portion of the collection, then you may be able to store everything and can therefore move on with your plans.

Otherwise, you're going to need to make some difficult decisions. The process of storing born-digital materials and the process of digitizing materials and then storing them are both tedious and time-consuming for varying reasons. You need to prioritize which parts of your collection need to be stored first, and chances are good that you won't be able to archive everything, and so you may need to determine what is not worth storing. There are a couple of ways to go about deciding what parts of your collection are the most important to digitally archive. Here are some good questions to consider:

- Is the item particularly useful to your patrons, or would it probably see a lot of use if it were part of your digital archive? Does it already get a lot of use? If so, then this is a high-priority item.

- Is the item unique in any way? Do many other people have a copy, or is it unique to your archive? The former would decrease priority, and the latter would increase it. If the information is unique, then it's important to archive because there are few or no backup copies in other archives.
- Is the item highly delicate? Is the item in danger of degrading beyond reasonable use? If it's a born-digital item, is it in danger of becoming obsolete? Protecting items from degradation or obsolescence should be a major goal for a digital archive.
- Has anyone else digitized the item? This might be difficult to determine, and it's not necessarily a bad thing for there to be two digitized copies of an item. If you definitely know that there is a digital copy of something already in existence, though, then the item probably drops on your priority list.
- Is the item too delicate for you to digitize? You may find that you have items that need to be given special treatment. Remember, scanners use beams of light, which may harm some items. In addition, with audio and video items, you may find that your items are in an odd format that needs special consideration.
- Is the original, nondigital item difficult to store? For instance, is it large, or does it require a special shelf or storage unit? Would digitizing the item remove difficulties in this respect or open up more physical space in the archive?
- Is the item difficult to retrieve? Would having a digital copy reduce this difficulty for your employees and your patrons?
- Is there something about the item that would require special equipment to digitize? You don't necessarily want to spend your funds on equipment that can digitize only a small part of your collection when you could spend the funds on something that could be used for a larger part of your collection.
- Is the item already catalogued, thereby making cataloguing the digital version simpler?

Some questions to consider for born-digital items in particular follow:

- Will this item potentially have historical or cultural significance? This is difficult to determine, but you can attempt to decide which items seem most useful by having protocols in place to make choices.
- Will the item be difficult to store? Will it be difficult to use and retrieve? This is a potential complication if you wish to store software that is designed to work with a specific operating system or piece of equipment.
- Will it be difficult to convert a file to a more archive-friendly format?

While you're pondering these questions, you'll probably think of more that are relevant to your particular situation—so write down ones that seem significant to you. You can use these to officially determine which items in your collection are most important to digitize or to help with discussions if you are making these decisions in a group.

Another important consideration to make is what your patrons might like to see. If you have anything that is particularly fun or interesting, you might want to make it part of your collection to draw patrons to your archive. Even if an item would otherwise be low priority according to these questions, an item that patrons will like is probably an important one to digitize. Items that are simply fun can put your archive into a positive light, draw more patrons in, and even help if you want to demonstrate your project to anyone who might be interested in funding your archive's efforts.

Dividing Your Collection

When deciding what to digitize first, you might want to divide your collection into parts. For example, suppose that your collection has local maps, books on civil war history, and books by local authors. Your maps don't get a lot of use, and you know that there are already digital copies of the books by local authors. You also know that there's an active historical society in town and that your civil war collection includes some unique primary resources. You therefore decide that your project will digitize all the civil war books first. By saying that anything in the category of "civil war history books" should be digitized, you can make things easier on anyone working on this project by making the important choices ahead of time.

You can also make the process of storage and digitization easier this way. For instance, you may decide that all the civil war books are going to be photographed and that the images will be converted to grayscale, regardless of whether or not they are in good condition, while another part of the collection will be scanned with a flatbed scanner. Having a consistent procedure in place also makes the work easier. For example, you may decide that, after ripping tracks off your CD collections, all files will be converted to an AIFF for storage.

If you approach your project in this manner, don't make categories mentally. Write down what parts of the collection you think are most important, as well as instructions for how to determine whether or not an item falls into the category. You might have blurred categories; for instance, a book that is on civil war history by a local author. You might also have items that don't fit tidily into your categories—for instance, a book on history that has only one chapter about the civil war. If everything is clearly written down, then anyone working on the project will have no trouble determining what to do, and the project can proceed without the need for you to constantly supervise or make decisions.

Regardless of what kinds of items you are storing, you'll probably need to deal with an important aspect of digital archiving before you proceed to actually creating your collection: legal issues.

⑥ Legal Issues

In chapter 13, you learned a bit about what kinds of legal problems can arise from archiving. The last thing that you want to do while you work to preserve information for the future is waste time and money getting tangled up in a legal dispute. You should therefore make an important part of your archiving process determining whether or not you have the right to store or digitize something or obtaining permission to store or digitize items.

Essentially, you need to determine if the work that you want to store is under copyright. Items that are not under copyright are free for you to digitize. If the item is in the public domain (i.e., has no copyright protection), then you're free to use it in your digital collection. Determining if items still have a copyright is a bit tricky, especially if you want to use something published in another country, since laws may be different there. As stated in chapter 13, in general if a work meets one of the following conditions, it's in the public domain and is free to use:

- The work was published in the United States before 1923.
- The work was published in the United States between 1923 and 1963 and has no copyright notice.

ITEMS THAT CANNOT BE COPYRIGHTED

- Any work that falls into the public domain upon creation
- Any work whose creator has given up his or her rights
- Slogans, titles, names, and other short phrases
- Lists of ingredients, processes, and methods
- Phone books and similar data
- News and facts
- Common or familiar symbols
- Common-property works, such as height or weight charts, calendars, or similar items

---

- The work was published in the United States between 1923 and 1963 and has a copyright notice, but that copyright wasn't renewed. This takes some investigating to determine.

Works published after 1963 had an automatic copyright renewal or had the copyright extended, depending on the year of publication. This means that if you want to use something published after this time, you'll probably need to obtain permission to use the work for your digital collection, especially if you want to display the item online or share it with your patrons and not simply store it.

Some people use alternatives to copyright law that might be of interest to you; these are typically used for born-digital materials. These alternatives limit the rights of creators and give more rights to the public, and so items that use these alternatives are probably safe for you to archive, although you should always consult legal counsel to be absolutely sure. Some of these types of licenses are listed in chapter 13.

Remember: archives and libraries do get some special treatment when it comes to copyright law. You should know what these are and what situations they apply to. For example, if you simply want to archive the data as a backup and not make it available to the public, then this is usually acceptable. Archives can also sometimes make copies of materials that are degrading when a new or better copy can't be obtained for a reasonable price.

This book can give you only general guidelines for addressing and avoiding legal problems with your archive. When in doubt, always consult an attorney. While your archive may have good intentions, copyright holders and their lawyers may not see it that way.

Once you have determined what needs storing first and what you have the right to archive, a good next step to take is to decide how you are going to store your data.

Storage

Once you know how much of your collection that you can or want to store, you can make a reasonable estimate regarding how much storage space you'll need and what will or will not be a practical method of storing your data. Deciding how you'll store your data can be difficult, and you should think of it as an ongoing process because whatever storage method you use will almost assuredly become outdated.

For example, suppose that you have a collection of photos of local historical homes. You decide that you want to store only this part of your collection, so you scan these particular photos. You then back up your scans on CDs and then make the photos available online. Your community really enjoys the photos, and you get some funding from a local historical society, so you decide to expand your project. Unfortunately, you determine that the next phase of your digitization project, which involves digitizing books about local history, is not going to be practical to store on CDs. You're going to need to change your policies and plans to accommodate this, and you'll need to decide what will be practical given the scope of your project now.

Replacing outdated or broken technology is something else that must be part of your plans. For instance, you might have three 500-GB external hard drives, giving you a total of a terabyte and a half of data, and you find that this works very well for your collection for many years. But 10 years from now, 500 GB might be an extremely small amount of storage, and this storage method might be considered highly outdated. You might be able to buy something that runs faster or is more reliable.

If you use cloud storage, you will need to research your options regularly to ensure that you're getting a good deal with your service and that you still agree to the terms of service, since they can change.

There are many, many ways that you can store your data. This book covers a few of the most commonly used ones today: optical disks, magnetic tape, hard drives, flash memory, and cloud storage. Your options will very likely change in the future as well, as people develop new or better ways to store data. Chapters 6–10 cover the different major choices that you have.

Your data storage device is an object that will itself require a method of storage; that is, you'll need to protect your storage devices to keep your data safe. An important general consideration to make is whether or not you have optimal storage conditions available for a particular data storage method. Magnetic tape, for instance, is rather delicate and needs a room that is ideally situated and has a controlled temperature and humidity. If you can't accommodate archival conditions, you might want to use flash memory devices, which are more accommodating to less-than-ideal conditions, or optical disks, which are fairly inexpensive to replace.

Each method of data storage has some pros and cons, and you should think carefully about what would be optimal for your archive in particular. You do not have to pick only one, and using more than one is a good idea if it's possible. That is, you might want to use a hard drive for patron access but have the same data backed up on CDs for storage and retrieval (or vice versa). Using multiple devices makes your data safer. If you put a CD collection off-site and something happens to your main archive that destroys the hard drive, then your data is still safe. If CDs were to, say, become obsolete, your data is still safe on the hard drive. Again, having multiple copies of your data on multiple devices is a good idea that will keep your data as safe as possible.

After deciding where you'll store your data, the next step that you should take is to determine what kinds of files and specifications you want to use.

◎ File Settings

Deciding what specifications you'll use for your files or determining what equipment you need are good steps to take after deciding how you'll store your data. However, determining what kinds of files you want to store and create may make it easier for you to decide what your equipment needs to be capable of, and so you might want to pick your equipment later.

For digitizing tangible materials, you'll need to decide what formats will most accurately represent the original or, in the case of items such as text, what settings you need to further process the data. For storing born-digital materials, you'll need to decide whether you want to convert to a more archive-friendly format.

You may decide that you'll need to outsource your project or that outsourcing is going to be more efficient. Even if this is the case, you should still decide what kinds of files you want and what settings you require, as well as what files the company that you choose will create for your materials and whether you find this satisfactory for your archive's needs.

Write down what formats you think will be best for your project; you may want to note why as well, especially if you need to discuss the matter with others. You may need multiple formats, either to protect the files against obsolescence or to make your collection optimal in varying situations. For example, you might want to have an image stored as a TIFF for archiving but have another copy saved as a PNG for sharing online, or you might want to store a recording as a WAV for archiving but have a second copy as an MP3 for sharing.

Images

When it comes to images, you need to make a few decisions about the most basic parameters of your images: whether or not to use color and what level of color to use, the resolution and the file formats, as well as how you will capture the images in the case of digitization and what software is necessary. How computers store image data is discussed in chapter 3.

Color

Images may be in color, grayscale, or black and white. Digital cameras typically capture images in color, and scanners often have several options. You can also convert color images to grayscale using photo-editing software. Remember: color requires the most data to store; grayscale requires less; and 1-bit monochromatic color requires the least.

You may want to have different policies regarding color level, depending on what kind of image is being stored and whether or not it is in color. This is fine so long as you are consistent and can clearly define which parameters for image capture are to be used for which situations to avoid confusion and inconsistent work. The sidebar contains some questions to consider.

DPI or PPI

After determining how you will handle the color level for your images, you must then determine what dpi or ppi you wish to use for your images. You should scan your images at the same dpi or ppi for consistency. As explained in chapter 3, it's better to work in ppi, or pixels per inch, whenever possible, rather than dpi, because ppi is technically more accurate. For archiving, a range of 300 to 400 ppi is usually adequate, but you may want a higher range for greater detail and resolution. Some archiving projects use 600 ppi, and you can use an even higher range.

QUESTIONS TO CONSIDER FOR IMAGE DATA STORAGE

- Are your images in black and white, or are they in color?
- Will you need to convert color images to grayscale?
- Do you have a variety of images to digitize? Would it be simpler for you to simply use the same settings regardless of the type of image, or would it be more efficient to customize your settings to the particular image?
- Do you benefit from having a ppi higher than 300–400?
- Will having a higher ppi make storage and retrieval of data too cumbersome for your archive?
- Do you want to change the ppi for born-digital images or always use the original format?
- Are you archiving images that require a specialized scanner?
- What is your budget for equipment?
- Which formats do you feel will make it easy for patrons to access your information?
- Do you want to share your data online?
- For born-digital materials, what is the original file format for the item?

If you want a higher range, you should remember that images with a high ppi require more room to store and take longer to store and retrieve, so you should take this into account when making a decision. A lower range may produce an image that is too low in quality to be of historical use. As with color, you can use different ppi ranges for different materials, but you should make it clear when a lower or higher ppi should be used for an image.

With born-digital images, you can reduce the ppi, but increasing it requires the computer to make "estimates" and guess what color information would be in the extra pixels, which is inaccurate. It's best in most situations to either reduce ppi only or always leave it in the original format.

Capturing Images

Unless your image is born digital, you'll need to use equipment to get a capture of the item, or to digitize it. The two main choices are to use a scanner or to use a camera. In most instances, the scanner is the simpler method, unless the item is too large to scan easily or the item is delicate. In these instances, a camera is the superior choice.

As discussed in chapter 11, you have a variety of choices for scanners. A flatbed scanner is a good choice for images in most situations but not all. You may need a specialty scanner if you want to digitize film or microfilm, for instance. If your archive wants to solely create high-quality archival captures of images, you may even find it worthwhile to invest in a drum scanner.

File Formats

Once you've created an image, you need to decide what format you require to store it. In general, the TIFF format is best for archiving, since this format captures a lot of information and uses lossless compression. However, TIFF files are typically quite large, and they are a poor choice for transmission over the Internet, so you should consider your options carefully. The JPEG, GIF, and PNG formats are better suited for use on the Internet. You can store an image in multiple file formats, having a format for storage purposes only and one for viewing online.

Even if you don't want to have your archive available via the Internet, having multiple file formats for your image helps to protect them from obsolescence. For instance, if you had the same image in both TIFF and JPEG formats and suddenly no one was making software that read JPEGs anymore—although this scenario is highly unlikely to happen anytime soon—then your files would still be safe because the other format, the TIFF, is still in use. A similar and more probable scenario would be keeping digital photo files in their native formats for the sake of posterity but also saving those same images in a more commonly used file format. In addition, if you're storing born-digital images, you might want to keep an image in its original format but also a copy in another format. Table 3.1 summarizes the various commonly used file formats.

Processing

After capturing your images, you may want to do some alterations. This typically involves rotating or de-skewing an image, cropping out unnecessary information, and improving the contrast or color levels. De-skewing an image can eliminate data around the edges of an image, so you should always do that first.

Write down the steps that you want to take to improve your captures; that way, everyone who works on the project does it the same way every time, thereby improving quality and consistency.

Text

Like photos, your text items may already be in a digital format, or they may need to be digitized. Each requires a slightly different approach. Storing text is covered in chapter 4.

QUESTIONS TO CONSIDER FOR TEXT DATA STORAGE

- Does your archive benefit from having text items in multiple formats?
- Will patrons be accessing this data?
- Do you lose significant amounts of data by converting to another format? Is the formatting of the text item important, or is the information itself more important?
- Do you want to keep a copy of the file's original format?
- Do you want to use a camera or a scanner or some mixture of both? What kind of scanner is best for your materials?
- What settings are optimal for capturing your text materials? Do you want to further process the images by making the text searchable?
- Are your text materials clear and easy to read, or are they faded? Does this affect what settings you choose for capture?

Digital Format

If your text is already in a digital format, then you essentially need to make one decision: is it better to keep the text in its original format or to convert it to something else? You can do both and keep both copies, which may be better from a preservation standpoint in that you have a copy of what the original item was like, even if there is no software to read it.

The biggest problem with items already in a digital format is the fact that many file formats for text are proprietary and may become obsolete if the software to read them becomes outdated. In this book, you learned about some formats that are relatively safe from becoming obsolete. TXT, RTF, and OTD are some fairly safe options. TXT allows for very little formatting; RTF allows for some more; and OTD has essentially the full range of word-processing formatting options available today.

HTML and XML are markup languages that work with plain text. HTML is generally useful for only web pages, but since it allows for formatting with plain text, you may find it useful for other purposes. A web page does not need to be online to be viewed in a browser program if the data for the web page is on the computer that you want to view it on. XML allows for metadata, which you might find useful, as it can generate information about your collection and help with patron access. Metadata is covered in chapter 12.

PDF files allow for "pages" and can feel like the original document to the user. The PDF/A in particular is a variation on the PDF format geared toward archiving. The PDF format is very user-friendly and is a good choice if you want patrons to use your archived documents.

Digitized Materials

If your text needs to be digitized, then you'll be taking a picture of it, through either a scan or a photograph. It will need to be treated in a similar manner to an image, and so you'll need to consider some of the same questions as you did regarding images. As with images, you will be using either scanners or cameras to capture your data. Cameras are good in most situations with text items, and flatbed scanners are good for text items that are either not bound or have a strong binding that can withstand rough handling. However, if you don't mind destroying the original object and the text is in good condition, a sheet-fed scanner is efficient with text and so is an extra consideration for your choices.

Precision is important with text. Like plain image files, TIFF files tend to be best for your original image captures, but you can use other formats if needed or desired. The JPEG format tends not to work as well with text, because the text can become fuzzy due to how JPEGs are encoded and compressed, but you can use this file type if desired. In essence, you need a lossless format that can capture crisp edges. You may want to use a higher resolution with text than ordinary images. This will allow the user to zoom in on words, and it may help optical character recognition software function better should you choose to use it.

If you want your text to be searchable, then you need to scan the original items with this in mind. As discussed in chapter 4, optical character recognition software "looks" for matches to an internal library of letters and characters. You need to scan items in such a way as to make this as easy as possible for the software. If you have clean, clear documents with no fading, damage, or images, then you should use 1-bit monochrome to get a plain black-and-white document with a small file size. If there are spots or faded areas that would show up as black splotches in a scan that has only two colors, then grayscale is better.

Once you have scanned your items, you can leave them as a sequence of images, but it's better to put them into something like a PDF format for convenience. PDFs can be made from text documents or images with equal ease and, as mentioned earlier, "feel" like pages in a book to the user. Storing the images like this will keep relevant items together as well, which is helpful to you as an archivist.

Audio/Video

Like text materials, your audio or video materials may already be in a digital format, or they may need to be digitized. Unlike text, the same file formats are suitable in either case. Audio and video formats for archiving are less straightforward than those for image and text items, and finding truly archival quality formats is a struggle. For example, although the MP3 format is a highly efficient and popular method of storing audio data, it is proprietary and uses lossy compression, which means that some of the audio data will be lost when the file is compressed to save space. Lossy and lossless compression methods are described in chapters 3 and 5, and audio and video data storage is discussed in chapter 5.

It's a good idea to save files using more than one file format. For example, WAV and AIFF are two common proprietary formats that are extremely similar in capability. You could store a single sound file in both formats, making it safe in the event that any of the companies or corporations who own these formats go out of business or their file format goes out of use. If your audio data already has a digital format, then one of the formats that you use should probably be the original format.

You'll face similar difficulties with video formats, since most are proprietary and use lossy data compression. You can use similar considerations with video formats, by storing more than one file format and choosing the formats with the least amount of data loss. With video formats, you'll need to compromise between lossy and lossless storage. Lossless storage methods are superior from an archiving standpoint but are uncommon for video. Lossy methods are much more common, and there are more choices for storing a video with lossy compression. You don't have to use a compression method at all, but this will create a very large file. In addition, while there are formats that are fairly friendly

QUESTIONS TO CONSIDER FOR AUDIO AND VIDEO DATA STORAGE

- Do you want your files to be available online?
- Do you want to offer a transcription of your audio and video files?
- Does it matter to you how well suited a file is toward digital archiving, if the file is originally in a digital format?
- Does it matter to you if a format or method of compression is lossy? Remember: lossy formats are more common and more efficient but are inferior from a pure archiving standpoint. You do not have to compress files at all.
- Is the software that you want to use compatible with the formats that you'd prefer? Will the software determine what formats you will ultimately save your files in?

for archiving, the less archiving-friendly formats are more likely to have more software options.

Once you know what kinds of files you need and what settings you want to use, you can go about selecting the optimal equipment for your project.

⚙ Equipment

The type of equipment that you need depends on what you're archiving. If you want to, say, digitize a collection of local photographs, you'll need more equipment than if you were archiving the websites of university professors. This book covers the type of equipment that you will most likely need in detail in chapter 11; this section reviews this information. No matter what you archive, though, you have to have two items: a computer and a monitor.

Choosing Computers

Although tablets and smartphones are highly prevalent today, you'll probably still want a dedicated desktop or laptop, at the least. This is largely owing to the greater computing power offered by these devices. Tablets and smartphones also have fewer and more specialized ports, which makes using equipment more difficult. This may change in the future, but for now, you should really consider a desktop or laptop for your project.

When you buy a computer, it can be difficult to compare one computer to another or to understand why one is better than another. The basic parts of a computer are described in chapter 2. Computers may have features that seem complicated or difficult to understand, or you may have trouble determining why two similar computers have different prices or why one computer might be better than another. Although it can be a little confusing and even though some merits of a computer are largely opinion, doing a general comparison does not have to be difficult. Here are some things to look for when you want to make a purchase.

Operating System

An operating system is essentially the general software that allows a computer to coordinate its own functions. This affects everything about a computer and how it runs. Operating systems change over time, with companies updating the systems to meet new customer demands. If you buy a new computer, it will probably have the latest operating

---

FEATURES TO LOOK FOR IN COMPUTERS

- Amount and type of RAM
- Number and type of ports
- Operating system, manufacturer
- Size of the hard drive
- Speed of the CPU

system. If you buy a used computer, be sure that you know what the operating system is. Sometimes old computers can be upgraded, and sometimes they can't.

The type of operating system and the company that made it will determine what software you can use with the computer. Software is not universal; that is, software is designed to run on certain computers and operating systems. The software that you want to use can determine what kind of computer you want to buy, although it's more common to select software based on what kind of a computer you have.

Different companies will sell computers with different operating systems. For desktops and laptops, Microsoft's operating system Microsoft Windows and Apple's OS X are the major choices. Remember: software designed for one of these operating systems won't necessarily work for the other. There are also other operating systems, such as Linux, but these are less commonly used.

Hard Drive

Another easy thing to look for is how big the hard drive is. Bigger is always better when it comes to hard drives; you'll be able to save more data on a bigger hard drive. Hard drive sizes are listed in either gigabytes (GB) or terabytes (TB). Remember, a terabyte is 1,000 gigabytes, so a 1-terabyte hard drive is twice as big as a 500-gigabyte hard drive.

CPU

The central processing unit, or CPU, is the part of the computer that handles all calculations and other requests made by the user. It's therefore an essential component. The speed at which the CPU operates is determined by the clock, which is a vibrating crystal inside the computer; this rate is usually designated in gigahertz (GHz). The bigger this number, the faster the CPU can operate, and the faster the computer can operate as a whole. You may want to see if any software that you want to use has a minimum CPU requirement to help you determine the optimal amount for your computer.

You may see terms such as "dual core" or "quad core" when it comes to CPUs. A computer can have more than one CPU or have CPUs with duplicate components, which also improves the speed.

In addition, the CPU has its own memory, known as "cache memory." More cache memory also helps improve the processing speed by having plenty of space to store the CPU's calculations. Finally, a term often connected with CPUs is the "front-side bus," or FSB, which is the portion of the CPU that allows for communication between the CPU and the rest of the computer. The speed of the FSB directly affects how fast the CPU can respond to the user's requests.

RAM

There are several types of RAM chips. For modern computers, SDRAM and DDR SDRAM are the common ones. DDR SDRAM is faster, so a computer with 4-GB DDR SDRAM would be faster than a computer with 4-GB SDRAM. You can often add more RAM, and it's not too difficult to do. If you can, it's better to purchase a computer with a sufficient amount of RAM just for the sake of ease. RAM chips are covered in detail in chapter 2.

A computer must have ports, or else it is not able to communicate with the outside world. The number and types of ports will be important to you. Most computer manufacturers advertise how many USB ports are available. Many types of equipment can use USB ports to communicate with the computer, so more USB ports are better. It's possible to buy a hub that plugs into a USB port and gives you more USB ports, though, so it should not be your only consideration.

FireWire ports have a similar function but are somewhat more specialized. If you want to use equipment that requires a FireWire port, then it will be important for you to have at least one on your computer.

Some other common ports are those for microphones and speakers, monitors or televisions (e.g., VGA, DVI, and HDMI ports), and those designed for mice and keyboards.

Choosing Monitors

Choosing a monitor is simpler in some ways than choosing a computer. In many stores, samples of the available monitors will be powered on so that you can see the difference between the monitors.

Computer monitors and flatscreen televisions are very similar, so you can potentially use a television instead if it's more economical. Remember: monitors should be calibrated to match real-world colors and contrast for best results. Bigger monitors are better, especially if you're going to work with images and video files, but don't get one that's too large to reasonably fit into the space you have to work.

While a computer and a monitor are the major items of equipment that you'll need, there will probably be others, such as speakers, mice, and keyboards. You'll also need more equipment as well as software if you will be digitizing materials. Some of this equipment can be used for projects other than digitizing materials as well.

Scanners and Cameras

With images, you need a way to record the image, or capture the image. You have two options: a scanner or a camera.

Use a scanner:

- If the images are small enough to fit on the scanner bed
- If the items are not delicate—or, in the case of a book, if they can be taken apart for the digitization process

FEATURES TO LOOK FOR WHEN PURCHASING MONITORS

Physical size of the monitor: expressed as the diagonal measurement

Resolution: number of pixels, or how clear and sharp the picture is

Ports: how it can connect to the computer

Other features: whether it has speakers or whether the monitor is adjustable, for example

Use a camera:

- If the item is large
- If the item is delicate or the item is a book that should not or cannot be taken apart

There are several types of scanners to choose from:

- Flatbed scanners are common and useful for most situations but are somewhat tedious to use.
- Sheet-fed scanners are partially automated and are faster than flatbed scanners. They are not suited for delicate items and can't scan a book, unless it is taken apart.
- Portable scanners don't produce archival-quality results, but they may still be useful because they are portable and allow for the user to be gentle with the item to be scanned.
- Drum scanners are useful for high-quality scans of photos. They produce the highest-quality scans but are far less convenient than your other options and are very large and expensive.
- You may need a scanner designed specifically for some items; negatives and microfilm are some items that really need a specialty scanner.

A good scanner will, at the minimum,

- Scan items at your archive's target dpi or ppi
- Scan items and convert the data into multiple formats, including those that you want to use
- Scan in color, grayscale, and monochrome
- Connect easily to a port on your computer

With cameras, you should be concerned mainly with the size of the sensor and how many megapixels the camera captures. Bigger is better in both instances. You need some extra equipment with a camera setup, such as a book cradle for books, a stand or platform for large images, something to hold the camera steady (e.g., a tripod or an arm), and something to discretely hold down pages.

Audio/Video

If your audio data is already on an optical disk, then you simply need to "rip" the music from it. A typical computer already comes with software that will do this for you.

If you need to digitize your data, then you basically require two things: something that can play the recording (a record player, for instance) and something that can connect the player to your computer so that it can capture the audio data. Chapter 11 describes what you need for this process.

Video data can also be directly copied, just like digital audio data. For video data that is on film reels, you'll need to treat it similarly to audio data in that you need to play and record the video simultaneously. You'll require appropriate equipment to play whatever kind of film you have. If you want to record a VHS tape, there are devices designed to capture and digitize such information. You will require one of these devices and a VHS player.

⊙ Processing

Once you've created your digital files, you'll then need to make them practical for use by the public or your staff. This will involve cleaning up captures, adding metadata, and creating catalog entries.

Cleaning Up Files

Once you've created your digital files, you need to decide what the next step is. Some questions you might consider:

- Are you going to adjust images for brightness/contrast, rotate or de-skew, or do any other digital cleanup or enhancement?
- Do you want text to be searchable?
- Do you want to divide audio or video captures into segments, such as individual tracks, or leave them as complete files?
- Should digital restoration be part of your project? For example, if you have a photograph with a tear in it, you could use a photo-editing program to remove it. Although this isn't "pure" from an archiving standpoint, your patrons might like it.
- Are the file names important? If they aren't, then you can save some time by numbering files or using another simple system rather than trying to think of a good descriptive title for each item.

Before coming up with an official plan, you might want to digitize a few items to figure out what process will be best. For example, suppose that you want to digitize some photographs. After digitizing about a dozen, you decide that the best procedure is to scan the photo, de-skew it in a photo-editing program, enhance the contrast, name the file using the photographer's last name and a number, save it as both a TIFF and a JPEG, add metadata, and then catalog the entry.

Metadata

As discussed in chapter 12, your files aren't useful if no one can find or access them. Typically, you'll want to add some kind of metadata to them. Software for images, audio, and video data in particular may give you the option to permanently add metadata to the

METADATA AND PATRON ACCESS

- Do you have programs suitable for adding metadata?
- How much metadata do you want to add, and what kind of information is important to put into the metadata?
- Are you digitizing items that already have a usable catalog entry?
- What type of metadata schema do you want to use?
- How much patron access do you want to allow?
- How will you prevent others from tampering with your files?

file, and whether or not software is capable of this might determine whether you want to use a certain type of software. There are ways to embed metadata in text files as well. You may or may not want your patrons to access your digital archive; you may want to limit the amount of access; or you may want to limit who can access the data.

Once you've created and stored your files, your work is not finished. Digital archiving is an ongoing process.

⊚ Maintaining Your Archive

As mentioned at other points in this book, digital archiving is different from regular archiving. Your collection will need to be monitored and maintained, to protect it against physical degradation and against obsolescence. Chapter 14 discusses some of the major issues with digital storage and digital archiving. You need to have a good plan in place for how you'll deal with changes in technology and hardware or software issues. Some thoughts to consider:

- How often do you think you should check your collection for corruption, errors, or physical damage or degradation? How will you go about this in an efficient manner? What will you do if you discover damage or errors? There is software available that can help with this.
- If you find that part of your collection is in danger of becoming outdated, what is the best way to move your files without losing any data?
- How will you monitor relevant developments in digital storage?
- What will your archive do in the event that your software is no longer usable for your project or in the event that a more efficient method of archiving is discovered?

⊚ Key Points

- Your collection may be very large or small, or you may want to digitize only part of a collection. In most instances, you will need to prioritize which parts you address first.
- Potential legal problems should be addressed before any digitization or storage takes place.
- You will need some way to store your digital files. Using multiple storage methods is the optimal choice. The ideal method depends on how much data you need to store and how much money your archive has.
- You may want to store your data in multiple file formats. You should always choose your formats based on what is optimal for your project's goals.
- You will require equipment; at the minimum, you need a computer and a monitor. Other equipment that you need will depend on what you want to store. Oftentimes, choosing equipment requires a compromise.
- You will need to add metadata to your items; the best way to accomplish this will depend on what kinds of files you are storing, your method of cataloging, and what software you have available, as some software can embed metadata.
- One of the primary considerations for your archive must be how you will maintain and upgrade your collection.

Without a doubt, the future of archiving will be digital and will require the use of computers. While the process of digital archiving may seem unfamiliar or intimidating, the amount of data that can be stored and shared will be highly beneficial for future generations. Your efforts now can benefit others for many years to come.

Index

defragmentation, 92

digital archiving: definition, 1–2; equipment, 130–43, 198–201; goals, 5–7, 188; vs. traditional archiving, 3–5; organizations, 7–8

direct access, 80, 92

display adapter. *See* graphics card

dots per inch. *See* DPI

DPI, 27

DVD 63, 182; construction, 64

EBCDIC, 38

FAT, 91, 106–7

Federal Agencies Digitization Initiative Still Image Working Group, 131

file allocation table. *See* FAT

file extension, 30

firmware, 16

flash drive, 105, 106, 107–8

flash memory, 103–14; advantages, 108–10; disadvantages, 110–12; storage, 113

floppy drive, 24

fragmentation, 92

frequency, audio, 52

front side bus. *See* FSB

FSB, 18

full-screen, 58

graphics card, 22, 131–32

hard drive, 17, 20–21, 89–101; advantages, 96–97; disadvantages, 97–98; storage, 98–100

hardware, 16

high color, 28

histogram, 34, *35*

HTML, 42–44, *43*, 45, 117, 148

hypertext markup language. *See* HTML

image data, 25–35; file types, 30–33

indexed color, 31

interlaced image, 31

interlaced scanning, 58

internal bus, 18

Internet, the, 116–19

Internet archive, 7, 184

IP address, 118

jump drive. *See* flash drive

keywords, 148–49

LAN, 116

laser rot, 70–71

Latin-1 Extended ASCII set, 39

LCD, 130–31, 132

Library of Congress, The, 7, 31–33, 41, 44, 45, 152, 184

liquid crystal display. *See* LCD

local area network. *See* LAN

magnetic tape, 75, 180, 181; advantages, 82–82; construction, 79–80; disadvantages, 83–84; history, 76; storage, 84–86

magnets, 76–78

mainframe computer, 119, 123

MAN, 116

memory stick. *See* flash drive

metadata, 145–55; schemas, 150–54; types, 149–50

metropolitan area network. *See* MAN

monitor, 26–27, 130; resolution, 131; size, 132

mono recording, 54

motherboard, 19

native formats: images, 32–33; video, 57–58

noninterlaced image, 31

nonvolatile, 106

OCR software, 46–48, 139

optical character recognition software. *See* OCR software

optical media, 64–65, 69, 181; advantages, 69–70; disadvantages, 70–71; dyes, 71; storage conditions, 71–73

outsourcing, 130, 193

pen drive. *See* flash drive

picture element. *See* pixel

pixel, 26–27

pixels per inch. *See* PPI

ports, 17, 21; audio, 22; DisplayPort, 132; DVI, 132; eSATA, 94; ethernet, 22; FireWire (IEEE 1394), 22, 94–95, 200; High-Definition Multimedia Interface (HDMI), 22, 24, 132; parallel, 23; PS/2, 22–23; serial, 23; USB, 22, 93, 94–95; VGA, 22, 132

POST, 20

power-on self-test. *See* POST

About the Author

Elizabeth R. Leggett is a freelance technical writer. She has bachelor degrees in English and psychobiology from Centre College and a master degree in library and information science from the University of Kentucky and has worked in libraries and archives at Centre College, the University of Kentucky, and Murray State University. She also began a local digital genealogical collection at the Calloway County Public Library. Her writing on the topic of digital storage and archiving appeared in the 2012 summer edition of *Kentucky Libraries*.